Licensing Parents

Licensing Parents

Family, State, and Child Maltreatment

Michael T. McFall

LEXINGTON BOOKS
A division of
ROWMAN & LITTLEFIELD PUBLISHERS, INC.
Lanham • Boulder • New York • Toronto • Plymouth, UK

LEXINGTON BOOKS

A division of Rowman & Littlefield Publishers, Inc.
A wholly owned subsidiary of The Rowman & Littlefield Publishing Group, Inc.
4501 Forbes Boulevard, Suite 200
Lanham, MD 20706

Estover Road
Plymouth PL6 7PY
United Kingdom

British Library Cataloguing in Publication Information Available

Library of Congress Cataloging-in-Publication Data

The hardback edition of this book was previously cataloged by the Library of Congress
as follows:

McFall, Michael T., 1978–
   Licensing parents: family, state, and child maltreatment / Michael T. McFall.
      p. cm.
   Includes bibliographical references and index.
   1. Family policy—United States. 2. Child welfare—United States. 3. Parents—
Legal status, laws, etc.—United States. 4. Child abuse—United States—Prevention.
I. Title.
   HQ536.M414 2009
   362.760973—dc22

                                                                    2008039289

ISBN: 978-0-7391-2913-5 (cloth: alk. paper)
ISBN: 978-0-7391-2914-2 (pbk.: alk. paper)
ISBN: 978-0-7391-3353-8 (electronic)

Printed in the United States of America

∞™ The paper used in this publication meets the minimum requirements of American
National Standard for Information Sciences—Permanence of Paper for Printed Library
Materials, ANSI/NISO Z39.48-1992.

Contents

Foreword

Without children, humanity has no tomorrow. For this very reason, the way in which we raise our children is absolutely key to there being a better tomorrow. No amount of progress in science or technology should be allowed to overshadow the importance of how we raise our children.

Michael T. McFall's *Licensing Parents: Family, State, and Child Maltreatment* is animated by these immutable truths. Writing with a passion sustained by rigor, McFall offers a philosophically beautiful account of the family as the fundamental institution in society. This is because the psychological and moral sense of self that underwrites the flourishing of children has its beginning in the family. Indeed, the sense of justice that makes for a stable society has its most secure moorings in none other than the family.

One aspect of the extraordinary power of McFall's argument lies in the universality of the argument. The family is equally important for all. Another aspect of the argument's power is that it reaches across every conceivable social construct. Surely this is the way it should be. This is because every child born is equally innocent; and every child is marvelously responsive to the salubrious effects of parental love.

In a most illuminating manner, *Licensing Parents: Family, State, and Child Maltreatment* underscores the simple but yet ever so profound truth that parental love is one of the greatest gifts that human beings can give. In terms of both self-respect and self-esteem, both of which are necessary in order thrive in the face of the vicissitudes of life, it is the foundation afforded by the family that makes the difference for the better in a child's life in a way that nothing else can.

Alas, the truth can be radical. So it is with the truths of *Licensing Parents: Family, State, and Child Maltreatment*. This is because insofar as we take the family seriously, then a just society is not one that merely maximizes liberty while underwriting mutual respect. It is also one that gives pride of place to the family as one of the most fundamental institutions in society.

McFall holds that if we are to keep alive the hope that no child should be left behind, then it is not to schools and other social centers that we must turn in order to achieve that end. Rather, we must turn to the family; for as the great philosopher Jean-Jacques Rousseau reminded us: The family is the most natural and the most basic of social institutions.

Licensing Parents: Family, State, and Child Maltreatment presents an eloquent and passionate argument, advanced with purity of heart, for undergirding the family in order that the most precious of all, namely children, will have from the very start of their lives the most majestic affirmation that is humanly possible.

The framers of *The Constitution of the United States* spoke of a "more perfect union." Quite simply, McFall's brilliant argument is that a more perfect union starts with none other than the family.

Laurence Thomas,
professor of political science in the Maxwell School
and professor of philosophy, Syracuse University

Acknowledgments

I have been extremely fortunate. Many people, even strangers, have placed a tremendous amount of trust in me. I frequently find myself listening to people share their deepest fears and most painful experiences. This has forced me to cultivate and refine the ability to listen carefully to what people say and how they say it in an attempt to unearth the true meaning of their words. I have thus come to understand better the importance of love, especially parental love, and grasp how devastating child maltreatment can be. I have learned that political theories that do not account for the role that love plays in human life are deeply suspect. I thank all of those who have trusted me with accounts of their most painful experiences. I hope that this project will spur society to action by helping to find ways to ensure that fewer children suffer maltreatment.

I have been blessed to be surrounded by extremely helpful people. I am indebted to the following at Syracuse University for reading and commenting upon earlier drafts of this book: Ken Baynes, Elizabeth Cohen, Ned McClennen, and Michael Stocker. I also thank the following for discussing this project with me, sometimes even reading through some of the chapters: Jeremy Dickinson, Jordan Dodd, Christina Hoffman, Nathan Hanna, Michael McKeon, William Merz, Adam Schechter, Matt Skene, and Josh Umar. I am also thankful to Jessica Bradfield, Patrick Dillon, Michael Sisskin, and an anonymous reviewer at Lexington Books. Each of these helped greatly. I presented parts of this book to the Ashland University Philosophy Club and to Syracuse University's Philosophy Department Dissertation Workshop. Both events yielded excellent feedback.

I am particularly indebted to three sets of people. The first is Laurence Thomas. He has served as an ideal mentor, and we have developed a beautiful friendship (insofar as a mentor and a student can be friends). He is the primary reason I was willing to take a chance to write this, and he encouraged me to stay with it. Laurence's work on the family has influenced me greatly. Most importantly, his patience and overwhelming generosity have enabled me to flourish.

Beth Vanderkooi read two earlier versions of this book. In addition to being a profoundly intelligent and tireless reader, she discussed and debated the issues in this book with me more than anyone else. I have learned much and benefitted enormously from her. Beth's love, friendship, and patience nourished me while writing.

I am most indebted to my parents. They have provided a constant source of love and affirmation from the moment that I was born, and they have been exemplary parents. My parents often worry that they somehow fell short in child-rearing, but I suspect that this is a natural, albeit irrational, concern that the very best kinds of parents have. This book is dedicated to my parents, Larry and Kay McFall. Thank you for everything; I love you both deeply.

Introduction

This book has three major objectives. The first is to discover what kind of egalitarianism best provides meaningful equality of opportunity. The second is to find a means to move from a mostly well-ordered Rawlsian society towards a stable and well-ordered society. The third is to discover how to reduce child maltreatment. Variations of the first aim are often discussed in political philosophy, but the latter two problems generally receive little attention. These problems cannot be answered successfully independently of each other. For example, the problem of child maltreatment must be addressed in order to reveal how to move from a mostly well-ordered society towards a stable and well-ordered society. Likewise, what constitutes meaningful equality of opportunity must be understood before identifying a means to move from a mostly well-ordered society towards a stable and well-ordered society.

When the above are considered together, more questions arise. One question is how best to instill citizens with good character, those which I call individuals with a sense of justice (ISJs), while minimizing the number of those with poor character, non-ISJs. To address this, I consider developmental moral psychology, which I argue should play a fundamental role in political philosophy. I argue that the family is the best environment to develop ISJs and minimize the number of non-ISJs. In fact, I show that a healthy family is the solution to all the above questions. In doing so, I raise two additional questions. First, what *kind* of family is necessary to provide equal opportunity, a means to progress towards a stable and well-ordered society, and an environment in which children are treated properly? Secondly, if this particular kind of family is necessary to solve the above problems, how can society ensure the existence of this family? This is complicated in a society where the government is largely *laissez-faire* about the family, especially about intra-family matters.

After considering various options, I argue that it would be best for children, adults, and society if parents were licensed, thereby preventing some people in our mostly well-ordered society from parenting.

This work manifests from a concern that political philosophy is moving in the wrong direction. In particular, it has been overly preoccupied with formal structures and means of distribution. Informal considerations, such as character, have often been overlooked. However, some formal structures might not be necessary, or as necessary, if citizens in society were to have a certain character. Likewise, distribution of goods and resources might be unnecessary if informal structures such as the family were healthy. Minimally, if ensuring a certain level of resources for everyone is sought by means of distribution, then serious consideration should be given to recognizing competent parents as the foremost equalisandum.

John Rawls's *A Theory of Justice* and Hugh LaFollette's "Licensing Parents" are the motivating influences of this book. Rawls's Original Position and Difference Principle are interesting, but I believe that Rawls's explicit use of developmental moral psychology within a theory of justice is his most significant contribution to philosophy. Rawls considers crucial matters of self-reinforcing mechanisms, and he does not forget that political philosophy deals with *humans*. Consequently, political structures must not overlook how human beings actually think and behave. LaFollette's essay is influential because it puts forth a counterintuitive conclusion that I cannot overcome with argument. This book began as a project to explain why LaFollette is wrong. I am now unsure that LaFollette is wrong, and I am convinced that he has revealed something profound in his defense of licensing parents.

This book consists of eight chapters. The first four outline a theory of developmental moral psychology and ask what implications this theory has for political philosophy if taken seriously. If convinced by the first four chapters, then one should accept what is put forth in the fifth chapter, which argues that we should license parents. Chapters 6 through 8 respond to the strongest objections that can be put forth to a system of licensing parents.

Chapter 1 frames the issue of ISJs and their relation to a stable and well-ordered society and explores the relationship between psychological and political stability. Rawlsian developmental moral psychology, which plays a foundational role in my book, is outlined. I seek a real-world solution; therefore, I suggest that we need to move beyond a hypothetical model where all are ISJs and consider the reality that many people are non-ISJs. I also examine what role envy and resentment have in political philosophy. Something like Rawlsian ISJs are necessary to move from a mostly well-ordered society (our society) towards a completely well-ordered society, but Rawls's account is inadequate.

Chapter 2 begins by asking why Rawls cannot eliminate envy in his system and how this problem is related to his concept of self-respect. I argue that this problem reveals that Rawls offers two distinct conceptions of the self. I survey both concepts and put forth my own ideal—a non-Rawlsian ISJ with self-respect, which differs importantly from a Rawlsian ISJ. I do so after examining what self-respect is, how it is developed, how it works, and how it is different from self-esteem. The self-respect of my ISJs will be developmentally and motivationally underwritten by proper child development in the family, not by recognized rights and liberties. My ISJs serve as the ideal selves that I seek for the rest of the book.

Chapter 3 continues the project of chapters 1 and 2 by asking how children best develop into ISJs and how contemporary political philosophy accounts for this. Political philosophy largely does not consider character development, and I ask why not. This develops into a discussion about what kind of harm results from child maltreatment and the political implications of this harm, especially for becoming an ISJ. I show that contemporary egalitarianism cannot provide adequate treatment to develop children into ISJs if it does not understand how harmful child maltreatment is. I note that we cannot compensate children when they are maltreated, unlike how we can often compensate adults for suffering either misfortune or injustice. I then examine whether the government should provide resources for children or whether it should guarantee that resources are provided by ensuring that children are raised by families. I argue for the latter because child development is predominately a matter of family structures and not something that can primarily be aided directly by the government or residually by means of economic assistance. I conclude by asking how we ought to invest in children.

Chapter 4 describes what *kind* of family is ideal for developing ISJs and preventing maltreatment. After all, not all families provide a healthy environment for child development. I examine various childcare structures, such as single-parent families, cohabiting families, and daycare. In doing so, it becomes apparent that only a particular kind of family provides the cooperation, modeling, stability, intimacy, and privacy that children need to become ISJs. I also discuss why this type of family, which I refer to as *neo-nuclear*, is different from the traditional nuclear family.

Chapter 5 seeks a means to *ensure* that children are raised in environments where they are likely not to be maltreated and are likely to become ISJs. Following chapter 4, it could be suggested that the neo-nuclear family should try to be ensured. However, this is implausible in the real world. Therefore, I seek a means to guarantee that all children are likely to have at least minimally competent parents, which is done by ensuring that those who are most likely to maltreat their children are forbidden from parenting. This chapter is concerned with establishing the conditions that must be met before parental licensing can be implemented justifiably, and it demonstrates that these conditions can be met. I argue for a system of minimal licensing which would preclude relatively few people from parenting. I demonstrate that parental licensing is superior to alternative approaches to protect children, provides equality of opportunity, and it can help move a mostly well-ordered society towards a stable and well-ordered society.

Chapter 6 responds to the objection that licensing parents is unjustified because all humans have a *right* to reproduce and raise children. I begin with a brief examination of parental rights throughout history. I argue that if a right to parent exists, this right is defeasible. More importantly, I argue that viewing the parent-child relationship only in terms of rights is dangerous. Instead, we should also think in terms of duty. We should recognize that the parent-child relationship consists of both rights and duties insofar as the rights of parents result from their duties to their children. I ask why it is generally accepted that prospective adoptive parents can be forbidden from parenting based largely on a system advocated in chapter 5, while it is generally not accepted that prospective biological parents should have to abide by the same system. That is, why do most accept the current licensing of adoptive parents but not the same kind of licensing for non-adoptive parents?

Chapter 7 examines legal precedent and asks when prior restraint can be violated justifiably. That is, when can we justifiably prevent someone from doing something that is potentially harmful to others, and how can we pre-judge a person while still respecting and not stereotyping him unfairly? I also examine how legal precedent unjustifiably biases adults over children and physical harm over psychological harm.

Chapter 8 confronts the objection that licensing parents is an example of protecting ourselves into oblivion. Even if it successfully eliminated child maltreatment, would licensing parents decrease social warmth and trust? This objection is important because increased social warmth and trust are integral and sought throughout this book. I also examine related objections concerning a right to privacy. Privacy is one of the virtues provided by the family because it creates space for intimacy. If the kind of privacy that is needed for proper child development is vitiated by licensing parents, then licensing is largely self-defeating. Lastly, I examine several utopian models of society. I reveal that licensing parents, or some kind of government interference in the family, is common in such models. However, my model is importantly different, and it is neither utopian nor dystopian.

1

A Sense of Justice and Political Stability

Commentators have considered many aspects of John Rawls's *A Theory of Justice*,[1] but his moral psychology has been given little attention. The moral psychology of part III, chapter VIII is usually considered only to examine further the argument for the congruence of (i) justice as fairness and (ii) goodness as rationality in part III, chapter IX and following. Consequently, the full force of Rawls's first stage of stability, where he engages in developmental moral psychology and searches for a sense of justice requisite in a well-ordered society, is often overshadowed by his second stage of stability, where he discusses whether justice as fairness and goodness as rationality are compatible.

I will examine the first stage of stability in relation to a sense of justice and a well-ordered society. I wish to consider the pragmatic elements of these features and will examine them, as much as possible, outside the context of individuals in the Original Position or behind the veil of ignorance. The moral psychology in relation to a sense of justice is not disjoint from the rational choice argument of the analytic construction.[2] I do not mean to imply that they are ultimately separable, but I wish to examine only the moral psychology and sense of justice.

I proceed in this manner because I seek to explore how, at the legislative stage, an actually existing society (more precisely, a nation) with a mostly just structure (but not a Rawlsian well-ordered society) could strive to approximate more closely a completely well-ordered society. To elucidate the kind of society from which I begin, one that is mostly just but not a completely well-ordered society in the Rawlsian sense, I will use the contemporary United States as a model. I do so while recognizing that a completely well-ordered society is an ideal society and that stability is only one element of a well-ordered society; Rawls requires stability to be combined with the

right reasons and be just. This examination will be useful to gain rightful appreciation of the force of Rawls's moral psychology and its need to be explored and improved. I use Rawls's work as a foundation because he puts
forth something about stability and a well-ordered society that needs to be
given serious consideration—something that most post-Rawlsians seem to
overlook. Edward McClennen is one of the few to note this:

> [Rawls's argument] strikes out on a path relatively untraveled by mainstream
> moral philosophers in this century. For the most part, philosophers have shown
> little interest in the problem of psychological stability. Most have been preoc-
> cupied with the issues of meaning and justification. The tacit assumption seems
> to be that if one can show certain principles to be justified, this will suffice to
> ensure that reasonable persons will accept these principles as regulative of their
> affairs. On this view, once the question of acceptable principles is resolved, one
> has, as a bonus, a solution to the problem of stability. Such a view relies on a
> dubious psychology, however.[3]

Similarly, Rousseau notes:

> Just as an architect who puts up a large building first surveys and tests the
> ground to see if it can bear the weight, so the wise lawgiver begins not by lay-
> ing down laws good in themselves, but by finding out whether the people for
> whom the laws are intended is able to support them.[4]

If a society's citizens are not psychologically stable, then that society cannot
be politically stable—regardless of the beauty of a society's constitution or
laws. Also, following Rousseau, laws should be carefully constructed to take
the character of a society's citizens into account.

The first section of this chapter outlines what Rawls means by stability, a
sense of justice, and a well-ordered society. This is critical for understanding
the second section, which explains how Rawlsian ISJs are created. The third
section brings the previous sections together by showing how an increase in
the number of ISJs is crucial to move towards a stable and well-ordered society. It is important to create and perpetuate a character in citizens that mostly
shields them from the dangerous emotion of envy. Consequently, I examine
what Rawls says about the nature of envy and resentment.

1. STABILITY, A SENSE OF JUSTICE, AND
THE WELL-ORDERED SOCIETY

A well-ordered society requires that (i) everyone has a sense of justice, (ii)
everyone accepts the same principles of justice and this is publicly known,

and (iii) the basic social institutions satisfy these principles of justice and this is publicly known.[5]

A sense of justice requires (i) the skill to judge what is just and unjust, (ii) being capable of supporting one's judgments about justice with reasons, and (iii) a desire to act according to the dictates of justice (which are chosen in the Original Position), thus giving to others that which they are entitled (and expecting a similar desire on their part).[6] What is most important about a sense of justice is how it is formed. Rawls explains, "In *Emile* Rousseau asserts that the sense of justice is no mere moral conception formed by the understanding alone, but a true sentiment of the heart enlightened by reason, the natural outcome of our primitive affections."[7]

A society is stable when (i) it is just, (ii) it generates its own support with principles that produce a sense of justice, (iii) everyone possesses a sense of justice, and (iv) everyone desires to do his part to maintain what justice requires.[8]

The above ideals are unattainable in the real world. Yet because I wish to make practical use of these concepts, I start with a mostly just society and ask what it would take to create more individuals with a sense of justice (ISJs). This is done with the presumption that producing and increasing the number of ISJs will help to approximate a stable well-ordered society. Rawls only discusses a well-ordered society, but I wish to offer a theory of transition from contemporary society to a well-ordered society and use the following terms. A society that only has just citizens is *informally well-ordered*, and a society that only has just laws is *formally well-ordered*. A *completely well-ordered* society is informally and formally well-ordered; it is also stable. I take our mostly just society to be formally well-ordered, but if it is to approach a completely well-ordered society then it needs improvement by becoming informally well-ordered. Because the starting point is not the Original Position, not all citizens in my model will already have a sense of justice. This project will be difficult because not all citizens have a sense of justice and there is no stable consensus from which to build; the principles of justice do not initially engender their own support universally.

In working with a mostly just society and towards a completely well-ordered society, it is important to have a society of ISJs, primarily because they will enable a greater degree of political stability; a theory of justice would generate its own support through ISJs. This is important to Rawls: "However attractive a conception of justice might be on other grounds, it is seriously defective if the principles of moral psychology are such that it fails to engender in human beings the requisite desire to act upon it."[9] Important within this concept are reciprocity and trust. Citizens would recognize each other as ISJs and be more likely to trust and cooperate with each other. Ideally, however, it is important that a theory of justice generate its own support with trust in a particular way—with actions motivated *internally* rather than *externally*.[10] That is, the trust that we have with others should not derive primarily from external threats. Society can function with varying degrees of trust, even with little trust. However, lack of trust requires costly economic and social externalities and is not ideal.

2. THE PRINCIPLES OF MORAL PSYCHOLOGY: HOW ISJs ARE CREATED

Rawls introduces three principles (or laws): the morality of authority, morality of association, and morality of principles, which are:

> First law: given that family institutions express their love by caring for his good, then the child, recognizing their evident love of him, comes to love them.
> Second law: given that a person's capacity for fellow feeling has been realized by acquiring attachments in accordance with the first law, and given that a social arrangement is just and publicly known by all others to be just, then this person develops ties of friendly feeling and trust towards others in the association as they with evident intention comply with their duties and obligations, and live up to the ideals of their station.
> Third law: given that a person's capacity for fellow feeling has been realized by his forming attachments in accordance with the first two laws, and given that a society's institutions are just and are publicly known by all to be just, then the person acquires the corresponding sense of justice as he recognizes that he and those for whom he cares are the beneficiaries of these arrangements.[11]

In addition to these laws, Rawls says, "I assume that the sense of justice is acquired gradually by the younger members of society as they grow up. The succession of generations and the necessity to teach moral attitudes (however simple) to children is one of the conditions of human life."[12] He assumes a principle of gradualism about moral development, which reveals a rejection of strong moral innatism, especially of the intuitionist variety. In other words, humans require external influences to develop a sense of justice. Consequently, the moral attitudes yielded by a sense of justice could become extinct if we were to completely fail to nurture or provide moral education for children. If innatist, Rawls's moral psychology must be innate in the weak sense that it is a potentiality that can only become actualized by the external influence of others through acts of affirmation, moral and non-moral, and moral education.[13]

Rawls believes that we gradually develop psychologically and morally, and this gradualism reveals recognizable stages. The boundaries of these stages sometimes overlap because they are not precise. Children who are nurtured properly will not only experience the morality of authority but will also experience the morality of association, and they eventually experience all three moral principles simultaneously. However, it is unclear exactly how gradual these stages are and whether experiencing an earlier stage is a prerequisite for entering a later stage of morality. For example, can a person enter the morality of association stage without first graduating from the morality of authority stage? More importantly for the purposes of this book, can a child derive a sense of justice from the morality of principles stage without previously having experienced, because of childhood neglect, the morality of authority? Likewise, can a child derive a sense of justice from the morality of principles stage if the child did not experience the proper morality of authority because of childhood abuse? Rawls leaves these questions unclear because he assumes that such abuses would not take place in a well-ordered society. But he does imply in his list of the three laws that the second and third laws do require fulfillment of antecedent laws. For example, the second law begins, "given that a person's capacity for fellow feeling has been realized by acquiring attachments in accordance with the first law," and his third law begins, "given that a person's capacity for fellow feeling has been realized by his forming attachments in accordance with the first two laws." One must experience earlier stages properly before successfully evolving to later stages of development. One cannot skip stages, and one must experience each stage in the *proper* moral sense.

I mostly agree with Rawls's order of stages, and I generally agree that one must experience an antecedent stage properly to progress to the next stage. However, I wish to moderate this thesis slightly by putting forth a less controversial one. I require only that it is *generally* true that one needs to experience earlier stages of morality properly in order to attain later stages of morality successfully. For example, it is possible for a child who does not experience the proper morality of authority from his caretakers to achieve a sense of justice successfully at another stage. This is possible if some alternative positive influences in the association stage overlap the authority stage. This is possible, but I will assume that it is extremely difficult to reach later stages of development if earlier stages have not been experienced properly. It would be incredibly difficult for a child who experienced neither the proper morality of authority nor morality of association stages, because of frequent abuse or neglect, to enter the morality of principles stages successfully and gain a sense of justice.

Having described Rawls's principles of morality and how they progress, I turn to an explanation of each stage. Rawls rightly associates the morality of authority as mostly relating to the child-parent relationship. He refers to the morality of authority, when dealing with children, to be in its "primitive form."[14] Non-primitive forms of authority (Rawls never provides a term for this) are experienced by adults, presumably in relationship to the government, police, educators, and religious leaders. The reason why the primitive/non-primitive distinction must be made follows from this analysis:

> [I]t is characteristic of the child's situation that he is not in a position to assess the validity of the precepts and injunctions addressed to him by those in authority, in this case his parents. He lacks both the knowledge and the understanding on the basis of which their guidance can be challenged. Indeed, the child lacks the concept of justification altogether, this being acquired much later. Therefore he cannot with reason doubt the propriety of parental injunctions.[15]

Children are not always at a stage where they lack the capability to assess whether authoritative acts imposed upon them are just, as opposed to merely displeasing. I thus propose an additional term—ultra-primitive morality of authority. "Ultra-primitive" applies to children at the earliest stages of authority where they *completely* lack a concept of justification. Children who are more developed and have a primitive form of justification but are still mostly under parental authority, whether or not they have begun to reach the early stages of the morality of association, will henceforth be referred to as simply being in a primitive (as opposed to an ultra-primitive) stage of morality of authority. The primitive and ultra-primitive stages of the morality of authority are particularly important because at these stages love is first learned through parents taking pleasure in the presence of their child (minimally, not abusing or neglecting the child) and supporting the child's sense of worth and sense of competence, which is important in conjunction with Rawls's Aristotelian Principle.[16] If love is shown by the parent and recognized by the child in the ultra-primitive stage, then the child will experience authority guilt and cease, at least after some time, activities when demanded by the parents. In the primitive stage when parents either demand that the child refrain from doing something or punish the child for doing something against parental dictates, especially if the parent also provides comprehensible justifications and rules for the child, the child will refrain from acting as such out of authority guilt. Acting out of authority guilt is different from refraining from fear because it is recognized by the child that it is the parent's love that motivates punishment.[17]

In the morality of association stage, the family becomes only one of many associations in a child's life. The child interacts with others in games, sports, school, and he becomes acclimated to his environment while also learning the virtues of being a good classmate, friend, and, eventually, citizen and spouse.

The psychological development that allows for this is a more mature ability and increased opportunities to experience the perspective of others. Rawls describes the acquisition of abilities as:

> First of all, we must recognize that these different points of view exist, that the perspectives of others are not the same as ours. But we must not only learn that things look different to them, but that they have different wants and ends, and different plans and motives; and we must learn how to gather these facts from their speech, conduct, and countenance. Next, we need to identify the definitive features of these perspectives, what it is that others largely want and desire, what are their controlling beliefs and opinions. Only in this way can we understand and assess their actions, intentions, and motives. Unless we can identify these leading elements, we cannot put ourselves into another's place and find out what we would do in his position. To work out these things, we must, of course, know what the other person's perspective really is.[18]

Until this point, children usually make judgments according to external actions rather than the complex motives behind those actions. They lack the insight necessary to assess the justice of an act properly. As adults, a refined development of this capacity is necessary to become an ISJ.

The last stage is the morality of principles. Individuals in the association stage are capable of understanding some principles of justice; however, the motive for acting according to such principles derives from societal approbation of parents, teachers, and classmates. At the principles stage, individuals achieve a greater understanding of how the principles of justice, as applied in social arrangements, have promoted their good and the good of others in a cooperative scheme. This knowledge leads citizens to bond from acceptance of the principles of justice—not simply fellow-feeling, as was the case in the previous stages. For this reason, citizens are willing to work towards just institutions and develop the capacity for principle guilt, which is guilt proper because it is a moral sense of guilt, when they violate principles of justice. Either this helps to maintain order by preventing violations of the morality of principles or, if broken, causes members to understand that punitive measures imposed upon them are just.

3. RECIPROCITY, ENVY, RESENTMENT, AND SELF-ESTEEM

One of the major threads that run through Rawls's principles of moral psychology is reciprocity: "we acquire attachments to persons and institutions according to how we perceive our good to be affected by them. The basic idea is one of reciprocity, a tendency to answer in kind. Now this tendency is a deep psychological fact."[19] Reciprocity yields great things when, as Rawls assumes, everyone possesses a sense of justice and this is sufficient motivation to restrict everyone's actions to those that benefit society. But what about when not everyone possesses a sense of justice? McClennen recognizes this problem and remarks:

> The characterization of the sense of justice as a disposition to respond *in kind* invites one to consider the sense of justice as more complex than this—as a disposition not only to do one's part when one expects that others will also, but to respond negatively and even aggressively to those who free-ride at one's expense. On this interpretation, anticipated defections by others can be expected to engender not only distrust (which has direct bearing on rational self-interest) but also attitudes of resentment and hostility.[20]

From this, one could derive that sometimes it is not in our best interest to resist or take aggressive action against those who take advantage of us because they may reciprocate with further aggressive actions, employing even more costly resources. A more fundamental lesson is that we should increase the number of ISJs to minimize free-riders and criminals in the first place. This view is compatible with McClennen's because even after minimizing the number of free-riders and criminals, *some* free-riders and criminals will inevitably exist and some policy will then have to be constructed to deal with them. One who maintains that it is sometimes not in our best interest to resist or take aggressive action against free-riders and criminals could also advocate first seeking to minimize free-riders and criminals via first increasing the number of ISJs and then implementing his policy at a later stage.

It could be objected that at a certain point, one where all or almost all citizens are ISJs, the likelihood of producing free-riders might actually increase. This objection is founded on the assumption that when more citizens become ISJs more citizens will trust and cooperate with each other. The incentive to defect might increase because citizens are unlikely to suspect each other of defection. Therefore, the temptation to take advantage of their fellow citizens may be unbearable for some ISJs. This becomes a sort of Ring of Gyges problem. One could argue that ISJs would be strong enough to overcome this temptation, but that response fails to recognize that ISJs are still human. ISJs will resist temptation much better than non-ISJs, but they will still yield to temptation if it is great enough. It is better to have more ISJs than fewer, and the above objection implicitly assumes something that need not be the case in a stable well-ordered society—the complete elimination of the criminal justice system. Despite needing less law enforcement as the number of ISJs increase, it would never be prudent to eliminate law enforcement—even if the entire population were ISJs. There must be a minimum level of security to adjudicate misunderstandings between ISJs and to provide disincentive to potential defectors. Also, as the number of ISJs increase, the number of criminals would decrease. Therefore, even though a smaller police force would exist, society would also have to police a smaller set of criminals. Lastly, other disincentives would likely replace formal disincentives. For example, the informal disincentive of shame (or guilt) would likely play a greater role in a society composed largely of ISJs. Though shame may not play a large disincentive in the mostly just society in which we now live, that does not mean that it could not emerge as a powerful tool when ISJs are more common.

If we wish to have a stable society that is just, we need to minimize envy, resentment, and hostility. Our current mostly just society is particularly susceptible to these sentiments, as Tocqueville noted,

> One must not conceal from oneself that democratic institutions develop the sentiment of envy in the human heart to a very high degree. It is not so much because they offer to each the means of becoming equal to others, but because these means constantly fail those who employ them. Democratic institutions awaken and flatter the passion of equality without ever being able to satisfy it entirely. Every day this complete equality eludes the hands of the people at the moment when they believe they have seized it, and it flees, as Pascal said, in an eternal flight.[21]

Tocqueville's observations are appropriate because our mostly just society is democratic, and it formally guarantees rights to all. Moreover, great disparities of outcome exist in our mostly well-ordered society. Rawls discusses envy in the sense that Aristotle and Kant spoke of envy—as a passion that does not admit of a mean and a vice of hating mankind.[22] Rawls explains, "We envy persons whose situation is superior to ours . . . and we are willing to deprive them of their greater benefits even if it necessary to give up something ourselves."[23] This differs from contemporary usage, which rarely differentiates between envy and resentment. When one envies, it is *always* with ill intent and the desire to deprive a person or class of persons of something even if it means one must give up something himself to ensure the deprivation.

Rawls makes four more distinctions concerning envy. First, persons experience *benign envy* when they affirm the value of things that others have without wishing others to be deprived of such things. For example, one might say to a friend, "I envy you for having that car." In this case, the friend is usually not envious—he simply wishes that he *also* had such a car. A category similar to that of benign envy is *emulative envy*, where one seeks to achieve what others have achieved. For example, Professor A remarks to Professor B that he is envious of the insightfulness of Professor C, but if

Professor A uses Professor C as a model without seeking to deprive Professor C of his noble trait, then this is not envy proper; it is emulative envy. A third distinction is between particular and general envy:

> The envy experienced by the least advantaged towards those better situated is normally general envy in the sense that they envy the more favored for the kinds of goods and not for the particular objects they possess. The upper classes say are envied for their greater wealth and opportunity; those envying them want similar advantages for themselves. By contrast, particular envy is typical of rivalry and competition. Those who lose out in the quest for office and honor, or for the affections of another, are liable to envy the success of their rivals and to covet the very same thing that they have won.[24]

Fourth, envy is not a moral feeling. The moral feeling closest to envy is resentment. Rawls explains, "If we resent our having less than others, it must be because we think that their being better off is the result of unjust institutions, or wrongful conduct on their part. Those who express resentment must be prepared to show why certain institutions are unjust or how others have injured them."[25] Resentment can be good or bad. Resentment can be bad if it is pervasive because this can reveal the existence of widespread injustice. In this case, it would be good to decrease levels of resentment if the primary reason for doing so is to eliminate the primary motivator of resentment, injustice. This relates to how resentment can be good. Adam Smith explains that justice is "the proper object of resentment," and Butler echoes this when he says, "*deliberate anger or resentment* is essentially distinguished, as the latter is not naturally excited by, or intended to prevent mere harm without appearance of wrong or injustice."[26] Smith explains this further,

> Resentment seems to have been given us only by nature for defence, and for defence only. It is the safeguard of justice and the security of innocence. It prompts us to beat off the mischief which is attempted to be done to us, and to retaliate that which is already done, that the offender may be made to repent of his injustice.[27]

Butler continues by saying how resentment can be a positive tool,

> The indignation raised by cruelty and injustice, and the desire of having it punished, which persons unconcerned would feel, is by no means malice. No, it is resentment against vice and wickedness: it is one of the common bonds, by which society is held together; a fellow feeling, which each individual has in behalf of the whole species, as well as of himself.[28]

In short, Butler says resentment "is to be considered as a weapon, put into our hands by nature, against injury, injustice, and cruelty."[29] When taken together,

Smith's and Butler's views reveal that resentment should have an important role in political philosophy because it is perhaps the primary emotion related to seeking justice. They also expose how resentment can be good or bad by describing the defensive and offensive nature of resentment, although Smith says that it is purely defensive. In the strictly defensive sense, resentment reveals where injustice exists and that we need to defend ourselves. This can lead to an offensive sense, as when Butler calls it a "weapon," when we are moved to act positively (or, more properly, react) to injustice. Therefore, I understand resentment to be only conditionally good. ISJs should be disposed to have resentment *if* exposed to injustice because this would protect them by triggering defensive mechanisms. However, rebelling against injustice would lead to political instability because ISJs would often mount an attack upon injustice that they would confront. Yet we do not wish to have only stability; we wish to have a stable *and* well-ordered society.

Resentment is still bad in a derivative sense because it reveals the existence of some injustice, and injustice should be minimized in a well-ordered society. When I argue that we need less resentment, I am actually saying that resentment reveals injustice, and we need less injustice. This view acknowledges that resentment is a positive and protective common bond of society. A completely well-ordered society will have less resentment than the current mostly well-ordered society. If injustice were ever to befall a well-ordered society, ISJs would be motivated by resentment and would try to return things to their proper order.

In thinking about resentment, it is also helpful to consider the role of gratitude in society. Smith merges resentment and gratitude beautifully when he notes, "Gratitude and resentment, however, are, in every respect, it is evident, counterparts to one another; and if our sense of merit arises from a sympathy with the one, our sense of demerit can scarce miss to proceed from a fellow feeling with the other," and "What chiefly enrages us against the man who injures or insults us, is the little account which he seems to make of us, the unreasonable preference which he gives to himself above us."[30] This may seem to exaggerate the relationship between gratitude and resentment, but a similar relationship is noted by Frederick Douglass, "If any one thing in my experience, more than another, served to deepen my conviction of the infernal character of slavery, and to fill me with unutterable loathing of slaveholders, it was their base ingratitude to my poor old grandmother."[31] Douglass may be wrong in locating lack of gratitude as the primary emotional response to the injustice of slavery, though I do not believe that he is. Even if lack of gratitude is not the primary emotional response to such an injustice, it is surely a powerful emotion. In minimizing the need for resentment, it is also important to note the power of gratitude as a self-reinforcing mechanism of ISJs.

In lessening the destructive influence of the widespread envy that threatens political stability, especially general envy, it also helps to examine the three conditions that Rawls believes encourage hostile outbreaks of envy:

> The first of these is . . . persons lack a sure confidence in their own value and in their ability to do anything worthwhile. Second . . . many occasions arise when this psychological condition is experienced as painful and humiliating. The discrepancy between oneself and others is made visible by the social structure and style of life of one's society. The less fortunate are therefore often forcibly reminded of their situation, sometimes leading them to an even lower estimation of themselves and their mode of living. And third, they see their social position as allowing no constructive alternative to opposing the favored circumstances of the more advantaged. To alleviate their feelings of anguish and inferiority, they believe they have no choice but to impose a loss on those better placed even at some cost to themselves, unless of course they are to relapse into resignation and apathy.[32]

Envy should not exist in a well-ordered society because the aforementioned sense of justice yielded by the principles of moral psychology would not permit it. ISJs could experience benign or emulative envy, but envy proper would not exist. Rawls says so explicitly, "A rational individual is not subject to envy."[33] This book begins not with a society that meets the principles agreed to in the Original Position, which would ensure a completely just system, but with a society that is *mostly* just. If the society is mostly just and most citizens are ISJs, then there should be little envy that derives from injustice. Moreover, we should be more concerned with resentment than envy because resentment is a moral feeling whereas envy is not. While the deleterious effects of envy and resentment both affect stability, it is only resentment that is directly relevant to justice because it is a moral feeling. Here lies an interesting problem: many people in the mostly just society that I am referring to *do* harbor great envy, much of which derives from their belief that the differences among citizens with respect to the distribution of goods, resources, and opportunities are unjust.

To adjudicate whether a claim of injustice is justified and to determine whether a feeling stems from resentment or envy, one must examine the particular society. Suppose that some citizens believe that they have insufficient resources or goods because wealth is fixed in an unchangeable zero-sum game where the disadvantaged are unable to obtain jobs or wealth, as they all have been taken by the rich. If a society had such a fixed economy, then those citizens would be entitled to some redistributions from the wealthy, and their feelings would be resentment—not envy. However, if society had a non-zero sum economy where opportunity, jobs, and resources were not fixed and were available to all, then hostility to the government would be envy—not resentment.[34] Determining whether hostility towards the government stems from envy or resentment may seem like epistemic pedantry with no pragmatic value because hostility in any form is a threat to stability. However, this distinction is important. Determining whether hostility arises from envy or resentment allows one to know whether the problem is the structure of society, such as its laws and institutions, or if the problem is the character of its citizens. If one lives in a society with a mostly just structure but its citizens are envious, then citizens simply lack the requisite sense of justice.[35] If the government is unjust and resentment is widespread, one must both produce more ISJs *and* change the structure of society. However, if the structure of society is mostly just but citizens lack the requisite sense of justice, then one only needs to produce more ISJs by changing the moral sentiments of citizens. The latter is difficult but less difficult than also changing the formal structure of society. I start with a society whose formal structure is already mostly just. Therefore, I will only consider how to produce more ISJs in the rest of this book. I do this because providing children with the capability to become ISJs will help society, but my program is not promulgated merely for the sake of moving towards a completely well-ordered society. Rather, I also seek to help children for their own sake because they are often neglected in both theory and practice. I hope also to show that this injustice is much deeper than most people recognize.

CONCLUSION

If we live in a mostly well-ordered society with a just constitution and system of laws, it is necessary to examine more closely the nature of its citizenry to better approach a stable and well-ordered society. This requires an examination of what makes human beings psychologically stable insofar as they can be internally motivated to be good people. Individuals who fit this description are called ISJs. However, creating ISJs is difficult because humans are psychologically complicated. For example, most humans possess a concept of self-respect that is highly dependent upon a comparison of oneself and others, which often leads to powerful emotions of envy or resentment. Furthermore, humans tend to value reciprocity; therefore, trust can be a fragile thing if cooperation does not exist. If high levels of distrust, envy, or resentment exist, then a society will likely be unstable—regardless of how formally well-ordered it is. That said, we do possess a good idea of how to produce ISJs. For those who doubt this, it is less controversial to acknowledge that certain types of behavior, such as child maltreatment, are unlikely to create ISJs. The key, then, to ensuring more ISJs is simple—nurture children properly. If nurtured properly, cooperation seems more likely because children will likely mature into more trusting and less envious individuals because of the love and education provided in being nurtured. Maltreatment often precludes developing the trust requisite for social cooperation and increases the chances that such children will become envious and threaten social stability. If ISJs are as important as I argue, then it is crucial to describe precisely how they develop and what their character is like. Rawls does an excellent job at this; however, his account is inadequate. I will expose its inadequacies in chapter 2 and offer a different concept of the self as an ideal, a non-Rawlsian ISJ.

NOTES

1. Revised edition, (Cambridge, MA: Harvard University Press, 2000). Hereafter referred to as *TJ*.
2. This important point is noted and argued for by Edward F. McClennen in "Justice and the Problem of Stability," *Philosophy and Public Affairs*, 18 (1989), 6–7.
3. McClennen, 5n.
4. Jean-Jacques Rousseau, *The Social Contract*, ed. Maurice Cranston (London: Penguin Books, 1968), 88.
5. See *TJ*, 4 and 274. Because what is just and unjust is so often in dispute, Rawls believes that existing societies are seldom well-ordered, 5.
6. See *TJ*, 41 and 274–75. Sometimes Rawls refers to "a" sense of justice, sometimes "the" sense of justice. He seems to use these articles interchangeably, but his use of "a" seems to appear more frequently in later works. Though he does not draw a distinction between the two, an important distinction could be made from such varied usage. "A" sense of justice seems to imply one of several possible senses of justice, while "the" sense of justice implies one sense of justice (thus an objectivist justice). Rawls seems, especially when he introduces the concept of an overlapping consensus, to wish only to use "a" sense of justice. As a moral realist, I believe "the" sense of justice to be more important (though I also believe that "a" sense of justice may very well lead to "the" sense of justice).
7. John Rawls, "The Sense of Justice," *The Philosophical Review*, 72 (1963), 281.
8. See *TJ*, 119 and 398.
9. *TJ*, 398. See also *TJ*, 119n: "An important feature of a conception of justice is that it should generate its own support."
10. Derek Phillips also notes this point in *Toward a Just Social Order* (Princeton, NJ: Princeton University Press, 1986), 241. However, Phillips's main account is primarily influenced by Allan Gewirth—not Rawls.
11. *TJ*, 429–30. Rawls cites seven sources of influence from psychology and sociology: Jean Piaget, Lawrence Kohlberg, William McDougall, E. E. Maccoby, Martin L. Hoffman, Albert Bandura, and Roger Brown. See *TJ*, 402n, 403n, and 404n for particular works of these thinkers that influenced Rawls.

12. *TJ*, 405. Also, "the sequence of stages represents a progressive development and not simply a regular sequence," 434.

13. The difference between what I call "weak" and "strong" moral innatism is that the former requires external influences to draw out moral principles, whereas in the latter principles reveal themselves without external prompting. This interpretation is strengthened when taking into account the following from Rawls's "The Sense of Justice," "In the instance of children, one supposes that the capacity for a sense of justice is there and only awaits development. Guardians must secure this development and they must decide for their wards in view of what a person is presumed to want and to claim once he reaches the age of reason," 303.

14. *TJ*, 405. Rawls assumes that in a well-ordered society children are legitimately under the authority of parents in a *family*. By this term, he often refers to "parents," not a "parent," with children. After *TJ*, Rawls loosened such conditions and, I think imprudently, abandoned the two-parent condition.

15. *TJ*, 405.

16. See *TJ*, 406. Rawls's Aristotelian Principle states, "other things equal, human beings enjoy the exercise of their realized capacities (their innate or trained abilities), and that this enjoyment increases the more the capacity is realized, or the greater its complexity," *TJ*, 364. See also *TJ*, 374. The companion effect of the Aristotelian Principle exposes the backdrop for Rawls's principles of morality, especially the first two stages: "As we witness the exercise of well-trained abilities by others, these displays are enjoyed by us and arouse a desire that we should be able to do the same thing ourselves. We want to be like those persons who can exercise the abilities that we find latent in our nature," 376.

17. See *TJ*, 407.

18. *TJ*, 410.

19. *TJ*, 433.

20. McClennen, 13.

21. Alexis de Tocqueville, *Democracy in America*, ed. and trans. Harvey C. Mansfield and Delba Winthrop (Chicago: University of Chicago Press, 2002), Vol. I, Part II, Ch. 5, 189. Max Scheler agrees. However, he says it of *ressentiment*, a notion somewhat different than envy: "*Ressentiment* must therefore be strongest in a society like ours, where approximately equal rights (political and otherwise) or formal social equality, publically recognized, go hand in hand with wide factual differences in power, property, and education," *Ressentiment* (Milwaukee: Marquette University Press, 1998), 33.

22. See TJ, 466n.

23. *TJ*, 466.

24. *TJ*, 466. Rawls is mostly concerned with general envy.

25. *TJ*, 467.

26. Smith, *The Theory of Moral Sentiments* (Amherst, NY: Prometheus Books, 2000). Part II, Sect. II, Ch. I, 114; Samuel Butler, *Fifteen Sermons* (Charlottesville, VA: Lincoln-Rembrandt Publishing, 1993), Sermon VIII, 95.

27. Smith, Part II, Sect. II, Ch. I, 113.

28. Butler, Sermon III, 95–96.

29. Butler, Sermon VIII, 97.

30. Smith, Part II, Sect. I, Ch. V, 108 and Part II, Sect. III, Ch. I, 139.

31. *Narrative of the Life of Frederick Douglass: An American Slave, Written By Himself*, ed. Benjamin Quarles (Cambridge, MA: Harvard University Press, 1988), 76. See also Laurence Thomas, "Gratitude and Social Equality," *The Hedgehog Review*, 3 (Spring 2001).

32. *TJ*, 469.

33. *TJ*, 464. I do not wish to debate whether envy is natural in human beings and thus whether it can be completely eradicated. Rather, I simply wish to argue that if envy is natural then we can at least minimize it, and we can minimize outbreaks that would otherwise result in political instability.

34. This mirrors, perhaps extrapolating a bit, *TJ* on 472. This also demonstrates how powerful economic presuppositions are in moral and political philosophy. If one believes that all economies are zero-sum games, then one will likely argue for extremely egalitarian principles. In the most extreme cases one gets something like Philippe Van Parijs's "Why Surfers Should Be Fed: The Liberal Case for an Unconditional Basic Income," *Philosophy and Public Affairs*, 20 (1991) or, less extreme, Robert E. Goodin's chapter in David Schmidtz and Robert E. Goodin, *Social Welfare and Individual Responsibility* (Cambridge, MA: Cambridge University Press, 1998), 99–195. If one believes that economies are not zero-sum games, then one is more likely, though certainly not necessarily, to support economic libertarian positions. I assume that the mostly just society in consideration has a non-zero sum economy.

35. This is possible in societies that begin as mostly just (or become mostly just), prosper by means of a just structure, especially materially and concerning defense, and then lose an appreciation for the structure that got them to that level, thereby causing the society to collapse or decline. Political philosophy has progressed in developing concepts of a just state and how to attain such a state, but it has been quiet about what happens when a just state is had and it is the citizens, not the state, that are the problem to stability. Rawls approaches this question with his remarks about a self-reinforcing system (see McClennen's observation on 2n of this chapter), but this topic needs more exploration.

2

Non-Rawlsian ISJs and Self-Respect

In chapter 1, I outlined how a Rawlsian well-ordered society, a sense of justice, and political stability are related,[1] and I examined how individuals with a sense of justice (ISJs) are formed.[2] This was done while praising Rawls for requiring that a well-ordered society have just laws *and* just citizens. I refer to societies with only just citizens as *informally well-ordered* and societies with only just laws as *formally well-ordered*. A *completely well-ordered* society is informally and formally well-ordered. In this book, I undertake a theory of transition from the real world to an ideal world, I assume that our society is formally well-ordered, and I inquire how it can be better informally well-ordered to approach a completely well-ordered society. I argue that this necessitates more ISJs in society. In addition to trying to discover how to create more ISJs and prevent non-ISJs, my major objectives are to reveal what type of egalitarianism best provides equality of opportunity and to understand how best to reduce child maltreatment.[3]

This chapter begins with the observation that Rawls does not entirely eliminate envy. Despite assuming that envy does not exist and later arguing that it cannot exist in a stable society, Rawls concedes that disparities beyond certain limits may cause envy. I shall explain why this is puzzling, and a closer examination of envy will reveal a problem concerning Rawls's notion of self-respect. Several commentators have noted that Rawls equivocates between or conflates "self-respect" and "self-esteem." I push the examination further and argue that Rawls actually develops two conceptions of the self. These conceptions differ greatly at the level of origin and motivation. The first is an account where self-respect is founded upon recognized rights and liberties. The second is an account of ideal child development. Rawls favors the first account to describe how self-respect originates and is motivated, whereas I show that his account of self-respect should be founded on and motivated by something like his account of ideal child development.

In developing the latter account, I describe an ISJ that is immune to *Rawlsian* envy because he has deep self-respect. This contrasts with Rawlsian ISJs, who are closely linked to their self-esteem and whose foundation of "goodness as rationality" is not as motivationally firm. If my ISJs are as robust as I allege and can be developed as I claim, then many of Rawls's sophisticated mechanisms become unnecessary. In particular, either condition (a) of his Difference Principle[4] is unnecessary or the set of who constitutes the least advantaged needs to be reevaluated. This arises by asking what would happen if Rawls were to recognize the potential power of his developmental moral psychology and its link to self-respect while taking self-respect, not self-esteem, to be the most important primary good.

Critiquing Rawls is only a means to an end. In critiquing him, I seek to explain the conception of the self embodied in my ISJs. This will be integral for the rest of this book because I later ask how we can approach a completely well-ordered society by producing more ISJs. In doing so, I will gradually identify what the focus of contemporary egalitarianism should be—promoting good character and decent families. Producing ISJs and maintaining healthy families will also help to reduce child maltreatment, which I will later argue is devastating to those maltreated and to society.

1. RAWLS AND ENVY

Rawls uses "envy" in a technical sense, so I will explain what he means by it. I will then show why Rawls needs to eliminate envy, that he does not, and why this is a problem. Rawls says envy is "the propensity to view with hostility the greater good of others even though their being more fortunate than we are does not detract from our advantages . . . we are willing to deprive them of their greater benefits even if it is necessary to give up something ourselves."[5] He believes that this is how Aristotle and Kant spoke of envy; it is a passion that does not admit of a mean, and it is a vice of hating mankind.[6] Concepts close to envy exist, but they are not envy proper because they are not vices: *benign envy* and *emulative envy*. Benign envy occurs when one affirms the value of things that others have without wishing others to be deprived of them. Emulative envy occurs when one affirms the value of things that others have and wishes to have them as well, without wishing that other be deprived of them.[7] Envy is not a moral feeling for Rawls. The moral feeling closest to envy is resentment: "If we resent our having less than others, it must be because we think that their being better off is the result of *unjust* institutions, or *wrongful* conduct on their part. Those who express resentment must be prepared to show why certain institutions are unjust or how others have injured them."[8]

Rawls disallows envy in his system because he does not want it to motivate his principles of justice, "since envy is generally regarded as something to be avoided and feared, at least when it becomes intense, it seems desirable that, if possible, the choice of principles should not be influenced by this trait."[9] Also, envy causes political instability. Rawls justifiably claims, "envy tends to make everyone worse off. In this sense it is collectively disadvantageous."[10] Benign and emulative envy are permissible, but in *A Theory of Justice* Rawls assumes that envy proper does not exist because rational individuals are not subject to envy. I agree with both of these claims, at least when using Rawls's strong notion of envy. Yet Rawls often qualifies these claims. For example, he writes, "The special assumption I make is that a rational individual does not suffer from envy. . . . Or at least this is true as long as the differences between himself and others do not exceed certain limits."[11] In fact, Rawls says that *excusable* envy exists "When envy is a reaction to the loss of self-respect in circumstances where it would be unreasonable to expect someone to feel differently."[12] I am not interested in Rawls's non-envy stipulation for the sake of keeping his principles of justice untainted, but I am concerned about the pragmatic ramifications of envy insofar as they affect political stability. Rawls seems unconcerned with allowing some genuine envy to exist in society. This is clear when he writes, "the principles of justice are not likely to arouse excusable general envy (nor particular envy either) to a troublesome extent. By this test, the conception of justice again seems *relatively* stable."[13] Furthermore, he believes that the principles of justice restrain envy, "when the principles adopted are put into practice, they lead to social arrangements in which envy and other destructive feelings are not likely to be strong."[14]

These concessions to the existence of envy, though merely *some* envy, are worrisome. Rawls recognizes envy as the vice of hating all mankind. I take the vice of hating all mankind, even moderately, to be a threat to a stable society. But even here Rawls retreats and is content with a *relatively* stable society. If nothing else, envy reveals the existence of egoism. One who is willing to deprive another of greater benefits even if it is necessary to give up something himself is the worst kind of egoist. This is problematic for Rawls because he *tries* to remove egoism from his system.[15] It is also unclear why differences between people beyond certain limits cause envy. Likewise, it is unclear what makes this justified in his system, where he otherwise recognizes its danger and assumes it does not exist. Rawls seems to assume that envy is reduced by the principles of justice because the principles of justice promote affirmation of equality. However, the assumption that equality re-duces envy is contestable.[16] Even more interesting is Rawls's claim, from his definition of excusable envy, that envy is a reaction to a loss of self-respect. This is not an anomalous claim; he later states, "the main root of the liability to envy is a lack of self-confidence in our worth combined with a sense of im-potence."[17] A lack of self-respect will make one vulnerable to envy, but I would have thought that Rawlsian ISJs would have self-respect and thus not be prone to envy. This is one of several places where Rawls reveals his belief that self-respect derives from experiencing the principles of justice. This mer-its more treatment, which is given in the next section.

2. RAWLS AND SELF-RESPECT

Self-respect is a primary good for Rawls. Primary goods are "what persons need in their status as free and equal citizens, and as normal and fully coop-erating members of society over a complete life."[18] They are "things that every rational man is presumed to want. These goods normally have a use whatever a person's rational plan of life."[19] Self-respect is conspicuous amongst social primary goods such as rights, liberties, opportunities, income, and wealth. It is particularly conspicuous because Rawls describes self-respect as a "very important," "essential," "main," and "perhaps the most im-portant" primary good.[20] He even says of self-respect, "Without it nothing may seem worth doing, or if some things have value for us, we lack the will to strive for them. All desire becomes empty and vain, and we sink into apa-thy and cynicism."[21] Self-respect should be given such praise, but it is doubt-ful that Rawls is talking about self-respect here. If Rawls is referring to self-respect, he does not properly locate how self-respect develops in humans.

Rawls's clearest articulation of what he means by self-respect occurs in section 67. He identifies two aspects of self-respect:

> [I]t includes a person's sense of his own value, his secure conviction that his conception of the good, his plan of life, is worth carrying out. And second, self-respect implies a confidence in one's ability, so far as it is within one's power, to fulfill one's intentions. When we feel that our plans are of little value, we can-not pursue them with pleasure or take delight in their execution.[22]

Furthermore, Rawls notes that goodness as rationality allows him to better characterize support for the first aspect of self-respect, "(1) having a rational life plan of life, and in particular one that satisfies the Aristotelian Principle; and (2) finding our person and deeds appreciated and confirmed by others who are likewise esteemed and their association enjoyed."[23] Rawls discusses something closer to self-esteem than self-respect, but more importantly Rawls improperly identifies how self-respect is developed. He writes, "The basis for self-respect in a just society is not then one's income share but the publicly affirmed distribution of fundamental rights and liberties. And this distribution being equal, everyone has a similar and secure status when they meet to conduct the human affairs of wider society."[24] Income share should not be a basis of self-respect, but it is unclear how the basis for self-respect is the publicly affirmed distribution of rights and liberties. This is plausible to Rawls because he also believes, "our self-respect normally depends upon the respect of others."[25] Public affirmation of rights and liberties *is* a good thing. Furthermore, there is a sense in which equal status exists when equal distribution and affirmation of rights and liberties exist. Indeed, much of our self-confidence often depends upon how others respect and treat us. However, these concessions are compatible with self-respect arising from a place other than recognition of rights and liberties. As I defend in section 3 of this chapter, self-respect is developed as human beings mature, ideally in a family that bestows parental love. Before developing my thesis concerning self-respect, I show why self-respect cannot originate as Rawls believes it does.

Because Rawls believes that public affirmation of rights and liberties is the basis of self-respect, it is difficult to understand how he can account for people whose actions seem to manifest from self-respect despite lacking public affirmation of their rights and liberties. Consider women or blacks in an earlier part of U.S. history when neither had full public affirmation, especially concerning voting rights. I imagine that many sought equal rights because they believed that they deserved public affirmation of their rights and liberties. Consequently, I presume that many fought for equal public affirmation of rights and liberties because they had self-respect. However, this is precluded in Rawls's account because public affirmation of rights and liberties is the basis for self-respect.[26]

Public affirmation of rights and liberties is largely a good only if one *already has* self-respect. Consider a child who never received love or affection from his parents. His parents need not have been physically abusive; they simply failed to raise him with love or affection. Unless other people provided him with love and affection, the child is unlikely to develop self-respect, as will be shown later in this book. He may have the freedom to exercise his rights and liberties and flourish, but he will unlikely have self-respect and the motivational structure to make use of his rights or liberties.

A society that publicly affirmed one's rights and liberties might even, *at least while using Rawls's sense of self-respect*, cause one to *lose* self-respect. This could happen to one who lived in a society that did not affirm his rights and liberties but now does. If he is a failure in most aspects of life, he may have had "self-respect" prior to affirmation of his rights and liberties because he justified his failures as being the consequence of others not affirming him. If he cannot push blame elsewhere, his "self-respect" will be diminished in a society that now recognizes his rights and liberties.

Rawls's misunderstanding of what self-respect is and how it originates also permeates his theory of happiness and a meaningful life. Assuming Rawls's Aristotelian Principle is true, one would prefer playing chess to checkers. One aspect of having self-respect is "having a rational plan of life, and in particular one that satisfies the Aristotelian Principle."[27] Imagine a person for whom playing chess is a large part of his life plan. Suppose some of his rights and liberties are usurped, and he is now only allowed to play checkers. It is overly dramatic to say that he would lose his self-respect simply because he cannot play chess. If he claimed a loss of self-respect, one might question whether he ever had self-respect. He may be less happy or even depressed, but to say that he would lose self-respect does not accurately capture what is lost.

3. SELF-RESPECT EXPLAINED

I noted, and many have observed,[28] that Rawls equivocates between or conflates "self-respect" and "self-esteem." I have yet to propound a model of self-respect or how it differs from self-esteem, but I will now. This account is not exhaustive; such would require extensive treatment outside the scope of this book. I also introduce a notion of *deep self-respect*, which my ISJs have but Rawlsian ISJs lack. This leads to an examination of how respect is developed and clarifies how self-respect and self-esteem are related. I consider the role of social comparison and social affirmation in developing and maintaining self-respect. A comparison with Rawls's concepts occurs in section 4 of this chapter.

Respect towards persons is a mode of perceiving that others have intrinsic worth, acknowledging this, and acting accordingly.[29] This differs from stipulating that one respects another if he treats that person as a person. Stipulating the necessity of perceiving and acknowledging this value, in addition to acting upon it, is necessary because one could treat another as if he had intrinsic value while believing that he lacked this value.[30] Self-respect is respect for oneself and, residually, others.[31] The need for respect is generated by an object or feature that all persons have—intrinsic worth. Subjects have no control over this feature; all have it regardless of their character. The subject does not generate respect; a subject's interests, plans, desires, hopes, fears, and character have no bearing on his intrinsic worth. Respect is non-evaluative and non-comparative. As such, one *always* ought to respect himself and others; one can never be morally justified in withholding respect. In the sense that I am using respect, one should even respect murderers. Respecting them does not mean approving of their character or deeds; respect is a non-evaluative concept that yields neither approval nor disapproval. One can respect a murderer while punishing or even killing him, assuming proper motivation and means.

Esteem is an evaluative and, often, comparative concept. Non-intrinsic features of the subject are esteemed. However, different subjects have different features, abilities, and character. Accordingly, esteem can be bestowed or withheld subjectively. Indeed, esteem *should* be bestowed or withheld in some cases.

Before clarifying these concepts further, I will compare my respect/esteem distinction with contemporary accounts. This contextualizes my concept better and establishes that my distinction is not purely *ad hoc*. Two popular approaches are used to clarify the concept of self-respect. The first, employed by Stephen Darwall and Stephen Massey, is to stipulate different kinds of respect. The second, favored by David Sachs and Laurence Thomas, is to stipulate between respect and esteem. I use the latter approach. There is nothing wrong with the former approach; of the accounts mentioned, I prefer Darwall's overall. The two approaches overlap, but the latter account best exposes Rawls's error. It also establishes more distance between the concepts of self-respect and self-esteem, which I believe is needed. Most importantly, I believe that *healthy* self-esteem relies upon self-respect. However, speaking only in terms of different kinds of respect results in one kind of respect resting on another kind of respect, and this gets confusing quickly. Darwall distinguishes *recognition self-respect* from *appraisal self-respect*, saying, "the sort of regard involved in recognition respect is a regard for a fact or feature having some weight in deliberations about how one is to act."[32] Persons are owed something by virtue of being persons, and this demands that we should take them seriously in a certain way and tailor our behavior accordingly. By contrast, "Appraisal respect is an attitude of positive appraisal of a person either judged as a person or as engaged in some more specific pursuit."[33] This distinction allows us to say consistently that (in one sense) all people are entitled to categorical respect while (in another sense) they may not deserve respect. My notion of respect is close to recognition respect; Rawls's is close to appraisal respect. Massey also distinguishes between two kinds of respect by asking whether self-respect is a moral (objective) or psychological (subjective) concept. He argues, "If it [self-respect] is an objective notion, then a self-respecting person must not simply value himself, but properly value

himself, however, the notion of 'properly' valuing oneself is defined."[34]
Massey has four criteria for subjective self-respect:

1. A person who respects himself identifies with a project, activity, or status which he regards as having value. . . .
2. Identification with a project, activity, or status provides both a standard of worthy or appropriate conduct and a desire to act in accordance with it. . . .
3. A person with self-respect believes that he has acted in accordance with his conception of what is worthy. . . .
4. A self-respecting person is confident that he will continue to act in accordance with his standards of worthy behavior.[35]

Massey's subjective self-respect is extremely close to Rawls's self-respect, and my concept of self-respect overlaps Massey's objective self-respect.

Laurence Thomas also draws a moral/psychological distinction, but he makes a distinction between self-respect (moral) and self-esteem (psychological). He appeals to William James's formulation that self-esteem equals successes divided by aspirations.[36] Thomas states that self-respect "consists in having the belief that one has and is worthy of full moral status," and "is a sense of worth which we are justified in having in virtue of the fact that we are persons."[37] James's account of self-esteem roughly corresponds to Rawls's notion of self-respect, but Rawls's is more sophisticated. Thomas's notion of self-respect is close to mine, but it seems less robust; he requires *belief* of intrinsic value without requiring that *behavior* follow from this recognition. David Sachs makes a respect/esteem distinction akin to Thomas's, but Sachs does not provide a clear definition of either concept. Nonetheless, Sachs seems to embrace a notion of self-respect close to mine.

Having outlined my account of the distinction between self-esteem and self-respect and framed this within contemporary work on the subject, I will try to elucidate the distinction with some examples and further considerations. One may object that my account does not allow for praise or blame. One should always respect oneself and others, and this sort of respect is for persons as persons. Praise or blame can be issued in the realm of esteem. Narrowly defining respect entails that different kinds of esteem will exist, such as *character esteem* and *ability esteem*. Therefore, we can make judgments about character, and this often even includes making judgments about whether oneself or others have self-respect. A component of the set of things that most people esteem is respect. If a man demonstrates a lack of respect because he beats his wife, we evaluate him negatively. We can accurately remark that he lacks self-respect and respect for his wife. We should not, however, say that we lack respect for him; he maintains intrinsic value despite his poor character. Stating that we do not respect him denies his intrinsic value. We should instead observe, "he lacks self respect" or "I do not esteem his character."

It may be objected that in my account it is impossible to disrespect somebody. However, it is true that people can disrespect others; I conceded this in the wife-beating scenario. However, to disrespect is not simply a matter of not evaluating another highly. It is to not perceive another's intrinsic value, to not acknowledge this, or to not treat the other as if he had intrinsic worth. Likewise, one can lack self-respect. This does not simply mean feeling unhappy or unsatisfied. Lacking self-respect means not perceiving one's intrinsic worth, not acknowledging it, or not treating oneself as if one had intrinsic worth. If a person lacks self-respect, then he should be respected but not character esteemed. The reason for this is that his lack of self-respect does not diminish or extinguish his intrinsic value. Likewise, if one disrespects another then the other's intrinsic worth is unaffected.

Some persons make for interesting cases in my taxonomy. Newborn babies presumably cannot perceive intrinsic value in themselves or others; they lack the requisite cognitive structure. This precludes them from respecting in any way. Yet their lack of being able to respect does not entail that they lack intrinsic worth. Presuming that newborns have intrinsic worth, they ought to be respected—even if they cannot yet (or ever) respect. Older children are difficult because intrinsic worth is a vague concept, and it is unclear when children perceive such a thing. Nonetheless, most children eventually attain a semblance of the notion and could then be said to respect themselves and others.

Most of the ambiguity in my model will reside within the realm of esteem, and this is because there are different kinds of esteem. However, I conjecture that this ambiguity will have to exist somewhere. There is one more thing about respect which may not be clear. That is, it is important to distinguish the name of the object of value, intrinsic worth, from the name of properly recognizing this value, self-respect. Consider the following: "in order to have self-respect, a person need not have a morally acceptable character. For the belief that one is deserving of full moral status is certainly compatible with the belief that one's moral character is not up to par. And this underscores the fact that self-respect, as I conceive it, does not turn upon a person's abilities."[38] I believe Laurence Thomas equivocates here by using "self-respect" and "full moral status" interchangeably. As it is, this passage does not make sense on my model. However, it makes sense if what is meant is: "in order to have full moral status, a person need not have a morally acceptable character." Phrased this way, the passage makes sense and is true. If Thomas does not make this mistake and believes what was originally written, then I take the passage to be false because persons *do* need to have morally virtuous character to have self-respect. Full moral worth and intrinsic value have nothing to do with ability, but self-respect does. If Thomas maintains his claim, then he can continue to justify it by remarking that people vary in their abilities to carry out acts of respect. He continues along these lines, "Consider, for example, such moral virtues as honesty and kindness. The former calls for a considerable measure of resoluteness, a strong will one might say; the latter is intimately connected with the capacity for sympathetic understanding."[39] I concede all of this independently; however, Thomas's overall position commits him to accepting, say, that an irresolute serial child rapist can maintain self-respect because he recognizes his own moral worth and the moral worth of children but lacks the character structure to prevent him from raping children. In fact, on the above account it is difficult to imagine what would count as lacking self-respect. Those who perceive and acknowledge their intrinsic worth and that of others have excellent reason to treat people as if they had intrinsic moral worth. However, those without self-respect have little reason, other than pragmatic ones such as the law, to treat people as if they had intrinsic value. It thus makes sense that those with self-respect will also have good moral character and not infringe upon that which respecting the moral worth of others dictates. Likewise, it is unsurprising that those who are unable to act as if others do not have intrinsic worth do not have good moral character, a condition that results from lacking self-respect. I understand intrinsic value to be unearned and inalienable, but I take self-respect to be something earned and alienable, which is what makes it a virtue. We might give the irresolute rapist a lighter sentence for his offense if his irresoluteness was genuine and of no fault of his own (presuming that he could be successfully treated), but that does not negate the fact that his act demonstrated a lack of self-respect. Of course, Thomas may merely be making an error of equivocation.

4. THE ESTEEM SET, ENVY, AND SELF-RESPECT

I will now develop the concept of an esteem set because it illuminates the relationship between respect and esteem. An esteem set is the set of all things that one esteems. This involves different kinds of things esteemed. For example, I have already mentioned character and ability esteem. My esteem set is compatible with Sachs's understanding of the relationship between respect and esteem. He notes, "The possession of one's self-respect, I am taking it, then, is in every case a ground for self-esteem, and, in the usual case, contributes to it," and "retaining one's self-respect supplies a ground or reason for self-esteem; and that any loss or lack of respect is a ground for self disesteem."[40] If a person has self-respect then he must esteem himself to some degree because self-respect requires perceiving and acknowledging one's intrinsic value. Properly acknowledging one's intrinsic value is to value it, though to what degree will be discussed shortly. Having self-respect entails having some self-esteem, but having self-esteem does not necessarily entail having self-respect. This explains how some criminals can esteem themselves but lack self-respect. Most believe Sachs's passages above uncontroversial while finding their complement controversial:

> [N]either a lowering of one's self-esteem nor any enhancement of it furnishes any ground or reason whatsoever for one to come to possess less or more self-respect. Thus if a man no longer takes pride in something, upon which he had once esteemed himself—realizing he was not, for example, quite the gymnast or algebraist he once thought he was—his lower estimate does not in itself constitute a ground for lessening self-respect.[41]

By definition, one's intrinsic value is unaffected by disesteem. It is less clear, though I believe true, that self-respect cannot be affected by disesteem. Minimally, this needs an explanation. Rawls repeatedly claims that a lack of things that we esteem, such as affirmation from others or the ability to do things we enjoy and value, can diminish our self-respect. My disagreement with Rawls might be thought to be due to a terminological difference, but that is not the case. For example, Moody-Adams, who recognizes that Rawls uses 'self-respect' when he means 'self-esteem,' still maintains, "while self-esteem—confidence in one's life plan—is distinct from self-respect—a due sense of one's worth—severe diminutions in self-esteem many nonetheless have devastating effects on self-respect."[42] To explain why this is wrong, I will sketch how ISJs develop self-respect and then relate this to how self-respect works in an esteem set.

I do not take publicly affirmed rights and liberties as the basis for self-respect. Parental love is the foundation of self-respect. This overlooked thesis has recently been defended by Thomas: "Parental love, then, provides the grounding for the sense of worth bestowed by moral equality—such love provides the soil, if you will, in which the sense of worth afforded by moral equality may take root . . . parental love paves the way for having the proper appreciation of one's moral worth."[43] There are two major sources of human worth: self-respect and self-esteem (it is probably because both are modes of valuing that they are often used interchangeably). I understand Thomas to be describing the foundation of the former and Rawls to be discussing the latter.

Parents ideally help to nurture self-respect, which results in good moral character, while also nurturing things other than perceiving, acknowledging, and
properly acting in accord with one's intrinsic worth, such as developing various abilities. When esteem is nurtured but self-respect is not, the result is an
incomplete human being with little motivation to regulate his thoughts and
behavior according to the intrinsic value of himself and others. When this
happens, children are highly unlikely to become ISJs.

Helping a child become proficient in performing tasks is extremely important, but it is meaningless and even dangerous if not coupled with nurturance
of self-respect. Thomas notes, "parental love engenders and sustains in the
child basic psychological security, which we understand simply as a sense of
worth that is in no way tied to performances. As a result of their displays of
love, the child believes that his parents' acceptance of him and their desire to
support him is not tied to performances."[44] It is here that children come to understand the gift of intrinsic value; they themselves are loved *unconditionally*.
This provides a shield for them because they know that even if they fail in a
task or are not treated properly by others they still have the love of their parents. Children generally become increasingly competent in tasks, and they
generally move away from their parents. They will not always have directly
expressed categorical love from their parents. If raised properly, this love will
become clear to them frequently and deeply. Just as past successes may soften
the blow of present failure, the deeply rooted experience of categorical love
will remain a foundation for children as they become autonomous and experience the vicissitudes of life. This will encourage them to have self-love and
develop fellow feeling. The fellow feeling developed in the parent-child relationship serves as a foundation for how one relates to peers and, later, fellow
citizens. Parental love can provide a sustaining source of worth that exists regardless of performance, and this engenders *deep self-respect*. Deep self-
respect involves more than merely perceiving, acknowledging, and acting in
a certain way in response to intrinsic value. It involves valuing one's self-
respect as the *predominant* value in one's esteem set. ISJs with deep self-
respect are the very individuals needed to move towards a completely well-
ordered society and maintain stability. Rawls astutely recognizes that to solve
the problem of instability justice must generate its own support.[45] Furthermore, he recognizes, "Self-respect is reciprocally self-supporting" because
"those who respect themselves are more likely to respect each other and con-
versely."[46] But Rawls yields only an account of self-esteem, and self-esteem
is not necessarily self-supporting. Others may affirm a person in many ways,
but a person who derives his worth entirely from others demonstrates a lack
of self-respect, and such a person will sometimes perceive that he has no
worth because some others may disesteem him completely. When ISJs with

deep self-respect are developed, their secure sense of value and fellow feeling will increase societal trust, an integral feature of stability in a free society.

Now that I have developed a concept of respect and its origin and have described what an esteem set is, the two can be brought together to show why my ISJs are not prone to envy and why their self-respect remains intact despite performance failure, being disesteemed, or being disrespected. Think of an esteem set as a large translucent rubber ball that can be held in front of oneself with two hands. Within this set exists the entirety of things that one esteems, from achievements to self-respect. If child development and its relationship to self-respect are as I describe, then self-respect is foundational in the life of a self-respecting person. Not only does a person derive much esteem from having self-respect, but having self-respect puts constraints upon what one can do in all areas of his esteem set. This is not to say that the moral life should be identical to the scope of one's entire life; the most fulfilling life generally consists, I take it, of partaking of moral and amoral (but not immoral) activities. I thus concede to Rawls that playing chess may be an important part of a meaningful life. All that I mean by the above is that such activities should be permissible according to the moral aspect that is founded upon self-respect. When looking at one's esteem set with hands extended in front of oneself, suppose that one can see all that one esteems at the same time through the translucent ball. Suppose further that the objects esteemed vary in size and shape because we value many different things in life, value them differently, and value them with different intensity. Because self-respect is the foundation of a person with deep self-respect, it will occupy a large space within the ball; it will also be located at the forefront of the ball, nearest one's eyes, and one will see all other things *through* it.

Suppose that one values cars. Despite valuing cars, a self-respecting person could not envy another's car.[47] That is, he would neither be hostile towards the owner for his possession nor be willing to deprive the owner of the car while being willing to give up something of his own to do so. He would be valuing the car through the lens of self-respect. Self-respect would dictate that there are certain things that he cannot do in other realms of value, and this would be deeply rooted in his psychology. Furthermore, he would have fellow feeling for the other and recognize the other's claim to the car. Lastly, he will realize that he still maintains a great deal of esteem as a self-respecting person despite not having the other's car. He may esteem himself more if he had the car because having it might make his life more complete and happier, but that decreased self-esteem has no relationship to his self-respect.

Actually, decreased self-esteem does have a relationship with self-respect. However, it does not have the relationship that most people might think that it has. Consider again Moody-Adams, "while self-esteem—confidence in one's life plan—is distinct from self-respect—a due sense of one's worth—severe diminutions in self-esteem many nonetheless have devastating effects on self-respect."[48] This position is held by many regardless of how they distinguish esteem from respect or how robust their notion of self-respect is. However, if a person develops deep self-respect in the way that I have described, Moody-Adams's view is incorrect. Rather, what follows is only that if something causes a severe diminution in self-esteem then this has a harmful effect on one's esteem set. This, however, does not necessitate losing one's self-respect. Consider a self-respecting person who suffers a severe diminution of self-esteem because his wife left him for another man (or he loses an enjoyable job, fails his Ph.D. defense, etc.). He will esteem himself less, at least for a certain time. He will likely value himself less following, especially immediately after, such events. He may become depressed. Suppose even that all of the above are experienced in the same week and the only thing left intact within his esteem set is his self-respect. Recognizing that he at least still has self-respect will not eliminate the pain, as maintaining self-respect is compatible with deep pain and even depression. It is often assumed that such emotions are incompatible with or reveal a lack of self-respect, but I fail to see why this must follow. Despite not allaying the pain fully, self-respect is a stronghold that is particularly important when one loses self-esteem.[49] Self-respect does not diminish pain partially because the object of disesteem is so valuable that the person has difficulty focusing upon little else. However, a self-respecting person sees even such things through an intrinsic lens, though the lens may be somewhat blurred by the pain. Self-respect remains a predominant part of one's esteem set, and it still shapes and constrains what an individual may do even if it temporarily appears partially diminished. To say that a person would lose self-respect in such situations is not simply to say that he will suffer pain or depression; it is to say that he will fail to recognize his intrinsic worth, fail to acknowledge it, or fail to treat himself or others as if they had intrinsic worth. It is unclear that a drop in esteem would affect self-respect thusly.

I do not wish to portray my ISJs to be so robust as to be non-human. I analyzed how the esteem set of an ISJ with deep self-respect would work if he were properly nurtured and provided with parental love. If my concept of the self appears too robust, I suspect that this may be because few people experience what I have described. However, recall that my larger project is to promote environments amenable to nurturance while preventing environments that provide neither parental love nor proper nurturance. In rare situations the depth of self-respect may be inadequate to maintain a moral character. Consider Bruno Bettelheim on life in a concentration camp:

To survive as a man, not as a walking corpse, as a debased and degraded but still human being, one had first and foremost to remain informed and aware of what made up one's personal point of no return beyond which one would never, under any circumstances, give in to the oppressor, even if it meant risking and losing one's life. It meant being aware that if one survived at the price of overreaching this point one would be holding on to a life that had lost all meaning. It would mean surviving—not with lower respect, but without any.[50]

This passage beautifully elucidates how deep self-respect works insofar as it, at the forefront of one's mind, limits what one may do. It also captures the importance of self-respect in a meaningful life. At the risk of losing self-respect, one should risk losing one's life. That being said, one cannot expect or blame an otherwise self-respecting person from acting disrespectfully in extreme situations such as being in a concentration camp. In conceding this, I disagree with Thomas's claim that "it is a virtue of having self-respect that a person will not go on living a morally virtuous life if all the world should treat her immorally."[51] Thomas bases this on the claims that "it cannot be reasonably expected that self-respecting individuals will not experience resentment when subject to continuous wrongdoing" and "built up resentment invariably gives rise to the concomitant feelings of rancor and anger" which might cause one to disrespect another because the other's vices are magnified even as one recognizes that the other deserves moral treatment.[52] ISJs with deep self-respect can harbor resentment; that is the proper moral emotion in response to injustice, per Rawls's definition. But not living a morally virtuous life is never a virtue; it can, at best, be what is reasonably expected of humans when pushed past a certain point, and Thomas is correct about this. There seems to be an implied premise that if pushed past a certain point one will revolt against the oppressor and such a revolt demonstrates a lack of self-respect. Revolting against one's oppressor can be done in a manner that demonstrates a lack of respect for the other, but it need not. I see, for example, no reason why trying to kill an oppressor in order to escape/revolt upon the verge of likely losing one's self-respect is necessarily incompatible with having self-respect. This is not to say that people who do not revolt in such extreme situations are to be blamed. Rather, it is to observe that resentment is compatible with self-respect; claiming that it is a virtue of self-respect that a person stops living a morally virtuous life is to describe the event improperly.

5. RAWLS'S SECOND CONCEPTION OF THE SELF

I have found Rawls's account of self-respect inadequate largely because it is actually an account of self-esteem. Some might take this to be devastating to

Rawls because an account that seeks only to increase self-esteem might yield the result that criminals or moral reprobates who either do not realize their wrongdoing or who recognize but value it can maintain "self-respect" because they have high self-esteem. However, Rawls's account cannot be disposed of so quickly because he provides a sophisticated account of self-esteem that is in accordance with the principles of goodness as rationality where one's life plans are rational. Therefore, "His rational plan of life is consistent with the constraints of right."[53] Rawls recognizes that self-esteem needs to be founded on something that would ensure that which is esteemed is in accordance with the good. Otherwise, he cannot avoid the problem of criminals having "self-respect." However, rationality without the sufficient affectational structure does not ensure pursuit of the good. Neither goodness as rationality nor affirmation of rights and liberties provides the proper motivational structure for individuals to have self-respect. Rawlsian goodness as rationality only stipulates that rational deliberation will yield the good, and public affirmation only provides a space for self-respect (which must be developed elsewhere). Rawls develops his account of self-respect in his chapter, "Goodness as Rationality," but his following chapter, "A Sense of Justice," would have provided a better place to provide its foundation. I will show here how Rawls has the essential elements for an ISJ with self-respect, but he discards them in preference of an ISJ tied more closely to self-esteem and an account that cannot explain why individuals would acquire and be motivated to have self-respect.

Rawls's second conception of the self, revealed in his chapter "A Sense of Justice," recognizes the fundamental element of my ISJs—parental love. He writes that a child is "made aware that he is appreciated for his own sake by what are to him the imposing and powerful reasons in his world. He experiences parental affection as unconditional," and

> Their [parents] love is displayed by their taking pleasure in his presence and supporting his sense of competence and self-esteem. They encourage his efforts to master the tasks of growing up and they welcome his assuming his own place. In general, to love another means not only to be concerned for his wants and needs, but to affirm his sense of worth as a person.[54]

Rawls then builds from this foundation and puts forth an account whereby parental love is the foundation for fellow feeling and fellow feeling then engenders confidence and trust. Incidentally, this would evade Rawls's worries about free-riders because what motivates free-rider problems are egoists; Rawls's second account does a superb job of producing altruists. Yet Rawls ultimately backs away from fellow feeling and instead favors rules as the motivational structure for adult ISJs. He says, "It would seem that while the individual understands the principles of justice, his *motive* for complying with them, *for some time at least*, springs largely from his ties of friendship and fellow feeling for others, and his concern for the approbation of the wider society," and "the citizen body as a whole is *not* generally bound together by ties of fellow feeling between individuals, but by the acceptance of public principles of justice."[55]

The principles of justice, public affirmation of rights and liberties, and self-esteem are important, but they should be understood in the proper context. If individuals are given the freedom to enjoy equal rights and liberties, then this provides excellent space for those with self-respect to flourish. However, rights and liberties are unlikely to enable those without self-respect to flourish. Formal rules or their public affirmation do not yield self-respect. Self-esteem is important, but it is only good if founded on self-respect. Likewise, high self-esteem derived from one's life plans often indicates a meaningful or happy life. However, such esteem and life plans need to be founded upon having self-respect in a certain way. Self-respect provides a considerable amount of self-esteem. Only saints are content with morality alone in their esteem set, so things such as chess complement the moral life by making it more meaningful. A life of only chess would lack in fullness for most psychologically healthy humans. Lastly, just because others do not respect themselves or us does not mean that we cannot respect them and ourselves. It may be difficult, but in most instances it is reasonable to ask of a self-respecting person.

6. FINAL OBJECTIONS AND CONSIDERATIONS

Having sketched my account and located some deficiencies in Rawls's account, I will consider related concerns. The first is that, in trying to yield more ISJs to create a better society, my account demonstrates the idealism of ivory tower philosophy and has no use for improving actual society. In particular, many may be suspicious of my elimination of envy. Helmut Schoeck objects,

> Nearly all utopias in which ultimate and universal peace and contentment reign, as well as all markedly 'practical' progressive programs for a harmonious humanity, assume that it is somehow possible to 'de-envify' human beings. If only all were housed and fed, in good health and educated to at least a minor university level, all conflict, prejudice, and crime attributable to envy-motives would disappear.[56]

Schoeck is correct in that external leveling-down (or at least equalizing in some way), which is what his argument seems to attack, is often imprudent and dangerous.[57] I concede that one can be housed, fed, in good health, and educated and still be envious; Schoeck's observations attack many egalitarian theories forcefully and successfully. However, I do not believe that his list of what people value is exhaustive; in fact, his list omits that which is or can be the most important in a completely well-ordered society. Thomas Scanlon recognizes the proper space of valuing:

> The degree to which the accomplishment and rewards of some people under-mine the grounds of other people's sense of self-worth depends upon the degree to which particular forms of ability and accomplishment are regarded as having pre-eminent importance. Even a highly differentiated meritocratic system of of-fices and rewards might not undermine the self-respect of those who are not suc-cessful in it if the attainments which it recognizes and rewards are regarded as less important indices of self-worth than good moral character, conscientious-ness as a citizen, and devotion to the well-being of one's family and friends."[58]

Education and wealth may yield envy in a non-informally well-ordered so-ciety, but it is less clear why disparities would yield envy if a society pri-marily valued other things. Envy would be less prevalent in a society where ISJs primarily valued being good citizens, parents, or friends. Fur-thermore, in a society that valued good citizenship or good parenting, it is difficult to imagine what envy would look like. Schoeck does not consider that envy can be reduced *internally* via character formation in individuals. He is preoccupied with equalizing things *external* to persons as a means to reduce envy. My view of human nature may seem to presuppose supererogation about one's emotions, but I suspect that the reason for such a suspicion is that non-ISJs exist in our society and cause much harm. Also, when I state that ISJs should not have any envy, I carefully stipulate that they lack envy proper. However, when most people speak of envy and its widespread nature, they refer to benign envy or emulative envy, which I concede ISJs will have.

I take a middle path in the debate between realists who understand humans mostly as egoists and idealists who mostly understand humans as altruists. Many people are egoistic, and we ought to provide formal mechanisms so that they cannot take advantage of others. I agree that government would not be necessary if men were angels but men are not angels; therefore, government and laws are necessary. I also agree with Rawls that, "The need for the en-forcement of rules by the state will exist even when everyone is moved by the same sense of justice."[59] Yet a free society requires that people have good character, fellow feeling, and trust. It is better to have a society with an ex-cellent constitution and laws with virtuous citizens than to have a society with an excellent constitution and laws with immoral citizens. I do not believe that it will ever be possible that *all* citizens in a society will be ISJs. Yet this is compatible with the thesis that society would be better if *more* citizens were ISJs. In the realm of fairness, society should have an interest in trying to provide all of its citizens with the capability to become ISJs and have an environment where they can develop self-respect. This entails the need to re-think the role of children in society because child development is of the utmost importance to being an ISJ. Realists of the *laissez-faire* variety should also be attracted to the idea of having as many ISJs as possible in society because such individuals internally regulate themselves and require less external regulation by the government. Self-interest is innocuous if it is founded on an altruistic foundation. That is, as long as one's self-interest is pursued while respecting oneself and others. This parallels the need for self-esteem to be founded on self-respect.

Lastly, it may be asked in what sense self-respect is the most important good and what this means. Massey poses this question and notes that problems arise when trying to make either subjective or objective notions of self-respect the most important primary good, and Henry Shue provides an analysis concerning whether liberty should be given priority over self-respect.[60] Thomas and Yanal argue that self-esteem cannot be distributed as a primary good, at least not equally.[61] Catriona McKinnon and Jeffrey Moriarty derive arguments for an unconditional basic income and a living wage from Rawls's argument that self-respect is the most important primary good.[62] And Nir Eyal argues, "for Rawls, justice mandates that each social basis for self-respect be equalized (and, as a second priority, maximized). Curiously, for Rawls, that principle ranks higher than Rawls's two more famous principles of justice—equal liberty and the difference principle."[63] "Correcting that confusion [between respect and esteem]," Eyal notes, "forces Rawls to accept objectionable and illiberal politics. Surprisingly, a *consistent* Rawls must endorse absolute economic equality, deny liberty any priority whatsoever, or sponsor still other illiberal political views."[64] I am confident that Rawls does not mean to give lexical priority to self-respect over his two principles of justice. He is fairly clear about this: "The best solution is to support the primary good of self-respect as far as possible by the assignment of the basic liberties that can indeed be made equal, defining the same status for all."[65] Rawls here emphasizes the extreme importance of self-respect in the sense that it provides stability and glues everything together. Recall that for Rawls justice should generate its own support, and self-respect is integral in the sense that it is the self-supporting mechanism.

Because I assume formal well-ordering, I simply note that the two principles of justice *and* self-respect are necessary in a completely well-ordered society. My project tries to ensure, though it cannot guarantee (certainly not equally), that all will have the capability to become an ISJ. Recall that

Rawls's first principle states, "Each person is to have an equal basic right to
the most extensive source of liberties compatible with a similar scheme of liberties for others."[66] The second principle states, "Social and economic inequalities are to be arranged so that they are both (a) to the greatest expected
benefit of the least advantaged and (b) attached to offices and positions open
to all under conditions of fair equality of opportunity."[67] The first principle is
clearly necessary, and I accept (b) of the Difference Principle, though I believe that the "economic" clause is probably unnecessary (the reason for this
becoming clear in later chapters). The real question, then, is what (a) means.
If it is necessary at all, in light of this chapter, I take it that the set of the least
advantaged should be identical to the set of children because if a society can
ensure that children are provided with the requisite nurturance then such children will likely become ISJs. A society of ISJs in a formally well-ordered society would yield a completely well-ordered society. What matters concerning lexical priority is that self-respect should be given lexical priority over
self-esteem. In fact, self-respect should be given exclusivity because self-
esteem will likely be yielded, and in a good way, once self-respect is ensured.
This only works, however, when a notion of self-respect stronger than
Rawls's is used and when a notion of ISJs that is stronger than Rawlsian ISJs
is employed.

NOTES

1. A *well-ordered society* requires that (i) everyone have a sense of justice, (ii)
everyone accept the same principles of justice and this is publicly known, and (iii) the
basic social institutions satisfy these principles of justice and this is publicly known.
See *TJ*, 4 and 274. A *sense of justice* requires (i) the skill to judge what is just and unjust, (ii) being capable of supporting one's judgments about justice with reasons, and
(iii) a desire to act according to the dictates of justice (which are chosen in the Original Position), thus giving to others that which they are entitled (and expecting a similar desire on their part). See *TJ*, 41 and 274–75. A society is *stable* when (i) it is just,
(ii) it generates its own support with principles that produce a sense of justice, (iii)
everyone possesses a sense of justice, and (iv) everyone desires to do his part to maintain what justice requires. See *TJ*, 119 and 398.
2. "First law: given that family institutions express their love by caring for his
good, then the child, recognizing their evident love of him, comes to love them. Second law: given that a person's capacity for fellow feeling has been realized by acquiring attachments in accordance with the first law, and given that a social arrangement is just and publicly known by all others to be just, then this person develops ties
of friendly feeling and trust towards others in the association as they with evident in-
tention comply with their duties and obligations, and live up to the ideals of their sta-
tion. Third law: given that a person's capacity for fellow feeling has been realized by

his forming attachments in accordance with the first two laws, and given that a society's institutions are just and are publicly known by all to be just, then the person acquires the corresponding sense of justice as he recognizes that he and those for whom he cares are the beneficiaries of these arrangements," *TJ*, 429–30.

3. What counts as child maltreatment is complicated. Here I refer to maltreatment as abuse or neglect that would justify some sort of legal action against a parent in our society today. I focus on physical abuse and neglect because, though it is sometimes controversial what these are, they are less controversial than other things, such as indoctrination. For example, is it abusive to raise one's child as a neo-Nazi, a religious fundamentalist, or an atheist? Similarly, is it abusive to not allow one's child medical treatment or what is deemed by most to be an adequate education? These latter sets of questions are so important that they merit treatment in a book of their own. Consequently, I do not give them treatment here but refer the reader to the following sources if interested: I. A. Snook, ed. *Concepts of Indoctrination: Philosophical Essays* (London: Routledge & Kegan Paul, 1972); Will Kymlicka, *Liberalism, Community, and Culture* (Oxford: Clarendon, 1989); Chandran Kukathas, "Are There Any Cultural Rights?," *Political Theory*, 20 (1992); William Galston, "Two Concepts of Liberalism," *Ethics* 105 (1995); Joshua Cohen, Martha Nussbaum, and Matthew Howard, eds. *Is Multiculturalism Bad for Women?* (Princeton, NJ: Princeton University Press, 1999).

4. Condition (a) says that social and economic inequalities are to be arranged so that they are to the greatest expected benefit of the least advantaged. *TJ*, 72.

5. *TJ*, 466.

6. See *TJ*, 466n5.

7. See *TJ*, 467.

8. *TJ*, 467, emphasis added.

9, *TJ*, 465. Rawls is sensitive to this, aware of the common objection that egalitarianism is simply founded on envy.

10. *TJ*, 124.

11. *TJ*, 124. See also *TJ*, 464.

12. *TJ*, 468. See also *TJ*, 464.

13. *TJ*, 471, emphasis added.

14. *TJ*, 125.

15. It may be objected that one might be willing to deprive another because one is entitled to it or justice permits such a taking, but this is a concern of resentment, not envy.

16. David Hume notes, "'Tis worthy of observation concerning envy, which arises from a superiority in others, that 'tis not the great disproportion betwixt ourself and another, which produces it; but on the contrary, our proximity," in *A Treatise on Human Nature*, 2nd ed., ed. P. H. Nidditch and index by L. A. Selby-Bigge (Oxford: Oxford University Press, 1978), Bk. II, Pt. II, Sect. VIII, 377. Aaron Ben-Ze'ev also beautifully argues that, at multiple levels, increased proximity and equality often *intensifies* envy. See his "Envy and Inequality," *The Journal of Philosophy*, 89 (1992).

17. *TJ*, 469. Rawls also often equivocates self-confidence with self-respect and self-esteem.

18. *TJ*, xiii.
19. *TJ*, 54.
20. *TJ*, 79, 91, 477 and 386. See also *TJ*, 54 and 348.
21. *TJ*, 386.
22. *TJ*, 386.
23. *TJ*, 386.
24. *TJ*, 477. See also *TJ*, 156 and 478.
25. *TJ*, 155.
26. Much hinges on what counts as *public* affirmation. Rawls seems to require formal recognition by state sanctioned rules. However, if he conceded *informal* recognition as sufficient, such provided by communities, families, and friends, then this could explain how self-respect can arise when *formal* public affirmation is not given.
27. *TJ*, 386.
28. Stephen L. Darwall, "Two Kinds of Self-Respect," *Ethics*, 88 (1977); Michael Bernick, "A Note on Promoting Self-Esteem," *Political Theory*, 6 (1978), 113; Laurence Thomas, "Morality and Our Self-Concept," *Journal of Value Inquiry*, 12 (1978), 259n; Laurence Thomas, "Rawlsian Self-Respect and the Black Consciousness Movement," *The Philosophical Forum*, 9 (1978-9), 304; Stephen J. Massey, "Is Self-Respect a Moral or Psychological Concept?," *Ethics*, 93 (1983), 250; Robert J. Yanal, "Self-Esteem," *Noûs*, 21 (1987), 364; Michele M. Moody-Adams, "Race, Class, and the Social Construction of Self-Respect," in Robin S. Dillon, ed. *Dignity, Character, and Self-Respect* (New York: Routledge, 1995), 275; Nir Eyal, "'Perhaps the Most Important Primary Good': Self-Respect and Rawls's Principles of Justice," *Politics, Philosophy & Economics*, 4 (2005), 195.
29. I assume that people have intrinsic worth. This is also what I mean by 'persons as persons.' The existence of intrinsic worth is contestable, but a defense here would require too much room. I assume that the reader, even if he does not concede the existence of intrinsic worth, at least has a vague notion of what the concept means.
30. I also follow Thomas Hill that, "If the motive is a morally commendable one, or a desire to avert dire consequences to oneself, or even an ambition to set an oppressor up for a later fall, then I would not count the role player as servile," "Servility and Self-Respect," *Monist*, 57 (1973), 96. That is, in my account one can maintain self-respect if he fails to demand something owed to him if his failure meets these conditions.
31. That is, it is residual in the sense that if one has self-respect then he is likely to have respect for others. Minimally, those who lack self-respect have less reason to respect others than those with self-respect.
32. Darwall, 41.
33. Darwall, 44. Stephen Hudson's *directive respect* roughly parallels recognition respect, and Hudson's *evaluative respect* roughly parallels appraisal respect. See Hudson's "The Nature of Respect," *Social Theory and Practice*, 6 (1980).
34. Massey, 247.
35. Massey, 249. John Deigh does not create a distinction between respect and esteem. However, he consistently refers to Rawls as writing about self-esteem. I cite Deigh's concept of self-esteem here because it is remarkably close to Massey's subjective self-respect and Rawls's self-respect: "one *has self-esteem* if, first, one regards

one's aims and ideals as worthy and, second, one believes that one is well-suited to pursue them. With reference to the first we say that one has a sense that one's life has meaning with reference to the second we speak of a confidence one has in excellence of one's person," "Shame and Self-Esteem: A Critique," *Ethics*, 93 (1983), 229.

36. "The Consciousness of the Self," in *Principles of Psychology*, Vol. 1 (New York: Dover, 1950), 310.

37. Laurence Thomas, "Rawlsian Self-Respect and the Black Consciousness Movement," 309 and 308.

38. Laurence Thomas, "Self-Respect: Theory and Practice," in Dillon, ed. *Dignity, Character, and Self-Respect*, 254. By "full moral status," I understand Thomas to mean something like intrinsic worth, which is suggested in his earlier-cited passages.

39. Thomas, "Self-Respect: Theory and Practice," 254.

40. David Sachs, "How to Distinguish Self-Respect from Self-Esteem," *Philosophy and Public Affairs*, 10 (1981), 355 and 356.

41. Sachs, 356–57.

42. Moody-Adams, 275.

43. *The Family and the Political Self* (Cambridge: Cambridge University Press, 2006), 36. Before reading Thomas's book, I was trying to formulate such a thesis regarding development and the conception of the self. Reading it has clarified and affirmed what I was trying to do; I have little original to add to it. However, I seek to borrow it and apply it in ways that I believe Thomas has yet to do.

44. *Living Morally: A Psychology of Moral Character* (Philadelphia, PA: Temple University Press, 1989), 61.

45. See *TJ*, 119 and 230.

46. *TJ*, 156 and 156.

47. One may have *fleeting envy*, a brief *thought* about wishing to take something away from another. Such thoughts are rare and non-efficacious. Fleeting envy is thus an innocuous kind of envy, akin to benign and emulative envy.

48. Moody-Adams, 275.

49. It may sound odd to talk about a self-respecting person with greatly diminished esteem. This is probably because 'self-respect' is often used as a long-term character trait. It would be odd for a self-respecting person to have long-term diminished self-esteem. However, it would be common for the esteem of a self-respecting person to increase and decrease in the short-term in response to the vicissitudes of life.

50. Bruno Bettelheim, *The Informed Heart: Autonomy in a Mass Age* (Glencoe, IL: Free Press, 1961), 167.

51. *Living Morally: A Psychology of Moral Character*, 164.

52. *Living Morally*, 164 and 163.

53. *TJ*, 383.

54. *TJ*, 406.

55. *TJ*, 414 and 415, my emphases.

56. Helmut Schoeck, *Envy: A Theory of Social Behavior* (Indianapolis, IN: Liberty Fund, 1987), 304.

57. Rawls concedes this: "it is not in general to the advantage of the less fortunate to propose policies which reduce the talents of others," 92.

58. T. M. Scanlon, "The Diversity of Objections to Equality" in Matthew Clayton and Andrew Williams, eds. *The Idea of Equality* (New York: St. Martin's Press, 2000), 55.

59. *TJ*, 256.

60. Massey, 258–61 and Henry Shue, "Liberty and Self-Respect," *Ethics*, 85 (1975).

61. Yanal, 379n16; Thomas, "Morality and Our Self-Concept," 259; Laurence Thomas, "Morality and Human Diversity: A Review of Owen Flanagan's *Varieties of Moral Personality*," *Ethics* 103 (1992), 129n.

62. Catriona McKinnon, "Basic Income, Self-Respect and Reciprocity," *Journal of Applied Philosophy*, 20 (2003); Jeffrey Moriarty, "Rawls, Self-Respect, and the Living Wage," *Unpublished draft.*

63. Eyal, 195.

64. Eyal, 195.

65. *TJ*, 478.

66. *TJ*, 53.

67. *TJ*, 72. Some commentators refer to (a) as the Difference Principle, whereas some refer to (a) + (b) as the Difference Principle. I use the latter and make distinctions by appealing to whether something is an (a) or (b) condition of the Difference Principle.

3

Family Egalitarianism

$\mathbf{R}$awls did not sufficiently articulate a theory of transition from the actual world to an ideal world; he presumably left this to be decided at the legislative stage. However, he did broadly outline it by describing a well-ordered society and its components. An important feature of this is that society requires citizens with a certain character structure, ISJs. I follow Rawls in recognizing the need for ISJs, but per the previous chapter I favor my ISJs over Rawlsian ISJs. The key to producing my ISJs is to nurture children properly. Social cooperation seems more promising when children are properly nurtured because they will likely mature into more trusting and less envious individuals because of the education and love provided to them. As will become clearer in this chapter, the easiest way to create non-ISJs is to maltreat children. Maltreatment often precludes children from developing the self-respect and trust requisite for social cooperation, and it increases the chances that children will eventually threaten political stability. Therefore, I ask how best to produce ISJs and how to prevent non-ISJs. If a good family is the best place to raise a child to become an ISJ, then, as I will show later, this complicates how much government may intervene for the sake of protection and progress.

These considerations are not novel. Adeimantus told Socrates,

[W]e've been waiting all this time supposing you would surely mention begetting of children—how they'll be begotten and, once born, how they'll be reared—and that whole community of women and children of which you speak. We think it makes a big difference, or rather, the whole difference in a regime's being right or not right.[1]

Ever since this demand was put forth, many philosophers (especially Aristotle, Locke, and Rousseau) have taken children, their education, and their rearing seriously. That is, until the twentieth century. What is most important about Rawls is that he sought to bring back this tradition in part III, chapters VIII and IX of *A Theory of Justice*. He recognized the link between psychological stability, especially how children develop into ISJs, and political stability in a well-ordered society. Unfortunately, most philosophers after Rawls seem to overlook this and discuss distributions of goods and resources without adequate consideration of children and their role in the stability of society. My goal is to fill some of this void. I primarily examine how properly raising children in society fits into the framework of contemporary liberal egalitarianism. This involves taking a closer look at the relationship between child maltreatment and ISJ status. It should become apparent that families should be at the center of egalitarianism because families have the most important influence over how humans develop—for better or worse. I argue that ensuring competent parents for children, so that children can develop into ISJs (for their own sake and for the sake of society), should be the most crucial equalisandum.[2] I also argue that we need to examine what the family is, what it can be, what it provides, what it can provide, and what role it should play in political philosophy.

The first section of this chapter considers ISJs and the family in the context of egalitarianism. It uses Elizabeth Anderson's survey of political philosophy to demonstrate that egalitarians need ISJs, though they largely overlook this. Section 2 describes why it is important to consider what happens in societies where ISJs exist and how child maltreatment helps to vitiate children becoming ISJs. In particular, the negative effects of the cyclical nature of maltreatment is described. Section 3 takes stock of the current state of child maltreatment literature by empirical psychologists, showing what is needed for this field to advance and how empirical psychologists and political philosophers could benefit from each other. The fourth section examines models of economic and resource investment by the government and argues that these models either do not sufficiently value the role of childrearing in the family or do not fully understand child development. The final chapter asks if we should abolish the family. Furthermore, it gleans useful information from economists and evolutionary theory about how we ought to invest in children.

1. EGALITARIANISM

While I critique egalitarianism for not properly accounting for the need of ISJs in a completely well-ordered society, it is not the only political theory that falls short. Many libertarians, for example, presuppose robust citizens either while assuming that most citizens are ISJs or that the formal system of libertarianism will somehow turn them into ISJs.[3] A stable libertarian society requires, to a great degree, that citizens have self-respect and fellow feeling. A society of free but non-virtuous citizens who lack self-respect is not ideal. However, the formal system of libertarianism itself does not yield ISJs; liberty does not create ISJs. Rather, ISJs are created in informal structures such as the family. Unless libertarians have a means to underwrite ISJs, then nothing within the formal structure of the theory can compensate for this in a way such that society can maintain both stability and freedom. Like egalitarianism, libertarianism needs a means to produce and maintain ISJs to be plausible as a political theory.

Egalitarians tend not to presuppose robust ISJs for their theories. Rather, they tend to provide a concept of the self that is fragile, if not sometimes overly fragile. To survey contemporary egalitarian views, I refer to Elizabeth Anderson's "What Is the Point of Equality?"[4] Anderson's major concern is that "agendas defined by much recent egalitarian theorizing are too narrowly focused on the distribution of divisible privately appropriated goods, such as income and resources, or privately appropriated goods, such as income and resources, or privately enjoyed goods, such as welfare."[5] I agree with this general assessment, but I do so for different reasons than Anderson.

I consider equality of outcome approaches to be the least sophisticated. They generally demand little, if any, responsibility on the part of citizens and offer a far too weak conception of the self. More importantly, for the purposes of this book, equality of outcome approaches do not explain how to create ISJs. They never seem to try to create ISJs because they only ponder how to design formal systems that will closely yield an equality of outcome. Numerous objections against equality of outcome approaches are made elsewhere in the literature, and I will not review them. Yet Anderson notes the following trend: "luck egalitarians have moved from an equality of outcome to an equality of opportunity conception of justice: they ask only that people start off with an equal share of resources. But they accept the justice of whatever inequalities result from adults' voluntary choices."[6] Luck egalitarianism is Anderson's main target, and I will now consider it.

Anderson says that luck egalitarianism relies on two moral premises, "that people should be compensated for undeserved misfortunes and that the compensation should come only from that part of others' 'good fortune' that is undeserved."[7] Luck egalitarians have a sophisticated account that seems to come closer to confronting my question about how to create ISJs, as they often seek to improve the well-being of children. Seeking to improve the well-being of children, whether through equality of opportunity, resources, or welfare, is a healthy step towards producing ISJs. Yet luck egalitarians do not satisfactorily answer my question concerning how to produce ISJs. Luck egalitarian accounts that are compensatory in nature, where individuals are only compensated for having had bad "brute luck," may be sufficient for adults but are insufficient for children. Luck egalitarianism may be sufficient for adults because their moral and developmental psychology is usually mature. When adults harmed by bad brute luck are compensated for bad brute luck, they can generally resume their normal lives. However, in many cases no amount of compensation can appropriately compensate a child when he suffers bad brute luck because the moral and developmental psychology of children is not mature, especially in cases where the child has been severely abused or neglected.

Luck egalitarian approaches are often starting-gate theories, where the ideal is that people enjoy fair shares at the start of life. Anderson objects: "equality of fortune is essentially a 'starting-gate theory': as long as people enjoy fair shares at the start of life, it does not much concern itself with the suffering and subjection generated by people's voluntary agreement in free markets."[8] Anderson's dismissal is too quick. She does not seem to consider whether *some* fair shares at the beginning of life are capable of providing significant things that last throughout one's life regardless of one's luck later in life. I am also dissatisfied with most existing starting-gate theories, but I am dissatisfied for a different reason; they generally do not address my concern about ISJs. Many starting-gate theories are sophisticated and have many attractive features, but no amount of goods, resources, welfare, or opportunity given to a child after being maltreated will be helpful. Because his formative psychology will be disrupted, he is unlikely to become an ISJ. Starting-gate egalitarians need to confront the question of how to prevent child maltreatment. Unless maltreatment is prevented, starting-gate approaches are unlikely to be of any real assistance because those who are maltreated are likely to lag behind quickly after exiting the starting gate. As Anderson notes, simply providing fair shares at the beginning of life does not necessarily entail justice or fairness. I agree. However, I later show that if we provide a certain kind of fair share at the beginning of life, a decent family, then we have all that we need in a mostly well-ordered political society that is already formally well-ordered. There is nothing intrinsically wrong with starting-gate theories; their worth depends upon the substance of the particular fair shares provided.

After surveying the evolution of egalitarian theories, Anderson puts forth a theory of "democratic equality," which guarantees "all law-abiding citizens equal effective access to social conditions of their freedom at all times" and "effective access to a package of capabilities sufficient for standing as an equal over the course of an entire life. It is not a starting-gate theory, in which people could lose their access to equal standing through bad option luck."[9] I have two objections to this. The first objection is that Anderson's theory takes a step backwards. One of the positive aspects of moving from equality of outcome to luck egalitarian approaches in political theory is that citizens are given more responsibility.[10] However, ensuring "effective" access to things in life, which I understand as being equivalent to guaranteed access to things needed even if the need is a result of bad "option luck" as an adult, seems to enable citizens to become less responsible for their own life choices.[11] The more important objection is that Anderson seems to assume that bad luck must, or can easily, change one's standing in society. This seems to imply that nothing can provide citizens with equal standing regardless of their luck. However, I believe that something *does* exist which provides permanent equal standing. If Anderson's concern is with the equal standing element of social justice, she needs ISJs because societal standing is largely contingent on a particular society's values. What we value in our current formally well-ordered society need not be valued the same way in the future. ISJs would value things like money and power, but they would predominately value family, friends, and fellow citizens. Their values would form due to how they were nurtured and their subsequent development of a strong inclination towards reciprocity. Their robust self-respect would preclude them from lacking equal standing if they chose to have equal standing. Their self-respect and recognition from society would be strong enough to prevent them from becoming envious or hostile to inequalities that arise justly.

Being an ISJ provides individuals with the greatest capability — self-respect. Because early experiences in life largely determine our capabilities, it is important to foster this capacity from the very start of life. Anderson's account of democratic equality fails to answer my concern about how ISJs are developed. However, she seems to approach an answer to my concerns about ISJs when she stresses that individuals ought to have access to *capabilities*. A capabilities approach seems to be the best way to address the problem of how to create ISJs because the very thing that one nurtures in producing ISJs is capabilities. Yet I am reluctant to accept Anderson's version of "effective access" to capabilities due to concerns about responsibility. Anderson elaborates, "Following Sen, I say that egalitarians should seek equality for all in the space of capabilities. Sen's capability theory leaves open a large question, however. *Which* capabilities does society have an obligation to equalize?"[12] Sen does leave this important question open, but in an important sense it does not matter that he leaves the question open. It would not matter which capabilities he sought to equalize if we could find the best way to nourish the most basic human capabilities, ensure that each human being received that which nourished those capabilities, and if the said capabilities were so powerful as to be self-reinforcing throughout one's lifetime. These conditions are met, as will become clearer later in this chapter, when children are nurtured properly by parents in a family.

One of Anderson's passages does lead indirectly to what I consider a powerful answer to the question that I have posed about ISJs. She states:

> Recent egalitarian writing has come to be dominated by the view that the fundamental aim of equality is to compensate people for undeserved bad luck— being poor with native endowments, *bad parents*, and disagreeable personalities, suffering from accidents and illnesses, and so forth. I shall argue that in focusing on correcting a supposed cosmic injustice, recent egalitarian writing has lost sight of the distinctly political aims of egalitarianism. The proper negative aim of egalitarianism is not to eliminate the impact of brute luck from human affairs, but to end *oppression*, which by definition is socially imposed. Its proper positive aim is not to ensure that everyone gets what they morally deserve, but to create a community in which people stand in relations of equality to others.[13]

We should not seek a system that necessarily compensates individuals for what they morally deserve, and we should strive for a system where people stand in relations of equality to each other. Yet I am concerned by how Anderson treats remedying bad parenting as only a luck egalitarian concern of bad brute luck. She thus implies that child maltreatment is not a form of oppression. However, a society that permits children to be abused or neglected by their parents is a form of oppression; more precisely, it is an oft-overlooked case of societal ageism. The use of 'oppression' may sound odd here because our mostly just society does not condone child abuse or neglect, but it often intervenes only *after* abuse or neglect has taken place. So, saying that we *permit* children to be abused or neglected seems to be on par with saying that a mostly just society permits crime because the legal system does not intervene until after the crime is committed. Minimally, these cases are disanalogous: children are vulnerable and cannot protect themselves. It is also important that children advance through one stage of development properly before arriving at the next stage. If trying to produce more ISJs in order to approach a stable and well-ordered society, then our primary focus should be ensuring that children arrive at the morality of principles stage and become ISJs. However, I may be exaggerating the importance of raising children properly. Perhaps I am also overestimating the damage that is done by child abuse and neglect. After all, in the rare instances that children are mentioned in political philosophy, it is even rarer to encounter mention of child maltreatment. I shall now consider child maltreatment and its relationship to ISJ status.

2. MALTREATMENT AND ISJ STATUS

Rawls stipulated, "Let us assume that each person beyond a certain age and possessed of the requisite intellectual capacity develops a sense of justice under normal circumstances."[14] If Rawls is granted this assumption, he can achieve many positive things with his ISJs. However, this cannot be assumed in my theory of transition—development must be accounted for. When this is done, I believe that the concept of needing ISJs for a completely well-ordered society is intuitively strong. However, I believe that the importance of ISJs in society becomes even more evident when it is also shown what happens in a society where non-ISJs largely result from something that Rawls did not discuss or allow in his system, child maltreatment. The most obvious cases where ISJs are not likely to form are when children are parented by abusive or neglectful parents.

Finkelhor and Browne note three major effects of child sexual abuse, and these are generally applicable to non-sexual abuse as well,

> *Betrayal* refers to the dynamic in which children discover that someone on whom they were vitally dependent has caused them harm. . . . *Powerlessness*—or what might better be called disempowerment, the dynamic of rendering the victim powerless—refers to the process in which the child's will, desires, and sense of efficacy are continually contravened. . . . *Stigmatization*, the final dynamic, refers to negative connotations—for example, badness, shame and guilt—that are communicated to the child around areas of molestation and that can become incorporated into that child's self-image . . . reinforced by attitudes that the victim infers or hears from other persons in the family or community.[15]

Feelings of betrayal, powerlessness, and stigmatization are all large impediments to becoming an ISJ. *Betrayal*, particularly by close authority figures such as one's parents, attacks what is needed to become an ISJ because it disallows the healthy developmental roots of reciprocity required in Rawls's first law of developmental psychology. Betrayal also short-circuits the likelihood of positively reciprocating with fellow feeling amongst later social groups, such as one's peers and, later, citizens in general. In addition to being directly harmed by particular acts of betrayal, children are likely to be negatively affected by residual effects of witnessing a poor behavioral model. In this vein, Locke noted,

> Having under consideration how great the influence of *company* is and how prone we are all, especially children, to imitation, I must here take the liberty to mind parents of this one thing, viz. that he that will have his son have a respect for him and his orders must himself have a great reverence for his son. *Maxima*

debetur pueris reverentia. You must do nothing before him which you would not have him imitate.[16]

Not only is one harmed immediately by the direct particular harm of experiencing maltreatment and by a more general harm of being less likely to respect and trust authority figures, but a child is also at increased risk to imitate abusive behavior himself.

A *sense of powerlessness* directly attacks a sense of justice—having a *desire to act* according to the dictates of justice and give to others that which they are entitled. A sense of powerlessness can stultify the will to act properly when coupled with betrayal because reciprocation has not developed properly. A sense of powerlessness can also work directly insofar as even if one wished to act positively he may choose otherwise because he feels his worth is so little that he does not possess the ability to be efficacious. *Stigmatization* can also be harmful because ISJs need to have self-respect and recognize themselves as having equal social standing. However, it is extremely difficult to maintain self-respect if one's formative developmental stages are strongly connected with feelings of badness, shame, and guilt.

No major child development theory has proposed that child maltreatment is good for children, or, for that matter, for parents. It is debated *to what degree* and exactly *why* child maltreatment is harmful, but *that* it is harmful is not disputed. Most theories also agree that harm will continue to manifest into adulthood. It is also uncontroversial that a maltreated child, no matter how robust, will be unable to respect and trust in the complete and healthy sense required in a society where stability depends upon reciprocity, respect, and trust.

Before transitioning from largely theoretical conceptions about what happens to maltreated children to empirical findings about child maltreatment, I wish to be clear that I am not simply concerned about whether children develop a proper conception of justice. I am mostly concerned about this conception becoming efficacious. For this reason, I use an ISJ model but not a rational agent model. Rational agents may cognitively recognize what they should rationally do but fail to do so for many reasons—perhaps they are akratic. Assuming that it is rational to be just, being a rational agent is only the first condition of being an ISJ (the skill to judge what is just and unjust). More important here, for political purposes, is the third Rawlsian ISJ condition: a *desire* to act according to the dictates of justice and giving to others what they are entitled. This is captured at its best by Rawls when he frames it in Rousseauian terms, "the sense of justice is no mere moral conception formed by the understanding alone, but a true sentiment of the heart enlightened by reason, the natural outcome of our primitive affections."[17] This is particularly important because developmental moral psychology is often faulted for only considering cognitive development via posing hypothetical moral questions to children without also exploring what, if any, effect this has on their behavior. Little work has been done taking these considerations into account, and even less that considers the variable of maltreated versus nonmaltreated children, but it seems that there is a gap between maltreated children's abstract knowledge of what is right and their performing right actions. One of the best studies on this comes from Smetana and Kelly who report:

> [C]hildren who have been maltreated do not internalize different standards of behavior . . . [yet] abused and neglected children are more aggressive than their nonmaltreated counterparts. Thus, the findings point to an apparent discrepancy between children's moral valuations and their aggressive behavior.[18]

This observation takes into account that children are more likely to judge hypothetical than actual transgressions as wrong, regardless of maltreatment status. Maltreated children are not necessarily any less knowledgeable than their non-maltreated peers about what actions are just. However, maltreatment is likely to extinguish the intermediary spark that turns knowledge into action. In other words, maltreatment likely often precludes the requisite desire to be formed in order to make moral knowledge efficacious.

There are many negative effects of child maltreatment, but they can be reduced to three major categories: self-harm, mental disorder, and antisocial behavior. Self-harm is serious, but I set it aside because I wish to emphasize the negative *social* problems that result from maltreatment. I will only treat self-harm insofar as it related to antisocial behavior. Likewise, mental disorders caused by maltreatment are terrible, but I only wish to consider the negative social effects of maltreatment. Of course, mental disorders can sometimes cause negative social effects. I am mostly interested in the antisocial behavior which child maltreatment can cause. There are numerous antisocial behaviors that result from maltreatment, but these are usually divided into two major groups: aggression and withdrawal. In early studies that did not differentiate between abuse and neglect, data revealed that maltreated children usually were either significantly more aggressive or socially withdrawn compared to non-maltreated children. However, abuse has been more correlated with aggression,[19] and neglect has been correlated less with aggression and more with social withdrawal.[20] Child abuse has been given much attention over the past forty years, but neglect has been given little attention as a separate kind of maltreatment. Only very recently, with rare exceptions, has neglect been researched and treated independently of abuse.[21] Yet some good research clearly separates abused and neglected subjects.[22] In one sense, the abuse-neglect distinction is important because they are different kinds of harms. However, much recent work separating them may not be as helpful as one might think because it has also been found that a high number of maltreated children often experience multiple kinds of maltreatment. Those who are abused are often also neglected and vice-versa.[23] Chronicity and severity of maltreatment also matter in examining the effects of maltreatment. All other things equal, a child who suffers more maltreatment than another is more likely to be affected more negatively (older studies were based upon whether one was maltreated or not, treating a child who was maltreated once the same as a child who was maltreated every day of his childhood).[24] However, it is still debatable whether chronicity or severity has more of a negative effect.[25] In absence of a clear answer to this question, perhaps it is best to talk about *degree* of maltreatment, where "degree" refers to the frequency *and* severity of the maltreatment experienced and degree is perhaps the most important factor because of the overlap of different kinds of maltreatment.[26]

Regardless of whether abuse leads to aggression or neglect leads to social withdrawal (or vice-versa, or both lead to either aggression or withdrawal depending on the child), maltreatment is dangerous due to the effects that it has upon children as they enter a social world with their peers. If early aggressiveness and social withdrawal derived from maltreatment were overcome by the socialization process, maltreatment would not be a problem for political stability, though it would remain a serious ethical problem. According to all major child development theories, abused and neglected children are at high risk to maladaptive peer relationships.[27] Furthermore, early aggressiveness is predictive of later serious antisocial behavior, such as criminal behavior, spousal abuse, and physical aggression.[28] Part of this is due to early childhood aggression being significantly linked to peer rejection and lower peer status through a child's life.[29] This is important because friendship has been shown to moderate chances of peer victimization, where a high number of friends is important but peer acceptance of one's best friend is more important.[30] When aggressive children do interact, even with friends, they have higher rates of negativity, conflict, and betrayal; they also have lower rates of caring, cooperation, and reciprocity.[31] Forming healthy peer relationships early is important. For many children, poor peer adjustment presents a higher chance of difficulties in later life, especially concerning criminality.[32] This is to be expected if we accept a developmental model that places heavy importance on the necessity of a healthy relationship between children and parents as a foundation for the later stages of positive interaction with peers. This is also important because in my model those who do not develop properly and interact positively with their peers are unlikely to be able to become ISJs or possess the requisite fellow feeling to be a good citizen. Rawls also argues that completing his second stage is important for developing later intimate relationships.

Research backs this claim because early childhood victimization has been linked to later violence against partners for both men and women and has been significantly linked to unhealthy intimate relationships.[33]

The factor that underlies both the effects of aggression and social withdrawal seems to be an unhealthy self-esteem caused by maltreatment.[34] Not only do maltreated children have significantly higher rates of unhealthy self-esteem, mothers who maltreat their children are much more likely to have unhealthy self-esteem.[35] This is important because self-respect is a primary good of importance for Rawls. In particular, having self-respect (or a healthy self-esteem) is necessary for the affective structure of ISJs.

The above may be conceded while still questioning whether child maltreatment should be the primary concern of egalitarianism and public policy. After all, it has been estimated that 4 percent of parents are incompetent (insofar as they maltreat) and 3.6 million children have been neglected.[36] This number is too high in the sense that no child should ever be maltreated, but most children are not maltreated. However, two important things must also be considered. First, it is within the small subset of children who are maltreated that the greatest threat to political stability exists. For example, over 80 percent of incarcerated criminals were abused by their parents when they were children, 66 percent of institutionalized delinquents had child neglect and abuse histories, and one-half of maltreated children died at an early age, became alcoholic or mentally ill, or have been convicted of a serious crime.[37] The second concern is that child maltreatment is cyclical in nature. Maltreatment can lead to long-lasting negative effects through a person's life, including an increased risk of maltreating one's children. Child maltreatment is not determined in the sense that maltreatment necessarily arises from parents who were maltreated as children, but it was thought so when empirical research on the topic started in the 1960s. The intergenerational transmission of child abuse has since been established to be about 30 percent $+/-5$ percent, about five to six times higher than the rate of abuse in the general population.[38] Though not 100 percent, the figure of approximately one-third is high enough to fit the intergenerational transmission hypothesis that children of parents who have been maltreated are at a much higher risk of maltreating their own children compared to children of non-maltreated parents. In general, it has been found that "the greater the overall burden of poor parenting experienced, the greater risk of poor parenting provided to the next generation of children."[39]

3. PHILOSOPHERS AND EMPIRICAL PSYCHOLOGISTS

Gelles advanced child maltreatment research when he opposed the dominant position that maltreatment is the result of one factor—the abuser is psychopathological.[40] He argued that things such as education, poverty, and social isolation also play an important role in child maltreatment. Following Gelles, Sameroff and Chandler rejected the single-factor (or "main effects") explanation of abuse models of those who sought single-factor causal models other than the psychological condition of parents (such as poverty, socioeconomic status, stress, and number of parents) and instead developed a transactional model able to take into account multiple transactions/factors of abuse.[41] In particular, psychobiological factors had to be considered—such as how the characteristics of children increase or decrease their chances of being maltreated. The transactional model was then modified to even broader ecological models, and an increasing number of studies examined what role the characteristics of children increased their risks of being abused (i.e., being born premature, mentally retarded, or handicapped).[42] After establishing the accepted rate of transmission of abuse, Kaufman and Zigler were then justified in their claim that "The time has come for researchers to cease to ask 'Do abused children become abusive parents?' and ask instead 'Under what conditions is the transmission of abuse most likely to occur?'"[43] This call has yielded many excellent studies on the etiology of maltreatment. I wish to extend and modify this call for research.

Because so many different correlations to high rates of maltreatment have been established, I believe that an ecological theory of maltreatment, which concedes that maltreatment is incredibly complex and multiply determined, is the best etiological theory of child maltreatment. Furthermore, I believe that there is little more that can be established by the current trend of undertaking empirical research that only yields correlation claims due to the complex and multiply determined nature of maltreatment. A major reevaluation is needed to progress effectively at this point in empirical psychological studies on child maltreatment. The first thing that is necessary is to shift to *positive* research. Rather than examining exactly what causes maltreatment (a negative thing), studies of what best prevents maltreatment and promotes healthy development (a positive thing) are necessary. This has already begun to happen to some degree in studies on child resilience, studies that examine why some children flourish despite being expected to fail due to adversities such as poor health or poverty.[44] Rawls's ISJ model provides a powerful model for such research. This may seem odd because Rawls's account is largely built on early work in developmental moral psychology. However, it was built mostly upon theories of developmental psychology that had little empirical backing—certainly not as rigorous as the current research that examines what causes people to flounder. Likewise, political philosophy needs to reevaluate itself in order to progress effectively. It needs to take into account what has already been learned in a negative sense from the past forty years of child maltreatment research to construct a positive model. In doing so, it will better root itself in reality and come to understand the vast and destructive political implications of poor parenting in order to make its normative models more plausible and powerful.

Political philosophy and developmental psychology need each other now to progress. Empirical psychologists and political philosophers need to devote more energy to examining what environments are healthy for child development and why these environments are healthy. I explore this in the next section because many political philosophers and psychologists seem to be in agreement about how to make social progress. In particular, they largely agree that we should focus our energies on people of low socioeconomic status either by distributing goods or resources in order to avoid problems or compensate for harm after the fact. That solution is not ideal, and I think that empirical psychologists and political philosophers agree on a solution due to their respective weaknesses. That is, empirical psychologists deal with human behavior primarily as an unchanging thing; progress can only be achieved by appealing to modifications that can be made within the *status quo*. It is perhaps not their job to do so, but they generally seem unable to capture the big picture concerning the political implications of their work and do not attempt to recommend more idealistic solutions. At best, short-term solutions are put forth—providing therapy, money, food, daycare, and education. However, none of these solutions seem to confront the long-term and cyclical nature of child maltreatment effectively. Political philosophers seem more detached from reality and think more in terms of general normative ideals. They can skillfully ponder what people are owed as human beings and citizens. Yet how this *exactly* gets cashed out in the real world is not always clear because they lack the expertise of empirical psychologists in understanding how people actually function—even though most political philosophers, implicitly or explicitly, espouse some kind of theory of human nature. I hope to account for how humans actually function while also being an idealist in the sense that I consider of what humans are *capable*. This is important while working within an ecological framework of maltreatment because no single causal factor directly causes maltreatment. I will seek that which best short-circuits the cycle of maltreatment, even though it may not be the only factor in the cycle of maltreatment. Similarly, I will seek a factor that is a sufficient condition for yielding ISJs. Just as there are multiple factors that help lead to child maltreatment, there are multiple factors that help prevent child maltreatment. However, if a sufficient factor can be picked out then it will be preferable in the sense that it can better prevent child maltreatment.

4. MONEY AND PARENTS

Recall that the goal of this work is not simply to confront child maltreatment; it is also to find a means to promote political stability via confronting child maltreatment within an egalitarian system. That is, minimize maltreatment for its own sake but also provide, by means of competent parents, meaningful equality of opportunity to minimize the number of non-ISJs, increase the number of ISJs, and increase political stability. As mentioned earlier, many psychologists and philosophers tend to focus their energies on distribution of goods or resources, and they focus particularly on economically disadvantaged populations. This does not mean that they disregard the family as an important institution in society. However, it does seem to indicate that they believe that the *status quo* of families cannot be changed or that it is a better idea to reduce inequality or provide goods or resources to citizens instead of promoting families. By 'families' I mean here two competent and married parents and their children, and I will justify the importance of this kind of family later. In arguing for the primacy of the family, I do not want to discount that lacking money or resources can be difficult; I wish to argue that problems with money and other resources would not be as traumatic as they are now if more ISJs existed. To transition towards a completely well-ordered society, we should not focus on goods or resources; we should focus on promoting good parenting and preventing bad parenting. Goods and resources do not make good parents; rather, having a sense of justice is a foundation of good parenting. We can provide a parent with food, shelter, and schooling to provide for his child, but such goods are of little value if the parent maltreats his child. If a child is maltreated at an early age of development and it is terribly difficult to bypass stages of development to the morality of principles, then that child is at risk to himself and others; he is at considerable risk of not becoming an ISJ, particularly when maltreated at the earliest stages of development. If not an ISJ, he becomes a threat to the stability and progress towards a completely well-ordered society.

I earlier framed the political question in reference to Anderson's work, but I now also appeal to Jeffrey Blustein, who captures a common sentiment of many egalitarians today while also demonstrating that he understands the importance of the role of the family in society:

> Among the forces responsible for the transmission of a high degree of social and economic inequality from generation to generation, the advantages or disadvantages conferred by one's family of origin are especially strong. Children inherit the advantages (or disadvantages) or their parents' superior (or inferior) socioeconomic status in the form of material wealth, parental pull or connections, and the investments in books, tutors, preparatory schools, and the like to speed development in an enriched environment. Since children start life with the eco-

nomic status of their parents, we can positively affect the opportunities of children by reducing the extent of economic inequality among their parents.[45]

Poverty is a factor, but it is secondary to good parenting. Bad parenting and poverty are often strongly correlated. Despite this correlation, good parenting should be the primary focus even when children are in poverty because good parenting is sufficient to yield ISJs. However, not living in poverty is insufficient to yield ISJs. It is also not the case that poverty itself is harmful, although the residual effects of being poor can be harmful. Yet child maltreatment *itself* is harmful, as are the residual effects of maltreatment. Likewise, living in poverty with good parents is unlikely to yield harm; however, maltreated children are likely to be harmed regardless of their economic status. Only one-third of maltreated parents will maltreat their own children, but other effects (drug use, violence, and depression) also increase with abuse. Most importantly, regardless of how maltreatment manifests itself negatively, *healthy* trust is lost. It is unclear how simply being poor, especially if one has good parents, can erode trust (or self-respect). Likewise, an educated and wealthy individual who is not also an ISJ actually poses more of a threat to society than a non-educated and impoverished one because he lacks the internal mechanism to prevent him from being an egoist. However, poor and poorly educated ISJs are not threats to the stability of a society. Being an ISJ is a necessary condition for individual and societal flourishing; being wealthy or well-educated is not necessary for individual or societal flourishing.

4.1 Family Stress and Family Resource Models

In presenting a critique of arguments that give primacy to economic and resource concerns, it may seem that I have been unfair. After all, money and resources can help parents raise ISJs and strengthen families; they are not always understood as intrinsic goods. Therefore, distribution of goods and resources can sometimes be intended to strengthen families and create more ISJs. I will consider these arguments in more detail. There appear to be two major theses. The first is the family stress thesis, which I consider the weakest. The second is the family resource thesis, which I believe is stronger and will consider later. These two theses are not completely separable; they often overlap because a lack of available resources can cause stress. However, they are different enough to discuss separately.

4.1.1 The Family Stress Model

The family stress thesis roughly reduces to the following argument: (i) economic hardship, whether poverty or unstable work, negatively affects parents' psychological well-being, and (ii) the stress of negative parental psychological

well-being manifests in negative emotions and behavior; therefore, (iii) negative parental emotions and behavior residually have a negative affect on
children via poor parenting, especially maltreatment. This position is often
used as an explanation for high rates of child maltreatment in poor populations by many psychologists and sociologists.[46] I suspect most political
philosophers also hold a similar position. I concede that poverty *can* be stressful, and intense stress and/or a high number of stressors *can* increase factors
such as psychiatric risk and risk to maltreat one's children.[47] In particular,
deep and persistent poverty should be expected to have high correlations to
low ability and achievement in children, as it does. Furthermore, the belief
that increased stress causes higher risk of negative things is not just a folk
model; many studies have shown that increased numbers of stressors is highly
correlated with psychiatric risk in children (and the increasing number of
stressors fit an exponential, not linear, model of increased risk).[48] However,
the relationship between stress and maltreatment decreases significantly, becoming either absent or minimal, when important variables are controlled.[49]
For example, it seems that competent and loving married parents cope with
equal levels of stress better than other types of parents and families.

Recall that the family stress thesis is being considered independently of
the family resource thesis. As such, it will not be examined here why stress
occurs or how it should be addressed. Also, when discussing poverty, we are
talking about poverty in our current society. We are thus discussing relative
poverty. It is assumed that the poor being discussed may have fewer goods
and resources than most other people in society, but they do have access to
basic resources. In general, the stress is not about facing the potential of
starvation—a potential that many poor people in other societies face. It appears as though most of the stress comes from not being able to live according to the standards of society.

The *status quo* does not need to be maintained with regards to stress man-
ifesting from failing to live up to economic levels of most people. Many today are incredibly stressed by not living up to the standards of others, but
these standards would not have a large effect on ISJs. As long as ISJs were
able to provide a minimum standard for themselves and their children, the
stress produced from the socially constructed view that being poor is necessarily bad or demonstrates a character flaw would not manifest. What would
matter primarily would be being good parents, spouses, and citizens. In a
world with more ISJs, poverty would not necessarily be seen as anything bad
and thus would not cause those who are poor that kind of stress. Relatedly,
ISJs would generally be able to handle stress better than non-ISJs due to their
deep self-respect and the affirmation that they have received throughout their
lives. Correlatively, the stress would not have to be transferred residually to

children. If children did not understand a lack of wealth to be intrinsically bad, then there would be no reason for their self-images to be negatively affected by poverty. The warmth and care of their parents, while just making ends meet, would be sufficient to help them become fully functioning ISJs. In fact, children might even appreciate their parents, and life generally, *more* if they understood the extraordinary sacrifices made by their parents to raise them well.

Perhaps the best way to understand the above is in terms of resilience. Studies have been performed to understand why some children in populations with multiple stressors flourish despite being predicted to flounder. In perhaps the best study on resilience, a thirty-year longitudinal study starting at birth, Werner and Smith examined children at highest risk—those exposed to four or more stressors by age two but who coped successfully. Of the factors that promoted resilience, it was found repeatedly that high amounts of attention from primary caretakers early in a child's life strongly counteracted a high numbers of stressors. They also demonstrated that poverty is not a sufficient condition for maladaptation, as should be clear because most people in poverty do not maltreat their children. Werner and Smith state that the following characteristics seem to be shared by resilient infants across sociocultural boundaries:

> 1. They tend more often to be first born, especially the males. 2. They may have survived some birth complications (such as moderate to marked perinatal stress or low birthweight), but they have few congenital defects and draw on generous reserves of energy. 3. They are perceived by their caretakers as very active and socially responsive infants. 4. They elicit and receive a great deal of attention during the first year of life. 5. They rarely experienced prolonged separations from their primary caretaker during the critical time period for the development of attachment.[50]

Assuming that poverty need not be an important stressor to parents, it is helpful to examine what happens when children do have competent parents while in environments that would otherwise put them at high risk because of a high number of stressors. We do not need to stipulate being in a world of ISJs where it is socially acceptable to be poor. That is, we can gather such information in today's currently mostly just society by examining the role of competent parents in the lives of children. Competent parents seem to serve as a shield for children when other conditions in life become difficult. Just as empirical psychology has negatively established the existence of an intergenerational transmission of abuse, it has also been established positively that an intergenerational transmission of warm parenting also exists.[51] In a comparative study of women subjected to chronic stress and disadvantage as adults, those who had unstable parents became incompetent parents, while those who had competent and affirming parents overcame adversity and were competent parents themselves.[52] Likewise, economic disadvantage in one's childhood is a secondary factor in determining development. This was observed in a follow-up study of men who were economically disadvantaged but not delinquent in their childhood; the vast majority did not repeat their disadvantaged back-grounds in their adult lives and cited mothers who demanded hard work, a man who substituted for an absent father, and a supportive spouse.[53] In my framework, these are revealing because they relate to important stages of de-velopment. A demanding mother will provide affirmation in both the author-ity and association stages. A man substituting for an absent father can play a similar role. A supportive spouse can serve as a source of constant affirmation when one is already an ISJ.

If stress results from being in poverty, then this problem largely reduces to a problem of family structure. Children who live with married parents, espe-cially parents who remain married, generally live in more economically sta-ble families than children whose parents never married, are parenting alone, or cohabit without being married. Consider the median annual income of the following groups: not married ($9,400), cohabiting ($30,000), divorced ($23,000), and married in first marriage ($54,000). Consider also median net worth: not married ($350), cohabiting ($16,540), divorced ($27,800), and married in first marriage ($120,250). Finally, consider the percentage of these groups living in poverty: not married (67 percent), cohabiting (39 percent), divorced (31 percent), and married in first marriage (12 percent).[54] If the ar-gument is that poverty causes maltreatment, then it seems that promoting marriage, particularly marriages that last, might be a good investment. Sim-ply being married with children does not necessarily entail that one will have more money; being married with children is surely not a direct causal factor which yields wealth. However, being married does seem to provide ample op-portunity for a different kind of investment and savings that is simply not pos-sible in single-parent families. This is important because it seems that single-parent families are a threat to producing ISJs. Single parents are more likely to use abusive forms of violence towards their children than parents in dual caretaker households. Also, income seems to play a substantially more im-portant role in single-parent families than in two-parent families with regards to parental violence.[55] This is compounded by the fact that children born to teen-aged mothers are twice as likely to be raised in poverty than those born to older mothers.[56] Also, almost all of the increase in child poverty over the last two decades can be traced to the high number of single-parent families after 1970, a trend almost exclusively due to an increase in childbearing out-side of marriage.[57] Finally:

If we look at unmarried female-headed households in general, 60 percent receive public assistance . . . children raised in those homes were less likely to be employed, and more likely to form single-mother households in early adulthood than those from two-parent families . . . the poverty rate for the children of mothers who finished high school, got married, and reached the age of 20 before having their first child was 8 percent, whereas it was 79 percent for the children of mothers who did none of these three things.[58]

Family structure and parental age play an influential role in the role of financial prosperity.

4.1.2 The Family Resource Model

The second major thesis concerning poverty is the family resource model. Here, stress is not the main consideration. Rather, it is that parents without sufficient money cannot provide the resources that their children need. I am more sympathetic to this thesis because I also wish to assure that children will have the necessary resources to become ISJs. However, its emphasis is on providing resources, not parenting, implying that children will fare well so long as they have resources provided for them. Yet merely having resources, without considering *which* resources are the most valuable or *who* ought to provide them, can be insufficient for healthy child development. This is well-illustrated in studies of children of affluent parents.[59] These studies are important because they provide a class where one variable in question, resources, is non-constant, and another variable in question, incompetent parents, remains constant. This is further illustrated in a comparative study of high socioeconomic status (SES) suburban students and their low SES inner-city counterparts; the high SES suburban youth had increased levels of anxiety and elevated use of cigarettes, alcohol, marijuana, and hard drugs.[60] The affluent children perceived their parents as physically and emotionally unavailable to the same degree that children in poverty did.[61] In the case of the suburban youth, perceived isolation from one's parents, particularly low perceived closeness to mothers, was identified as highly problematic.[62] One might think that having greater wealth would permit greater familial closeness because reduced economic hardship reduces stressors. The opposite was found. Feelings of isolation probably resulted from little family time together due to their numerous after-school activities for children and their parents' demanding career obligations.[63] Greater resources do not necessarily translate into healthy child development. Furthermore, good parenting is a necessary condition for healthy child development across sociodemographic groups and perceived closeness to parents promotes healthy child development.[64]

It may be objected that comparing an affluent population to an impoverished one is unfair. The belief that the poor do not have the luxury to choose
between working and spending time with their family, whereas the affluent
do, demonstrates an underlying classism. It also misses the point: children of
affluent parents, just as the children of the poor, are innocent victims when
they lack proper parenting. One would be immediately dismissed if he were
to say that we should not bother with the children of the poor because their
parents should just get a job (or a spouse, etc.) and fulfill their obligations
properly. Likewise, we should not ignore the high-risk children of affluent
parents because of the life-decisions that their parents have made. To consider
this from another perspective, in both poor and affluent populations children
are at high risk when a very basic requirement is missing from their lives—
involved and competent parents. The question should then be what to do to
remedy this problem. I have already addressed the poverty case and how
more ISJs would eliminate the need to worry about others' financial status
and this having a reflection upon their self-worth. Oddly, this is also applicable to affluent parents on a hedonic treadmill: parents who try to outdo their
neighbors at the risk of neglecting their parental duties. Such a treadmill
need not exist if society were to place a higher value on familial obligations
and encourage the affluent to be more devoted to their families in a meaningful way. This is consistent with maintaining a competitive and dedicated
workforce.

I discussed how impoverished parents need to believe that lack of wealth
is not necessarily bad nor does it demonstrate a flawed character. In that
sense, poverty-induced stress is a social construct, but it is a social construct
with a potentially important effect on children simply by negatively affecting
them through their parents' stress. Adults' attitudes often determine how they
respond to certain situations or environments; this also extends to children. A
strong belief in one's abilities helps to preclude developing a negative self-
fulfilling prophecy, and this also extends to children. This was illustrated in a
study comparing resilient and non-resilient children in impoverished environments; belief in one's abilities to succeed largely differentiated the two
groups.[65] The ability to develop the self-assurance needed to foster resilience
is highly determined by how children are reared by their parents. Parents can
cope with poverty in different ways, and they can explain why they are in
poverty in different ways. It is unsurprising that children's experiences with
poverty are shaped by how their parents react to poverty.[66] If poverty is explained as a social injustice, a child will be less likely to be resilient; lacking
the confidence to overcome challenges, he is likely to think that he is destined
to fail.[67] Poverty may provide some obstacles to development, but the most
difficult obstacles that exist are how one perceives poverty and life. If chil-

dren are parented well and develop self-respect, they should be able to flourish. We should focus our energies on good parenting.

5. PROPER INVESTMENT

5.1. Should We Abolish the Family?

If children are affected by parents as I have argued and if good parenting is as necessary for their well-being and the stability of society as I have proposed, then the most important question society can ask is what nurtures children in a way that is best for children and society. This question takes into consideration the interests of children, the interests of adults, and the interests of society as a whole. It even considers one of the most basic matters of fairness in the egalitarian concern of equality. That is, persons ought to have meaningful equality of opportunity and the capability to flourish. Yet I have also implied throughout this book that being raised by parents in a family is the best means to supply that equality and flourishing. I have demonstrated that parents can pose an incredible threat to their children and to society. Furthermore, the family is the most powerful creator of inequality. So, an important question arises: should we abolish the family? An egalitarian theory must at least consider whether the family should be eliminated. Rawls recognized this:

> It seems that even when fair opportunity (as it has been defined) is satisfied, the family will lead to unequal chances between individuals (§46). Is the family to be abolished then? Taken by itself and given a certain primacy, the idea of equal opportunity inclines in this direction. But within the context of the theory of justice as a whole, there is much less urgency to take this course.[68]

Joshua Schwartz, unconvinced, argues, "Rawlsian justice does indeed call for the abolition of the family."[69] In one of the very best philosophical treatments of the family, Blustein writes:

> Should we, then, abolish the family? There is no simple answer to this question. If we want equality for children, the price must be paid in parental liberty. Some form of common upbringing, in which the physical, emotional, and intellectual development of all children is continually monitored and uniform standards of adequate care are imposed, seems to be the best way to accomplish this. If we want greater equality for children and only some sacrifices of liberty, we can try to affect the opportunities of children by, for example, requiring that prospective parents be licensed before they are allowed to start a family. If we want to retain liberty and yet do something to reduce inequality of opportunity among children,

we can offer loans to children in the form of tax credits to their families, create new and support existing child-care services, disseminate information about child care, or provide educational opportunities for parents. In order to decide whether the family should be abolished, we have to balance liberty against equality.[70]

Rawls, Schwartz, and Blustein are justified in recognizing the tension that arises between equality of opportunity and liberty when the role of the family is carefully considered.

I argue that the family should not be abolished. Families are the ideal institution for proper child development; alternatives do not provide the same loving and nurturing that parents provide. This seems to commit me to accepting child maltreatment by parents and the vast inequality of opportunity that must exist when families exist. However, I do not. In addition to arguing that families are essential for optimal child development, I also argue that it is the duty of society to promote families with competent ISJ parents and to discourage families consisting of single parents or non-ISJs. In fact, a political society may even be justified in promulgating laws to ensure that only prospectively competent parents can raise children. This could be done through a system of licensing, which will be discussed in chapter 5.

I will next discuss a particular kind of parental investment, why and how this kind of investment is necessary, and why it is better than alternative kinds of investment in children. I admire the earlier mentioned family resource thesis because it, unlike many other models, is child-centered. The resources provided to parents are explicitly an investment in children. Specifically, the resource thesis argues that parents who are poor cannot invest much in their children. Parents who lack investment in their children cannot expect a high rate of return. Using financial terms is helpful here because poverty does not have to affect the *kind* of investment that children need most—non-abusive and competent parents who nurture out of love. It is also vital to understand further how best to invest in children if children are to play a role in political theory. To better explain the type of investment I advocate, I will now discuss investment in the context of economics and evolutionary biology before discussing more comprehensively how the family serves as the means of investing in children in the next chapter.

5.2 The Economist and the Family

Some economic models focus on the implications of altruistic behavior in cooperative games. This approach corresponds well with my intent to increase the percentage of ISJs and decrease the percentage of non-ISJs for political stability. A society of ISJs would have more trust, fellow feeling, and cooperation than a society of non-ISJs. In this sense, ISJs seem to be what economists sometimes refer to as "altruists" in models of cooperation. However, few economic models have explored *how* the preferences of altruists or ISJs develop.[71] Parents have an enormous impact on preferences and whether one matures into an altruist or an ISJ. I should be careful because 'altruism' is a vague term, and economists and philosophers may use the term differently. For example, the economist Gary Becker believes that altruists maximize their own utility, but I am unaware of many philosophical definitions of altruism that necessitate this condition, though some may permit it. Becker explains:

> Since an altruist maximizes his own utility (subject to his income restraint), he might be called selfish, not altruistic, in terms of utility. Perhaps—but note that *h* [an altruist] also raises *w*'s [his spouse's] utility through his transfers to *w*. I am giving a definition to altruism that is relevant to behavior—to consumption and production choices—rather than giving a philosophical discussion of what "really" motivates people.[72]

This does not seem to be a strong enough account of altruism, even as a descriptive account of behavior. It seems to preclude the possibility of *h* losing utility himself for the sake of increasing the utility of *w*, especially when the overall utility of *h* and *w* (and *h* + *w*) is less than it was before *h*'s altruistic act. I note this because Becker later seems to allow *h* to lose some utility for sake of *w* if such a loss benefits (*h* + *w*) overall. This usage is not limited to Becker. Ermisch notes that in economics "a person is said to be *altruistic* toward someone if his (her) welfare depends on the welfare of that person."[73] The welfare of the altruist is not necessarily considered to be a factor in determining acts of altruism in philosophy; rather, altruism is largely contingent upon whether one's act adds (or is intended to add) to the utility of others. However, some definitions in economics do seem closer to what is used in philosophy. For example,

> In economics, an individual is said to have altruistic preferences toward another if she places a positive weight on the others' welfare in her utility function. Hence, such a person would be willing to give up some of her own consumption in return for an increase in the others' consumption.[74]

I generally understand altruists to (i) have regard for others and/or (ii) be devoted to the welfare of others. I will henceforth refer to those altruists who embody (i) to be weak altruists and those who embody (ii) to be strong altruists. All ISJs are weak altruists by virtue of having self-respect, but some ISJs

are also strong altruists. While ISJs are weak altruists in all spheres of life as
all of their actions demonstrate regard for others, even when they are ultimately acting for their own sake, I also presume that ISJs are strong altruists
in parent-child relationships. ISJ parents cannot have regard for their children
as though they were unrelated. Rather, ISJ parents are *devoted* to the welfare
of their children. By appealing to a multiple-sphere model that differentiates
between one's family and the rest of society, I am not trying to make ISJs be
Kavkavian Predominant Egoists (those who only rarely act unselfishly and
act unselfishly only when benefiting family, friends, or projects of one's own
interests—or when the gain to others is large while the sacrifice to oneself is
minimal).[75] Rather, I am trying to account for why most people's intuitions
tell them that we ought to give special value to family and friends when acting and that we *ought* to do this for good reason when dealing with children,
especially one's own children. I refer to Adam Smith for why altruism often
decreases with distance from oneself:

> Every man feels his own pleasures and his own pains more sensibly than those
> of other people. . . . After himself, the members of his own family, those who
> usually live in the same house as him, his parents, his children, his brothers and
> sisters, are naturally and usually the persons upon whose happiness or misery
> his conduct must have the greatest influence.[76]

What Smith provides here is a descriptive account of how humans behave; he
does not also argue that how humans behave is how they ought to behave. I
hope to show, in this chapter and the next, why humans also have good reason to act this way.

It is also odd to see comments like this from Becker: "The model assumes
utility-maximizing parents who are concerned about the welfare of their children."[77] In fairness, he also says, "I do not assume that other species calculate
the relative advantage of different behavior or 'try' to maximize. The economic approach does not even assume that humans consciously maximize."[78]
I have two responses, depending on the reading of the above. On the less
charitable reading of Becker, one where the *parents'* utility is maximized, we
ought not to take this as a model of proper parental investment. At the motivational level, this reduces children to commodities used as a means to their
parents' own ends, even if children are not being used *only* as a means. It is
also objectionable to maximize at the behavioral level because children are
unlikely to develop properly if their parents seek to maximize their own utility. Concerns still exist on a more charitable reading of Becker, one where the
utility of the child is maximized. It is unclear that speaking of parental investment in terms of 'utility' is the proper way to think about any of this
(though it is understandable in this context, perhaps, because economists need

some unit of measurement to work with). Also, we cannot *demand* that parents seek to *maximize* the utility of their children. Maximizing for the sake of one's children is a noble ideal, but we have no reason to issue blame for those who simply do a great job without worrying about whether maximization is attained. In fact, obsession about such maximization may use up resources that could be used for the sake of benefiting their children. Parents must not be *completely* devoted to their children insofar as they must give up all of their own needs and interests. That said, parents need to take into consideration the great needs of their children. Perhaps this is what Becker means. Rather than thinking in terms of maximizing the utility of children or parents independently, perhaps he means to maximize the joint utility of parents and children. This sort of utility maximization is terribly complicated. My objection is not to a system where both parents and children flourish in their relationship as much as possible; rather, my objection is to trying to harness this into a utility-maximization scheme where a unique solution might exist and all other solutions are suboptimal. Life is simply too complicated to address parents and children in such a way.

Economists also have different models of fertility that relate to investment. Two prominent models are that children serve as providers of labor or serve as providers of support when their parents grow old. Becker and Tomes write,

> In many societies, poorer and middle-income-level parents are supported during old age by children instead of by the sale of gold, jewelry, rugs, land, or other assets that could be accumulated by parents at younger ages. Our analysis suggests that these parents choose to rely on children instead of assets because rates of return on investments in children are higher than they are on other assets.[79]

In a completely well-ordered society, it would be unnecessary for parents to consider children as an investment for their retirement. Many other bad reasons are cited as a reason to have children: affirmation of manliness or femininity, attempts at salvaging a bad relationship, seeking a source of affirmation or love, etc. However, some parents have altruistic reasons for having and raising children. These include a desire to nurture and to love. Parents should be motivated to have children primarily by the strong altruistic desire to have children.

Some economists recognize two different kinds of investments in children: financial and human capital. From Luthar's earlier-cited studies on affluence, it should be clear that financial investment without human capital investment is insufficient for the well-being of children. Likewise, as illustrated by the aforementioned resilience and competent parenting studies, human capital investment is much more necessary than financial investment in raising children.

Lastly, the problem of imperfect information is pervasive in the realm of economics; it is also a problem for families. Manser and Brown argue:

> An essential feature of the marriage decision in a world with many men and women is imperfect information. Any unmarried individual must decide whether to accept a given marriage offer without perfect knowledge about alternative opportunities and, in addition, information about potential spouses must be obtained sequentially by means of a search process. Faced with a given offer of marriage, the individual will accept the offer if he or she expects a gain in utility over time from accepting.[80]

The above is based on the assumption that "The decision to form a household depends on the existence of utility gains to both individuals, relative to their threat points."[81] I note the marriage decision in order to show similarities and differences with the parent-child relationship. Marriage consists of agents with independent wills who enter into a relationship. They do so with imperfect information and, therefore, do so at risk. They are not forced to accept offers, at least in our current society. Either spouse may leave the relationship if it is unsatisfactory. When parents have children, they do not engage in the same kind of activity. There is no bargaining; the unborn cannot bargain. Children have no choice in the matter, and they are forced into the relationship. This point is important because in most instances a child cannot divorce his parents. Furthermore, children, or at least young children, have no conceivable threat advantage over their parents. The only similarity between marriage and the parent-child relationship seems to be that of imperfect information because parents do not know many things about an unborn child genetically: sex, weight, height, intelligence, emotional disposition, etc. Many of these things can be nurtured (or modified through artificial genetic selection), but parents still initiate the relationship with a great deal of imperfect information. Recognizing how truly vulnerable children are, we should reflect upon the practice of indiscriminately allowing any potential parent the ability to enter into such an asymmetrical relationship. Likewise, we should realize that childrearing is a rare example of a cooperative arrangement that is reached without the mutual consent of the involved parties. Parental power entails a great deal of responsibility—a kind of responsibility that is rarely, if ever, found outside of the parent-child relationship.

5.3 The Evolutionary Biologist and the Family

Evolutionary biology's treatment of parenting and the family will also help clarify what I mean by parental investment. I use Robert L. Trivers' "Parental Investment and Sexual Selection"[82] as a guide. Trivers writes:

I first define parental investment as any investment by the parent in an individual offspring that increases the offspring's chance of surviving (and hence of reproductive success) at the cost of the parent's ability to invest in other offspring. So defined, parental investment includes the metabolic investment in the primary cells but refers to any investment (such as feeding or guarding the young) that benefits the young.[83]

I demand more than investment for the sake of *survival* in humans. Some human children will die from accidental or natural causes or, more rarely, as a result of parental neglect, but *basic survival* is not out of reach for most children in our society. Most children live to adulthood in our mostly well-ordered society. When talking about parental investment, I take it for granted that children will usually not die prematurely. I am concerned that they survive in a particular way—that they develop in a healthy manner, are provided with basic capabilities from their parents, and can become ISJs.

Trivers continues:

[Parental investment] does not include effort expended in finding a member of the opposite sex or in subduing members of one's own sex in order to mate with a member of the opposite sex, since such effort (except in special cases) does not affect the survival chances of the resulting offspring and is therefore not parental investment.[84]

If I were only concerned with parental investment as a means to produce a high number of surviving offspring, then I would agree that the effort expended in mate selection should not be considered part of parental investment. The quality of the parent is largely meaningless with regards to producing surviving offspring by humans in our mostly well-ordered society. No matter how low the quality of the parent is, the child will likely survive. The child may lead an unhealthy life and be bereft of basic capabilities necessary to flourish, but he is nonetheless likely to survive. Finding another human being with whom one can procreate is not that costly or difficult. Because mere survival is an insufficient threshold, mate selection *should* be an integral part of parental investment. Human mates should be much more careful, selective, patient, and demanding before engaging in activity that may lead to children. This is possible in a world of ISJs because individuals will have self-respect and will exhibit higher levels of responsibility. Mates will not have to settle for whatever is offered to them, even if pressured. They can respect and protect themselves and their (potential) children enough to invest more diligently in a search for a mate who demonstrates likely investment in a family. If this happens, the cost of the search in finding a mate should increase.

Due to biology, females will predominately bear the burden of being highly selective on this model, not males. Trivers explains why females particularly need to be more selective in their search for mates:

> After a nine-month pregnancy, a female is more or less free to terminate her investment at any moment but doing so wastes her investment up until then. Given the imbalance in investment the male may maximize his chances of leaving surviving offspring by copulating and abandoning many females, some of whom, alone or with the aid of others, will raise his offspring. In species where there has been strong selection for male parental care, it is more likely that a mixed strategy will be the optimal male course—to help a single female raise young, while not passing up opportunities to mate with other females whom he will not aid. In many birds, males defend a territory which the female also uses for feeding prior to egg laying, but the cost of this investment by the male is difficult to evaluate. In some species, as outlined above, the male may provision the female before she has produced the young, but this provisioning is usually small compared to the cost of the eggs. In any case, the cost of the copulation itself is always trivial to the male, and in theory the male need not invest anything else in order to copulate. If there is any chance the female can raise the young, either alone or with the help of others, it would be to the male's advantage to copulate with her. By this reasoning one would expect males of monogamous species to retain some psychosocial traits consistent with promiscuous habits. A male would be selected to differentiate between a female he will only impregnate and a female with whom he will also raise young. Toward the former he should be more eager for sex and less discriminating in choice of sex partner than the female toward him, but toward the latter he should be about as discriminating, as she toward him.[85]

The above describes something that is often overlooked—patterns of investment may be influenced by biological differences between the sexes. In particular, females can bear children but males cannot. Whether this is fair or not, depending on one's view of whether biology can be unfair, the asymmetry entails other asymmetries. The foremost seems to be that females, not males, largely dictate the level of parental investment in children in society.[86] At the most basic level, females are responsible for the extremely important element of prenatal care because biologically only they can provide it. It may be argued that this is, or ought to be, also a concern for males because males should help in assisting with prenatal care. Yet in a society where females do not demand a high level of devotion from males, males may simply flee upon the news that they have impregnated a female. Such a lack of investment in their partners, not demanding more investment from males, may leave females and their children to fend for themselves both in the prenatal and postnatal stages. Females ultimately dictate how much investment will be provided to children because they decide how much to invest in a relationship with a male before having children. If females do not require a dedicated investment from males, then it is unsurprising, as in Trivers's example, that males will not stick around, especially in an environment where survival of the child is guaranteed. If females demand male fidelity before having children, especially if this becomes a societal norm, then females increase the chances that males will help raise children after birth.

It may be objected that the above argument is sexist or out of date because other options exist. For example, society can provide artificial means for females to provide for their children without support of a partner, such as daycare or government-provided welfare. However, such artificial means of support to females seems to provide, on Trivers's thesis above, even less of a reason for males to stay and invest in their children. If a male's children will be taken care of by another, then he can move from female to female without making any investment. In this sense, female reliance upon an artificial means of support via welfare seems to lead to a vicious cycle whereby females harm themselves and their children. The reason for this on the ISJ model is that two parents are necessary for optimal child development (this will be defended in chapter 4). By not demanding more from males, females learn not to expect males even to fulfill basic obligations such as taking care of their own children. Meanwhile, males are given sexual rein without consequences. Females thereby perpetuate a system where they are solely responsible for childcare *and* where children are raised in suboptimal environments. Females would be subjecting themselves needlessly to more work. Consequently, it might even be argued that such a cycle demonstrates servile behavior. Females may consciously be exercising a perceived right to procreate with knowledge of the likelihood that their partner will not invest anything other than that involved in the actual sex act, and they thus may not be servile in one sense. Yet females are asymmetrically harmed by exercising such a right when not also demanding investment from males. Females may be provided with financial assistance from the government, but this investment of financial capital, though it may be intended to be a residual investment in human capital, is inferior to a direct investment in human capital by ensuring that children have decent parents.

It may further be objected that the above is still sexist or out of date because biological fathers can be identified with genetic testing, thus we can add more artificial constraints to decrease the likelihood that males will not invest in females and children. The legal system can require male investment by requiring financial contributions (child support) and enacting civil or criminal penalties for those men who do not meet their financial obligations. This may force males into "fathering" roles for the wrong reasons, and their money or mere presence will likely not entail any meaningfully increased investment in children. Child support will not suffice if what children really need is competent and loving parents. If a male supports a female and their children merely to evade jail, then the investment and quality of care that he is likely to provide must be called into question.

CONCLUSION

While egalitarians and libertarians have been debating over their respective conceptions of the self in adults or debating theories while presupposing such conceptions, they have largely ignored the fact that *all* children have an extremely fragile psychology. If we do not understand the fragility of children, it does not matter whether adults are universally robust (according to most libertarians) or fragile (according to many egalitarians) or, more likely, that adults vary with regards to degree of fragility. A stable and well-ordered society requires citizens with good character, and good character in humans is largely contingent upon being nurtured properly as a child. ISJs represent the kind of character that is needed to attain and perpetuate a stable and well-ordered society. In particular, ISJs are altruistic in the sense that they have fellow feeling that manifests cooperativeness, trust, and helpfulness. The deep sense of self-respect that they have makes them resilient to things, such as poverty, that are inimical to proper development only in the sense that they are socially constructed to appear as a hindrance to proper development.

Too many non-ISJs exist in society. As has been shown, one of the easiest and most common ways to create ISJs is to maltreat children. This raises a problem that is independent of any political implications that follow from it, the injustice of child maltreatment. Children are the most vulnerable class of citizens, and the lack of a genuine effort to reduce child maltreatment effectively is indicative of societal ageism. Not only does child maltreatment yield immediate harm, it also often yields long-term harm. Those who are maltreated are also at great risk of maltreating their own children, thereby continuing the cycle of maltreatment. The deepness of this harm generates a threat to society because those who are maltreated are at higher risk of being non-ISJs, and non-ISJs threaten society in many ways. The set of non-ISJs may be small, but they can severely damage the infrastructure of society.

In addition to protecting children for their own sake and for the sake of society, I sought to frame things within an egalitarian system. I have roughly employed a capability theory within the formal framework of what Anderson might call a starting-gate theory. This is done to provide meaningful equality of opportunity. In doing so, I hope to have eluded Anderson's objection that starting-gate theories cannot assure an equality of social standing. I did this by searching for something that could be self-reinforcing in a deep sense, and the role of self-respect seems to fill this. This is particularly true in a society where ISJs become predominant and their value system ranks dedication to one's family, friends, and fellow citizens as increasingly important. Because self-respect begins early in one's life, it can last throughout life and allows one to flourish. However, this raises the question of how to nurture children in a way that they become ISJs. It should be clear that directly investing in human capital via the family is superior to investing indirectly in human capital via other measures. Goods and resources do not provide a means to optimal child development, but good parenting does. If we must think of things in terms of goods and resources, it should be clear that good parenting provides the best kind of goods and resources for children. In the next chapter, I will examine precisely what a family is and why the family uniquely provides fertile ground for ISJs to develop.

NOTES

1. Plato, *The Republic*, trans. and ed. Allan Bloom (New York: Basic Books, 1991), Bk. V, 449d.

2. I do not mean that we should seek to equalize parenting quality. Rather, I mean that we should try to secure a minimal baseline or threshold of decency below which people should not be able to parent.

3. Exceptions do exist. I particularly have in mind Jennifer Roback Morse's *Love and Economics: Why the Laissez-Faire Family Doesn't Work* (Dallas: Spence Publishing Company, 2001) and her "No Families, No Freedom: Human Flourishing in a Free Society," *Social Philosophy and Policy*, 16 (1999).

4. *Ethics*, 109 (1999). I use Anderson's essay because I believe it to be the best brief survey of egalitarianism, and I object to many of the same things that Anderson does but for importantly different reasons.

5. Anderson, 288.

6. Anderson, 291. Anderson is particularly referring here to Richard Arneson's "Equality and Equality of Opportunity of Welfare," in Louis Pojman and Robert Westmoreland, ed. *Equality: Selected Readings* (New York: Oxford University Press, 1997). In general, she critiques various aspects of egalitarianism in Ronald Dworkin, Philippe Van Parijs, G. A. Cohen, and Thomas Nagel.

7. Anderson, 290.

8. Anderson, 308.

9. Anderson, 289 and 319.

10. Anderson's worry about this seems to be that egalitarianism has recently developed an unhealthy fetish about what to do about irresponsible and lazy people, and

luck egalitarians have put such persons at the heart of their theories instead of more important concerns of social justice. See Anderson, 287–88.

11. There is also the problem of how to adjudicate between objective needs of citizens and their mere preferences. I seek only to increase objective well-being; therefore, I am willing to allow that many citizens will not have their preferences filled as they choose. Also, part of my ISJ plan, as seen in chapter 2, is to nurture preferences in such a way that they closely approximate that which is best for well-being.

12. Anderson, 316. G. A. Cohen makes a similar point: "Amartya Sen asked what metric egalitarians should use to establish the extent to which their idea is realized in a given society," and "there is substantial ambiguity in Sen's use of the term 'capability,' which makes it hard to be sure what his conception of equality implies," "On the Currency of Egalitarian Justice," *Ethics*, 109 (1989), 906 and 942. Richard Arneson espouses something similar to a capabilities approach in "Equality and Equal Opportunity for Welfare," *Philosophical Studies*, 56 (1989), 90. For a list of human functional capabilities that Sen *could* accept, see Martha Nussbaum's *Women and Human Development: The Capabilities Approach* (Cambridge: Cambridge University Press, 2001), 78–80. For Sen's most complete articulation of his capability theory, see *Inequality Reexamined* (Cambridge, MA: Harvard University Press, 2001).

13. Anderson, 288–89, my emphasis.

14. *TJ*, 41.

15. David Finkelhor and Angela Browne, "Assessing the Long-Term Impact of Child Sexual Abuse: A Review and Conceptualization," in Gerald Hotaling, David Finkelhor, John T. Kirkpatrick, and Murray A. Straus, eds. *Family Abuse and Its Consequences: New Directions in Research* (London: Sage Publications, 1988), 278–79.

16. John Locke, *Some Thoughts Concerning Education and Of the Conduct of the Understanding*, ed. Ruth W. Grant and Nathan Tarcov (Indianapolis, IN: Hacking Publishing Company, 1996), §71, 50.

17. Rawls, "A Sense of Justice," 281.

18. Judith G. Smetana and Mario Kelly, "Social Cognition in Maltreated Children," in Dante Cicchetti and Vicki Carlson, eds. *Child Maltreatment: Theory and Research on the Causes and Consequences of Child Abuse and Neglect* (Cambridge: Cambridge University Press, 1989), 636. In general, maltreated children are found to be deficient in affective and behavioral regulation compared to nonmaltreated children. This, furthermore, has a negative effect on their social competence. See Ann Shields and Dante Cicchetti, "Reactive Aggression Among Maltreated Children: The Contributions of Attention and Emotion Dysregulation," *Journal of Clinical Child Psychology*, 27 (1998); Ann M. Shields, Dante Cicchetti, and Richard M. Ryan, "The Development of Emotional and Behavioral Self-Regulation and Social Competence Among Maltreated School-Age Children," *Development and Psychopathology*, 6 (1994).

19. See C. George and M. Main, "Social Interactions of Young Abused Children: Approach, Avoidance, and Aggression," *Child Development*, 50 (1979); Debbie Hoffman-Plotkin and Craig T. Twentyman, "A Multimodal Assessment of Behavioral and Cognitive Deficits in Abused and Neglected Preschoolers," *Child Development*, 55

(1984); Dorothy Otnow Lewis, Catherine Mallouh, and Victoria Webb, "Child Abuse, Delinquency, and Violent Criminality," in Cicchetti and Carlson (1989).

20. See Hoffman-Plotkin and Twentyman (1984); Thomas J. Reidy, "The Aggressive Characteristics of Abused and Neglected Children," *Journal of Clinical Psychology*, 33 (1977).

21. See James M. Gaudin, Jr., Norman Polansky, Allie C. Kirkpatrick, and Paula Shilton, "Family Functioning in Neglectful Families," *Child Abuse and Neglect*, 20 (1996); Julie A. Schumacher, Amy Slep, and Richard E. Heyman, "Risk Factors for Neglect," *Aggression and Violent Behavior*, 6 (2001); Stephanie A. Stowman and Brad Donohue, "Assessing Child Neglect: A Review of Standardized Procedures," *Aggression and Violent Behavior*, 10 (2005); Murray A. Straus and Glenda Kaufman Kantor, "Definition and Measurement of Neglectful Behavior: Some Principles and Guidelines," *Child Abuse and Neglect*, 29 (2005). Distinctions between different kinds of neglect are also now being made: John F. Knutson, David S. DeGarmo, and John B. Reid, "Social Disadvantage and Neglectful Parenting as Precursors to the Development of Antisocial and Aggressive Child Behavior: Testing a Theoretical Model," *Aggressive Behavior*, 30 (2004).

22. See Kathryn L. Hildyard and David A. Wolfe, "Child Neglect: Developmental Issues and Outcomes," *Child Abuse and Neglect*, 26 (2002); Hoffman-Plotkin and Twentyman (1984); Amy L. Koenig, Dante Cicchetti, and Fred A. Rogash, "Moral Development: The Association Between Maltreatment and Young Children's Prosocial Behaviors and Moral Transgressions," *Social Development*, 13 (2004).

23. See Daryl J. Higgins and Marita P. McCabe, "Multiple Forms of Child Abuse and Neglect: Adult Retrospective Reports," *Aggression and Violent Behavior*, 6 (2001).

24. See Kerry E. Bolger and Charlotte J. Patterson, "Developmental Pathways from Child Maltreatment to Peer Rejection," *Child Development*, 72 (2001); Louise S. Éthier, Jean-Pascal Lemelin, and Carl Lacharité, "A Longitudinal Study of the Effects of Chronic Maltreatment on Children's Behavioral and Emotional Problems," *Child Abuse and Neglect*, 28 (2004).

255. See Bolger and Patterson (2001); Kerry E. Bolger, Charlotte Patterson, and Janis B. Kupersmidt, "Peer Relationships and Self-Esteem among Children Who Have Been Maltreated," *Child Development*, 69 (1998).

26. See Bolger and Patterson (2001); Daryl J. Higgins, "The Importance of Degree Versus Type of Maltreatment: A Cluster Analysis of Child Abuse Types," *The Journal of Psychology*, 138 (2004).

27. See Carollee Howes, "Abused and Neglected Children with Their Peers," in Hotaling, Finkelhor, Kirkpatrick, and Straus (1988), 100–01; Suzanne Salzinger, Richard S. Feldman, Muriel Hammer, and Margaret Rosario, "The Effects of Physical Violence on Children's Social Relationships," *Child Development*, 64 (2003).

28. See L. Rowell Huesman, Leonard D. Eron, Monroe M. Lefkowitz, and Leopold O. Walder, "Stability of Aggression Over Time and Generations," *Developmental Psychology*, 20 (1984).

29. See John Coie, Robert Terry, Kari Lenox, John Lochman, and Clarine Hyman, "Childhood Rejection and Aggression as Predictors of Stable Patterns of Adolescent

Disorder," *Development and Psychopathology*, 7 (1995); Bolger, Patterson, and Kupersmidt (1998); Bolger and Patterson (2001).

30. See Claire L. Fox and Michael J. Boulton, "Friendship as a Moderator of the Relationship between Social Skills Problems and Peer Victimization," *Aggressive Behavior*, 32 (2006).

31. See Mary E. Haskett and Janet A. Kistner, "Social Interactions and Peer Perceptions of Young Physically Abused Children," *Child Development*, 62 (1991); Suzanne Salzinger, Richard S. Feldman, Muriel Hammer, and Margaret Rosario, "The Effects of Physical Abuse on Children's Social Relationships," *Child Development*, 64 (1993); Tasha R. Howe and Ross D. Parke, "Friendship Quality and Sociometric Status: Between Group Differences and Links to Loneliness in Severely Abused and Nonabused Children," *Child Abuse and Neglect*, 25 (2001).

32. See Jeffrey G. Parker and Steven R. Asher, "Peer Relations and Later Personal Adjustment: Are Low-Accepted Children At Risk?," *Psychological Bulletin*, 102 (1987).

33. See Helene Raskin White and Cathy Spatz Widom, "Intimate Partner Violence Among Abused and Neglected Children in Young Adulthood: The Mediating Effects of Early Aggression, Antisocial Personality, Hostility and Alcohol Problems," *Aggressive Behavior*, 29 (2003); Rebecca A. Coleman and Cathy Spatz Widom, "Childhood Abuse and Neglect and Adult Intimate Relationships: A Prospective Study," *Child Abuse and Neglect*, 28 (2004).

34. I use "unhealthy" rather than "low" because those with high self-esteem are often the most aggressive. The subjective nature of self-esteem allows phrases such as "unhealthy low/high self esteem" to make sense, whereas it generally does not make sense to talk about "low/high self-respect" because self-respect is usually an objective notion. It is difficult to know exactly how the above distinctions relate to the ones made in the previous chapter. I suspect that parents who maltreat often have low self-esteem; however, I suspect that a lack of self-respect is a better indicator. Likewise, I think that phrases such as "unhealthy self-esteem" reveal the existence of a lack of self-respect. This distinction seems to have caused much confusion in data interpretation in self-esteem studies. See Christina Salmivalli, "Feeling Good about Oneself, Being Bad to Others? Remarks on Self-Esteem, Hostility, and Aggressive Behavior," *Aggression and Violent Behavior*, 6 (2001).

35. See E. M. Kinard, "Emotional Development in Physically Abused Children," *American Journal of Orthopsychiatry*, 50 (1980); R. Rohner and E. Rohner, "Antecedents and Consequences of Parental Rejection: A Theory of Emotional Abuse," *Child Abuse and Neglect*, 4 (1980); Stephen C. Anderson and Michael L. Lauderdale, "Characteristics of Abusive Parents: A Look at Self-Esteem," *Child Abuse and Neglect*, 6 (1982); R. Kim Oates and Douglas Forrest, "Self-Esteem and Early Background of Abusive Mothers," *Child Abuse and Neglect*, 9 (1985); R. Kim Oates, Douglas Forrest, and Anthony Peacock, "Self-Esteem of Abused Children," *Child Abuse and Neglect*, 9 (1985).

36. Jack C. Westman, *Licensing Parents: Can We Prevent Child Abuse and Neglect?* (New York: Insight Books, 1994), 2. See also Hotaling and Finkelhor, 26, who estimate that 6.9 million children are abused each year.

37. See, respectively, Hugh LaFollette, "Licensing Parents," *Philosophy and Public Affairs*, 9 (1980), 185, n.4 and Joan McCord, "A Forty Year Perspective on Child Abuse and Neglect," *Child Abuse and Neglect*, 7 (1983).

38. Joan Kaufman and Edward Zigler, "The Intergenerational Transmission of Child Abuse," in Cicchetti and Carlson (1989), 135. For an earlier version of this, see Joan Kaufman and Edward Zigler, "Do Abused Children Become Abusive Parents?," *American Journal of Orthopsychiatry*, 57 (1987). See also Katherine C. Pears and Deborah M. Capaldi, "Intergenerational Transmission of Abuse: A Two-Generational Prospective Study of an At-Risk Sample," *Child Abuse and Neglect*, 25 (2001).

39. Michael Rutter, "Intergenerational Continuities and Discontinuities in Serious Parenting Difficulties," in Cicchetti and Carlson (1989), 339.

40. Richard J. Gelles, "Child Abuse as Psychopathology: A Sociological Critique and Reformulation," *American Journal of Orthopsychiatry*, 43 (1973). It should be noted, though, that Gelles went too far because environmental factors are neither necessary nor sufficient conditions of maltreatment.

41. A. Sameroff and M. Chandler, "Reproductive Risk and the Continuum of Caretaking Causality," in F. Horowitz, ed. *Review of Child Development Research*, vol. 4 (Chicago: University of Chicago Press, 1975). The influence of transactional effects especially became evident in Werner and Smith's landmark study: "In our longitudinal study on Kauai, it soon became clear that to venture a guess at (or predict) the probabilities of developmental outcomes we had to consider *both* the child's constitutional make-up and the quality of his or her caretaking environment," Emmy E. Werner and Ruth S. Smith, *Vulnerable But Invincible: A Longitudinal Study of Resilient Children and Youth* (New York: Adams, Barrister, Cox, 1998), 4.

42. For the origins of ecological accounts, see U. Brofenbrenner, "Toward an Experimental Ecology of Human Development," *American Psychologist*, 32 (1977); J. Belsky, "Child Maltreatment: An Ecological Integration," *American Psychologist*, 35 (1980). For surveys of the many important variables considered in maltreatment at this time, see William N. Freidrich and Jerry Boriskin, "The Role of the Child in Abuse: A Review of the Literature," *American Journal of Orthopsychiatry*, 46 (1976); Edward Zigler and Nancy W. Hall, "Physical Abuse in America: Past, Present, and Future," in Cicchetti and Carlson (1989).

43. Kaufman and Zigler, 146.

44. For more on resilience, see Lois Barclay Murphy and Alice E. Moriarty, *Vulnerability, Coping, and Growth: From Intimacy to Adolescence* (New Haven, CT: Yale University Press, 1976); E. James Anthony and Bertram J. Cohler, *The Invulnerable Child* (New York: The Guilford Press, 1987).

45. 202, Though I critique Blustein's solution to the problem about how to counteract the negative effects of families in society, I should note that he is one of the very few philosophers who clearly understands the importance of the family in political philosophy. I have benefited enormously from his work.

46. See R. D. Conger, K. J. Conger, G. H. Elder, F. O. Lorenz, R. L. Simons, and L. B. Whitbeck, "A Family Process Model of Economic Hardship and Adjustment of Early Adolescent Boys," *Child Development*, 63 (1992); R. D. Conger, G. R. Patterson, and X. Ge, "It Takes Two to Replicate: A Mediational Model for the Impact of

Parents' Stress on Adolescent Adjustment," *Child Development*, 66 (1995); K. J. Conger, M. A. Rutter, and R. D. Conger, "The Role of Economic Pressure in the Lives of Parents and Their Adolescents: The Family Stress Model," in Lisa J. Crockett and Rainer K. Silbereisen, eds. *Negotiating Adolescence in Times of Social Change* (Cambridge: Cambridge University Press, 2000). For an overview of different positions, see W. Jean Young, Miriam R. Linver, and Jeanne Brooks-Dunn, "How Money Matters for Young Children's Development: Parental Investment and Family Processes," *Child Development*, 73 (2002).

47. For evidence that stress often works like this, especially in the case of maltreatment, see Jocelyn Brown, Patricia Cohen, Jeffrey G. Johnson, and Suzanne Salzinger, "A Longitudinal Analysis of Risk Factors for Child Maltreatment: Findings of a 17-Year Prospective Study of Officially Recorded and Self-Reported Child Abuse and Neglect," *Child Abuse and Neglect*, 22 (1998).

48. See Michael Rutter, "Early Sources of Security and Competence," in J. Brunner and A. Gaston, eds. *Human Growth and Development* (Oxford: Clarendon Press, 1978); Michael Rutter, "Protective Factors in Children's Responses to Stress and Disadvantage," in M. Kent and J. Rolf, eds. *Primary Prevention of Psychopathology: Social Competence in Children* (Hanover, NH: University Press of New England, 1979).

49. Murray A. Straus, "Stress and Physical Child Abuse," *Child Abuse and Neglect*, 55 (1983).

50. Werner and Smith, 59. See also E. E. Werner, "High Risk Children in Young Adulthood: A Longitudinal Study from Birth to 32 Years," *American Journal of Orthopsychiatry*, 59 (1989).

51. Empirical research on this in the twentieth century is virtually non-existent, but research is beginning to build in the twenty-first century. *This* is the kind of research that needs to be taken more seriously. See Zeng-Yin Chen and Howard B. Kaplan, "Intergenerational Transmission of Constructive Parenting," *Journal of Marriage and Family*, 63 (2001); Qing Zhou, Nancy Eisenberg, Sandra H. Losoya, Richard A. Fabes, Mark Reiser, Ivanna K. Guthrie, Bridget C. Murphy, Amanda J. Cumberland, and Stephanie A. Shepard, "The Relations of Parental Warmth and Positive Expressiveness to Children's Empathy-Related Responding and Social Functioning: A Longitudinal Study," *Child Development*, 73 (2002); Nancy L. Galambos, Erin T. Barker, and David M. Almeida, "Parents *Do* Matter: Trajectories of Change in Externalizing and Internalizing Problems in Early Adolescence," *Child Development*, 74 (2003); Jay Belsky, Sara R. Jaffee, Judith Sligo, Lianne Woodward, and Phil A. Silva, "Intergenerational Transmission of Warm-Sensitive Parenting: A Prospective Study of Mothers and Fathers of 3-Year Olds," *Child Development*, 7 (2005); Michael J. Cleveland, Frederick X. Gibbons, Meg Gerrard, Elizabeth A. Pomery, Gene H. Brody, "The Impact of Parenting on Risk Cognitions and Risk Behavior: A Study of Mediation and Moderation in a Panel of African American Adolescents," *Child Development*, 76 (2005).

52. See David Quinton and Michael Rutter, *Parenting Breakdown: The Making and Breaking of Intergenerational Links* (Aldershot, UK: Aveburg, 1988), 199; Michael Rutter, "Resilience in the Face of Adversity: Protective Factors and Resistance to Psychiatric Disorder," *British Journal of Psychiatry*, 147 (1985).

53. Janis V. F. Long and George E. Vaillant, "Escape From the Underclass," in Timothy F. Dugan and Robert Coles, eds. *The Children of Our Times: Studies in the Development of Resilience* (New York: Brunner/Mazel, 1989).

54. These statistics are from Patrick F. Fagan, Kirk A. Johnson, and Jonathan Butcher, "The Map of the Family," The Heritage Foundation. www.heritage.org/Research/Family/upload /76145_1.pdf (6 April 2008). These statistics derive from the Survey of Consumer Finance, 2001, and they refer to families with children under the age of 18.

55. Lawrence M. Berger, "Income, Family Characteristics, and Physical Violence Toward Children," *Child Abuse and Neglect*, 29 (2005).

56. See R. M. George and B. G. Lee, "Poverty, Early Child Bearing, and Child Maltreatment: A Nominal Analysis," *Children and Youth Services Review*, 21 (1999).

57. Andrea Kane and Isabell Sawhill, "Preventing Early Childbearing," in Isabell Sawhill, ed. *One Percent for the Kids: New Policies, Brighter Futures for America's Children*, ed. (Washington, DC: The Brookings Institution, 2003), 59; Also, from 1960 to 1990 the number of unmarried mothers increased from 240,000 to 4.5 million. Westman, 37.

58. Westman, 70.

59. Suniya Luthar is one of very few researchers who has done much work in this area. This is important because the affluent are rarely studied. Middle-class white males, infamously, predominated studies in the early and mid-twentieth century. Since that time, studies have been increasingly focused towards women, racial minorities, and those in poverty. If omission of these latter groups in studies represented classism, sexism, and racism, then it is fair to say that omission of the affluent represents classism. See S. Luthar, "The Culture of Affluence: Psychological Costs of Material Wealth," *Child Development*, 74 (2003); S. S. Luthar and B. E. Becker, "Privileged but Pressured: A Study of Affluent Youth," *Child Development*, 73 (2002); S. S. Luthar and K. D'Avanzo, "Contextual Factors in Substance Abuse: A Study of Suburban and Inner-City Adolescents," *Development and Psychopathology*, 11 (1999); S. S. Luthar and Shawn J. Latendresse, "Comparable 'Risks' at the Socioeconomic Status Extremes: Preadolescents' Perception of Parenting," *Development and Psychopathology*, 17 (2005).

60. Luthar and D'Avanzo, 1999.

61. Luthar and Latendresse, 2005.

62. Luthar and Becker, 2002.

63. Luthar and D'Avanzo, 1999; R. B. Shafran, "Children of Affluent Parents," in John D. O'Brien, Daniel J. Pilowsky, and Owen W. Lewis, eds. *Psychotherapists with Children and Adolescents: Adapting the Psychodynamic Process* (Washington, DC: American Psychiatric Association, 1992).

64. See M. A. Zimmerman, D. A. Salem, and K. I. Maton, "Family Structure and Psychosocial Correlates Among Urban African-American Adolescent Males," *Child Development*, 66 (1995); E. L. Cowen, P. A. Wyman, W. C. Work, J. Y. Kim, D. B. Fagen, and K. B. Magnus, "Follow-Up Study of Young Stress-Affected and Stress-Resilient Urban Children," *Development and Psychopathology*, 9 (1997); P. A. Wyman, E. L. Cowen, W. C. Work, L. Hoyt-Meyers, K. B. Magnus, and D. B. Fagan,

"Caregiving and Developmental Factors Differentiating Young At-Risk Urban Children Showing Resilient Versus Stress-Affected Outcomes: A Replication and Extension," *Child Development*, 70 (1999).

65. L. Bobo and R. A. Smith, "Antipoverty Policy, Affirmative Action, and Racial Attitudes," in Sheldon H. Danziger, Gary Sandefur, and Daniel Weinberg, eds. *Confronting Poverty: Prescriptions for Change* (Cambridge: Cambridge University Press, 1994).

66. See V. C. McLoyd and L. Wilson, "The Strain of Living Poor: Parenting, Social Support, and Child Mental Health," in Aletha C. Huston, ed. *Children in Poverty: Child Development and Public Policy* (New York: Cambridge University Press, 1991); V. C. McLoyd, T. E. Jayaratne, R. Ceballo, and J. Borquez, "Unemployment and Work Interruptions among African-American Single Mothers: Effects on Parenting and Adolescent Socioemotional Functioning," *Child Development*, 65 (1994).

67. This is particularly the case with the academic goals of children. See Velma McBride Murray, Gene H. Brody, Anita Brown, Joseph Wisenbaker, Carolyn E. Cutrona, and Ronald L. Simons, "Linking Employment Status, Maternal Psychological Well-Being, Parenting, and Children's Attributions About Poverty in Families Receiving Government Assistance," *Family Relations*, 51 (2002). For more on hope and children, see Kristine Amlund Hagan, Barbara J. Meyers, and Virginia H. Mackintosh, "Hope, Social Support, and Behavioral Problems in At-Risk Children," *American Journal of Orthopsychiatry*, 75 (2005).

68. *TJ*, 448. Francis Schrag similarly notes: "any conception of justice which includes a commitment to equality of opportunity eventually must collide with a commitment to the family," "Justice and the Family," *Inquiry*, 19 (1976), 193.

69. "Rights of Inequality: Rawlsian Justice, Equal Opportunity, and the Status of the Family," *Legal Theory*, 7 (2001), 84.

70. Jeffrey Blustein, *Parents and Children: The Ethics of the Family* (Oxford: Oxford University Press, 1982), 14.

71. H. Elizabeth Peters and A. Sinan Ünür note this in "Economic Perspectives on Altruism and the Family," in Arland Thornton, ed. *The Well-Being of Children and Families: Research and Data Needs*, ed. (Ann Arbor: University of Michigan Press, 2004), 263

72. *A Treatise on the Family* (Cambridge, MA: Harvard University Press, 1981), 174.

73. John F. Ermisch, *An Economic Analysis of the Family* (Princeton, NJ: Princeton University Press, 2003), 4.

74. Peters and Ünür, 262.

75. See Gregory Kavka, *Hobbesian Moral and Political Theory* (Princeton, NJ: Princeton University Press, 1986), 64–80.

76. *The Theory of Moral Sentiments*, Pt. VI, Ch. I, Sect. II, 321.

77. Gary S. Becker and Nigel Tomes, "Human Capital and the Rise and the Fall of Families," *Journal of Labor Economics*, 4 (1986), S1. It is unclear how Rawls's model compares to these. But Rawls does write, "The family, in its ideal conception and often in practice, is one place where the principle of maximizing the sum of advantages is rejected. Members of a family commonly do not wish to gain unless they can do so in ways that further the interests of the rest," *TJ*, 90.

78. Becker, x.

79. Becker and Tomes, S1.

80. Marilyn Manser and Murray Brown, "Marriage and Household Decision-Making: A Bargaining Analysis," *International Economic Review*, 21 (1980), 41.

81. Manser and Brown, 42.

82. In Bernard Campbell, ed. *Sexual Selection and the Descent of Man 1871–1971*, ed. (Chicago: Aldine Publishing Company, 1972).

83. Trivers, 139.

84. Trivers, 139.

85. Trivers, 145–46.

86. The observation that women can have such an incredible affect in society, especially over men, is not a new. This was captured beautifully in a story by Aristophanes in his *Lysistrata*, ed. Jeffrey Henderson (Oxford: Oxford University Press, 1990). If women are able to stop a war, then it seems that they have the power to demand a greater level of investment from males. My point is not that women only have power over men in matters of sex (or derivatively so). My point is that in the context of parental investment women possess something extremely powerful that men do not.

4

What is a Family?

Francis Schrag notes this about the role of the family in political society:

> Although modern states have moved far in their quest to equalize opportunity and in doing so have perhaps undermined the stability of the family, men and women have been exceedingly reluctant to abandon the family, especially to yield up their own children to the larger community even in the name of justice. Is there a reasonable basis for this reluctance, or is this simply another case where habit or instinct or self-love or weakness of will prevent us from doing what we ought to do?[1]

This question, and the stronger one of abolishing the family altogether by Rawls, Blumstein, and Schwartz, is important. Following chapter 3, I argue that every child ought to be raised in a family for the sake of protecting children, maintaining meaningful equality, and increasing political stability by decreasing the number of non-ISJs and increasing the number of ISJs. This raises two major questions. First, what do I mean by "family"? Second, why should every child be raised in a family? In particular, why are other child-rearing structures inadequate?

It is important to be clear that I have in mind a particular ideal conception of the self, ISJs. I wish to discover the environment that best develops such individuals. I do this out of concern for the well-being of children and to discover what is owed to them. I also do this with the hope that a particular existing society, our current one, can progress towards a completely well-ordered society with ISJs. In arguing for what structure of childrearing is best, I am only concerned with the structure that is best compatible with the above ideal. ISJs are sought in society largely because they have self-respect, possess the powers of self-regulation, and trust and cooperate effectively. The best means of rearing will thus need to provide the requisite space to develop these skills properly. The family uniquely provides the kind of love, stability, privacy, and intimacy that are needed for children to develop the self-identity requisite to become ISJs.

The first section of this chapter introduces my ideal family for raising ISJs, the neo-nuclear family, and compares it to the traditional nuclear family. Sections 2 through 4 examine different kinds of childcare systems: section 2 discusses single parents, section 3 discusses cohabiting parents, and section 4 discusses daycare. The fourth section is the most detailed because it further reveals what exactly the neo-nuclear family provides for developing ISJs in the areas of modeling, cooperation, communication, stability, love, intimacy, and privacy.

1. ISJs AND THE FAMILY?[2]

Based upon what has been written thus far, it may be reasonably inferred that I advocate a traditional nuclear family. If true, then it is important to heed this, "The nuclear family has represented for Western man, then, both an ideal society and a bar to the creation of such a society, a model of justice as well as a source of injustice."[3] The family that I advocate is unlikely to be a source of intra-family injustice. In a well-ordered society, all (or most) children will be raised in this kind of family. Therefore, the residual injustice of unequal opportunity (and, to a lesser degree, inequality of outcome) will not exist. However, in the contemporary family model (one where *any* family structure is permissible) this is a problem because of the fundamental inequality; some children are either maltreated or neglected whereas others are raised by nurturing parents. The difficult question of how to ensure that children are raised in decent families will be discussed in chapter 5. The family that I advocate is a refinement of the traditional nuclear family, which consists of a married husband and wife and their children. The family that I advocate consists of the following: two adult (over eighteen) ISJs who are married with (adopted or biological) children.[4] I believe, *ceteris paribus*, the formal structure of the traditional nuclear family is usually superior to all other family structures. However, the traditional nuclear family is not intrinsically good; this has important consequences.

My account refines the traditional nuclear family, and it might be best to describe the family that I advocate as a *neo-nuclear family*. I will occasionally refer to it as a neo-nuclear family to remind the reader that by 'family' I mean something slightly different than a traditional nuclear family. One difference between the traditional nuclear family and the neo-nuclear family is that I leave open the possibility that the parents in the neo-nuclear family can be of the same sex.[5] The major difference is that a neo-nuclear family requires both parents to be ISJs. On the traditional nuclear family model, it is not required that both parents, or even either parent, be ISJs. ISJ parents are necessary to ensure intra-family justice. This is important, as Okin notes,

> Without just families, how can we expect to have a just society? In particular, if the relationship between a child's parents does not conform to basic standards of justice, how can we expect that child to grow up with a sense of justice?[6]

Okin is referring to the injustice that women are faced with in the traditional nuclear family because of asymmetrical gender roles. ISJ spouses need not play symmetrical gender roles to serve as positive models for their children or for justice to exist. The reason for this is that although negative and destructive gender roles exist, innocuous and beneficial gender roles also exist. ISJs will not take part in the former, but they will likely sometimes take part in the latter. This may not allay Okin's concerns completely, but I am confident that she would recognize the neo-nuclear family as an improvement over the traditional nuclear family. Modeling justice is only one reason why ISJ parents are necessary. The other is that adult ISJs with self-respect are more likely to care for their children properly by regulating their behavior. I would, however, like to be more clear about the relationship between being an ISJ and being a competent parent. Recall that a Rawlsian sense of justice requires: (i) the skill to judge what is just and unjust, (ii) the capacity to support one's judgments about justice with reasons, and (iii) a desire to act according to the dictates of justice and giving to others what they are entitled. These, especially the first two conditions, may seem too demanding. However, I do not require that one be able to write a treatise on moral justification to qualify as an ISJ. A simple abstract conception of justice suffices. A good understanding and application of the Golden Rule would probably suffice to meet the first two conditions. One need not have an advanced degree or be a moral philosopher to be an ISJ—one could even be illiterate. After all, the actions of parents—not verbal or written guidelines—do most of the work in child-rearing, especially in the ultra-primitive stages of child development. Providing proper nourishment, sufficient physical contact, and proper guidance will teach the child to respond properly to positive and negative stimuli. Even when the child acquires more complex language capabilities, he is shaped by observing how others around him act—not simply by what they say. Primitive justification, as mentioned in chapter 1, is necessary at least at a basic level, and this is minimally necessary to provide a foundation for moral resolve when temptations to be unjust arise.

It is easy to cite otherwise just or knowledgeable individuals (statesmen, professors of moral philosophy, Nobel Prize winners, etc.) who are incompetent parents. Such persons might only meet condition (iii) of Rawlsian ISJs, which requires that one desires to act according to the dictates of justice and give to others what they are entitled. The sentiment of (iii) is importantly different from love, especially at the motivational level.[7] Love is a necessary but insufficient condition for competent parenting. One may love his child but lack conditions (i) or (ii) of ISJ status. Or other circumstances might cause one to act in an unloving manner, even though his love is genuine. For example, a parent may have been maltreated as a child and is thus sometimes uncertain about how to express his love properly. Perhaps the parent knows how to love properly but being abused has caused him to become impatient and violent; a misbehaving child might test his patience and trigger violence (even though, in a calmer state of mind, the parent realizes that such violence or abuse is wrong). Being a loving parent is a necessary but insufficient condition for being a decent parent. It may be questioned whether a loving ISJ would necessarily be a good parent. Perhaps not in rare instances. However, this emphasizes how difficult parenting can be and just how difficult it is for *non-ISJs* to be decent parents.

A neo-nuclear family also requires that both parents be adults (say, eighteen years old). Although society may worry about or frown upon a fourteen-year-old mother and father, they are usually considered heads of a family. Adulthood is necessary because maturity, patience, and stability are necessary to raise a child properly. Most young teens do not possess these qualities, at least not to the degree necessary to care for a child properly. Teens are also still developing, and their development may be prematurely halted by raising a child.

The final difference between the neo-nuclear family and the traditional nuclear family is that it is unnecessary for the children in the neo-nuclear family to have any biological relation to their parents. Some conceptions of the nuclear family allow for adoption, especially today, but others do not. An argument can be made that a marriage is truly not a marriage and a family is truly not a family until a husband and a wife have procreated. I do not subscribe to this because my primary concern is the well-being of children and society, and neither children nor society seem to be harmed by the practice of adoption. In fact, adoption often provides an incredible amount of good. The concept of "parents + adopted children = a family" has not always been as obvious as it might seem today. I mention this with the following observation from Aristotle in mind: "There are two impulses which more than all others cause human beings to cherish and feel affection for each other: 'this is my own,' and 'this is my delight.'"[8] It could be argued that parents will naturally love their biological children because such children are their own, whereas adopted children may not receive the same love because they are not biologically related. I concede that the actual biological relationship often creates enough affection in parents that they will not maltreat their children. However, biology does not necessarily do this; child maltreatment exists in families where parent and child are biologically related.

Though biology may be a factor for parental feeling, it is not the only factor. In fact, it can be argued that the act of adoption does not conflict with evolutionary theory. It is generally true that in nature parental feeling is discriminate towards one's own young. However, sometimes even wild animals adopt non-biologically-related young. Of course, animals usually only adopt if the adoption does not cause them to reduce or eliminate resources that their own young need. Because many human adopters often cannot reproduce, are infertile, or have children that are grown, adoption does not seem to preclude parents' young from surviving.[9] Even when humans have biological children of their own, it does not preclude parental feeling toward an adopted child; mothers who have both adopted and biological children report no difference in the parental feelings that they have for their children.[10] It is no surprise that parent-child attachments in biological families do not differ from those in adoptive families and that adopted children often test higher on measures such as self-esteem than their biological counterparts.[11] In fact, in predicting levels of self-esteem, identity processing, and parental bonding have been found to be more important than adoptive status.[12] Adopted children are also found to be at no significant risk for anti-social or problem behaviors.[13] Lastly, child maltreatment is more prevalent in biological families than in adoptive ones.[14]

The above is not meant to be an attack on Aristotle; I believe that he is largely correct. Rather, the problem resides in the ambiguity of what "my own" means. It is important that both adoptive and biological parents recognize children as their own. Having a primary responsibility to love and care for the child is more likely to develop a sense of belonging than any single biological act. This is true largely because of the extremely vulnerable nature of young children. When adopted children are given to their adoptive parents, it soon becomes obvious that they will neither survive nor flourish if their new parents do not take care of them as if they were their own children and belonged to them.

It may also be asked why I require children to qualify as a family. That is, why not allow married ISJs without children to be considered a family? This is both a minor and a major point. It is a major point in the sense that some people do require that children must result from a marriage in order to consider it a family. This point usually revolves around this kind of observation put forth by Aristotle:

> Children are regarded as the bond that holds them [parents] together, and that is why childless marriages break up more easily. For children are a good common to both partners, and what people have in common holds them together.[15]

Aristotle is correct that things held in common generally bond people together,[16] and children are certainly an exemplary case of this. To strip away the beauty of Aristotle's articulation, the exit costs of divorce are much higher when a child is shared by a married couple. A financial burden is usually borne by the parent who leaves, and the custodial parent is usually left at an economic disadvantage.[17] In addition, informal costs exist. For example, it is costly to bear in one's conscience that one's child is unlikely to develop in an ideally healthy way. Likewise, it is costly to bear the thought that one is not completely fulfilling one's obligations to a child and former spouse. Exiting the marriage relationship can draw particular disapprobation from friends, family, and society after a child is born (that is, more scorn than if divorce were to occur without children) and is costly. I concede to the forcefulness of Aristotle's point. However, it has also been found that children, for numerous reasons (money, time, disputes about how to parent, etc), often cause a great deal of tension in marriages, and these factors should not be discounted entirely because they are often strong enough to overcome the above-mentioned Aristotelian common-bond thesis and dissolve marriage.

The minor point is that I technically do not have a problem with calling a childless married couple a family—regardless of whether they are capable of producing children. However, for the sake of this chapter, it is helpful to stipulate that children are necessary to constitute a family. Childless parents will not be responsible for primary childcare and are thus not a primary concern of this essay.

2. SINGLE PARENTS

What remains constant between neo-nuclear and traditional nuclear families is a rejection of single-parent and cohabiting families. When I say that every child should be raised in a family, I do not mean that they should be raised by single or cohabiting parents. This is not based upon, say, religious dogma. Rather, these structures generally provide an environment for children that is suboptimal compared to the neo-nuclear family. Not only are children raised in single-parent and cohabiting families less likely to become ISJs, this decreased chance entails an important inequality of opportunity compared to children raised in a neo-nuclear family.

For those who are compelled by the thesis that poverty leads to child maltreatment, it would be sufficient to bar single parents on the grounds that they generally have less income and wealth than married families. This was shown earlier. I conceded that poverty can cause stress and that stress leads to a higher risk of maltreatment, but I dismissed the importance usually given to this thesis. I do not object to single-parent families on the grounds they fare worse economically than any other family structure. Rather, they generally provide for a less healthy environment for child development than my family model, as is evident by the asymmetrically high rates of maltreatment that occur in single-parent families.[18] This may be sufficient reason to exclude single parents as acceptable family structures in an ISJ system. It may be objected that single-parent families need not be harmful to children and would not be harmful if only universal daycare were provided. I will address the daycare consideration later.

Children require an incredible amount of attention, especially young children. It is generally difficult for two parents to provide the requisite resources, time, and attention to their children to flourish properly, but this is extremely difficult for a single parent. For this reason, when a single parent does provide in a way that his child develops properly then that parent merits great admiration. Yet these instances are exceptions to the rule, and such children may have developed even better if a second parent were present. In one sense, it may even be argued that single parents do not exist because they necessarily depend upon others (be it family, friends, or childcare) to supplement their parenting. The children of two-parent families may also be partly nurtured by those other than their parents, but it is usually to a far lesser degree and is less necessary.

In critiquing single-parent families, the following objection by Okin must be given weight: "Contrary to common perceptions—in which the situation of never-married mothers looms largest—65 percent of single-parent families are a result of marital separation or divorce."[19] This point is made within the framework of her overall objection that gender-structured marriages make women particularly vulnerable to multiple harms in many ways, and the high number of single parents is largely the result of gender-structured families. In particular, the high number of single parents is not primarily a problem of women having children without marrying; rather, the high number of single parents is attributable to gender-structured families, which lead to divorce. I concede that divorce is a problem. If my family model were implemented (insofar as only married ISJ adults had children) *and* a high divorce rate still existed, then my efforts would be in vain because many children would ultimately be raised by

single parents. I disagree, however, that high divorce rates and single-parent families are mainly the result of gender-structured structured marriages. The number of single parents created by divorce that Okin cites
were from the mid-1980s, when divorce was at a historical high and traditional gender-structured families were at a historical low. One can look at
any other time in U.S. history, be it the 1890s or the 1950s, and find lower
rates of divorce and children living in single-parent households as a result
of divorce, and these families were much more gender-structured than they
were in the 1980s.[20]

Who is to blame for divorce and single parents is of lesser importance for
this chapter than the fact that such families are more likely to not be able to
provide the kind of environment that children need to become ISJs. Children will be at a distinct disadvantage in life when compared to the opportunities provided to their counterparts with two parents. Okin's passage,
however, serves to show an important trend in divorce and single-parent
families. The relevant data that she cited in *Justice, Gender, and the Family*
was up-to-date at the time of publication, but much has changed in a little
less than twenty years. For example, the number of divorces has been declining. Yet as divorces have been declining slowly, the number of children
in cohabiting families has increased exponentially. Although still too high,
the number of children who live only with their mothers because of divorce
is now only about 36.5 percent—almost half of the number that Okin
cites.[21] Divorce is no longer primarily responsible for the high-number of
single-parent families.

3. COHABITING PARENTS[22]

It might seem that cohabiting parents would be able to provide a sufficient
level of care to be accepted as a family in a system that seeks to protect children and create ISJs. Unlike single-parent families, parents in cohabiting
families seem capable of being available to their children because childcare
can either be shared or a division of labor can be established. Furthermore,
cohabiting parents have higher incomes and net worth than single parents. It
might seem that they could provide resources that single parents would be
unable to provide. Again, I am unpersuaded by the thesis that income must
affect good parenting. Cohabiting families may have some advantages over
single-parent families, but cohabiting families generally cannot provide the
stability needed for children to develop properly. For example, it has been
found that compared to married parents, parents in cohabiting relationships

report lower levels of happiness with their relationships and express lower levels of commitment to their relationships.[23] Women in cohabiting relationships are also more likely to experience more violence than married women.[24] In addition to posing a threat to women, this also poses a threat to children. If proper relationships are not modeled in the very place where they should be best exemplified, then the chances of children being able to engage in relationships with a high level of commitment are lowered.

Cohabiting relationships are consistently found to be less stable than marriages.[25] This is complicated because different kinds of cohabiters seem to vary in their stability and safeness. For example, the union of cohabiters that intend to marry (already engaged, waiting to finish a final year of school, etc.) largely resembles the union of those who are married.[26] It is not exactly clear why cohabiting families are so unstable and violent. One thesis is that the institution of cohabitation attracts people who are more likely to either have negative characteristics or make bad candidates to be in healthy personal relationships.[27] Another thesis is that the experience of living in a cohabiting relationship changes the attitudes of the cohabiters.[28] A similar thesis states that the additional formalized and legal status that cohabiting relationships lack causes them to be less stable than marriages. That is, "the *exit costs* (a measure of commitment) of leaving a cohabiting relationship would be less than those associated with ending a marriage."[29] This thesis is powerful because it has also been found that "those who married after cohabiting appear more similar to those who married without cohabiting than to those who are currently cohabiting. This suggests that the formal and structural elements of marriage do largely account for the differences between cohabitation and marriage."[30] It may be objected that (i) perhaps the study did not take into account the potentially important consideration that children in married families are likely to be biologically related to their parents while children in cohabiting relationships are less likely to be biologically related to their parents, and (ii) the study only accounts for the well-being of parents and that I have had to extrapolate from this account to determine the effects that cohabitation has on children. However, it has been determined that children in cohabiting families where the cohabiters are their biological parents generally experience worse outcomes than children who live with married parents who are also their biological parents.[31] Differences between cohabitation and marriage are partly due to certain people being prone to cohabit (or adverse to marriage) *and* that marriage provides a structure with more stability. That said, it should be clear from my definition of the neo-nuclear family that marriage of two adults is insufficient—two ISJs are also needed. If two non-ISJs are married then it is unlikely that the structure and formal societal recognition of marriage will not significantly decrease the amount of instability and violence in the relationship.

Regardless of what causes the unstable outcomes of cohabitation to be different than marriage, there are more direct reasons why cohabiting families are inappropriate in an ISJ model, if elimination of child maltreatment is a goal. It has been found that a boyfriend in a cohabiting relationship is up to thirty-three times more likely to abuse a child in that family than a father in a married relationship.[32] Morse also notes, "The cohabiting but not married father has the same genetic interest in the child as does the married biological father. Nonetheless, cohabiting fathers are twenty times more likely to abuse their own children than fathers married to the mothers of the child. This suggests that a commitment between the parents contributes to the child's safety independent of biology."[33]

4. DAYCARE

Earlier, I anticipated the objection that family structures such as single-parent and cohabiting families need not prevent children from becoming ISJs if society instituted universal daycare.[34] This objection is based on the idea that all we need to do to move from a mostly well-ordered society towards a well-ordered society is provide ample daycare to families who would appear to benefit from it. I argue that daycare may be able to provide some of the things that parents provide in my family model, but daycare usually cannot provide for children with the same degree of effectiveness, cannot provide some important kinds of things which children need, and it requires that children have already had proper attachment relationships via the first stage of developmental psychology. I will now put forth five major reasons why daycare is inadequate compared to being raised in a family if we are trying to ensure that children become ISJs. In doing so, it should become more clear what makes the neo-nuclear family special. Some of these reasons also apply to why single-parent and cohabiting families are inadequate institutions for children to be raised into ISJs.

5. BENEFITS OF THE FAMILY

5.1 Modeling and Cooperation

A large part of how children learn to think and behave is by observing behavior. Two of the greatest philosophers on the topic of education state this emphatically. Locke writes, "Nay, I know not whether it be not the best way to be used by a father as long as he shall think fit, on any occasion, to reform anything he wishes mended in his son: nothing sinking so gently and so deep into men's minds as example."[35] Rousseau says, "put all the lessons of young people in actions rather than in speeches. Let them learn nothing in books which experience can teach them."[36] Daycare workers can model positive behavior. However, it is incredibly difficult for daycare workers to model cooperation properly and fully. Children can witness a daycare worker cooperating with another child, and this is important. This cooperation is asymmetrical in the sense that cooperation is between adult and child—between nurturer and the nurtured. However, children can observe how adults interact in a large daycare where multiple adults work. Children also need to witness symmetrical kinds of cooperation to later demonstrate similar cooperation. In a small daycare run by one daycare worker, this kind of modeling is impossible. Observation of such cooperative interaction is useful. However, even that kind of cooperation falls short of the kind of cooperation that children also need to observe. When daycare workers model behavior they do so in a controlled environment that does not accurately map onto the kind of modeling that children need to observe to develop fully. Even though they may be good people who love children and cooperate well with other adults and children in the daycare, daycare workers model only part of what children need to witness because they are doing a job. Therefore, children cannot, for example, observe how to respond properly to people who are sick because daycare workers do not go to work when sick. If daycare workers go to work while sick, they would be negligent. Watching a healthy spouse take care of his sick spouse, even at risk of getting sick himself, is a great lesson for children.

Children will not know much about the personal lives of their daycare workers. Daycare workers presumably do not spend much time discussing their personal problems with other adults in the daycare while on the job. If they do, such behavior would probably be deemed inappropriate. Minimally, it would be argued that they should instead be spending time helping children. It is important for children to observe some hardships and disagreements in life and learn how to deal with them positively from their parents.[37] This happens, for example, when a child witnesses one parent who has had a stressful day and sees how the other parent responds with warmth. Or, this happens when children witness parents disagree about a matter and yet resolve the problem. Daycare may provide many cases for children to observe adult integration and cooperation, but it is provided in a largely sterile environment. Minimally, it is in an environment that has a limited sphere and does not capture interaction and cooperation at its best.

When children witness interaction and cooperation in the family, they witness acts from love, and they largely experience altruistic acts in both the weak and strong sense of altruism mentioned earlier. When children observe daycare workers, they witness somewhat distanced professional caretakers. They may love their job and love children, but if things get difficult they can leave their job or transfer it to others. To build upon Locke and Rousseau, a companion effect to Rawls's Aristotelian Principle explains why modeling is so important:

> As we witness the exercise of well-trained abilities by others, these displays are enjoyed by us and arouse a desire that should be able to do the same thing ourselves. We want to be like those persons who can exercise the abilities that we find latent in our natures.[38]

Not only does modeling provide an example of how to behave, it often causes us to wish to emulate our models.

Suppose that daycare workers are effective in modeling behavior, so effective that they, not the children's parents, are the primary models of behavior for children. This is likely to cause resentment and feelings of inadequacy on the part of the parents. It is also possible that some dissonance will develop in the psychology of the child. The child may have to try to adjudicate between the demands of two different authority figures. If children are to become parents themselves, they need to observe good parenting. If a large portion of the parent-like behavior that they witness is in the environment of a daycare center, then they will probably not know how to act properly in the other spheres of life—those that are most important in parenting and in families.

5.2 Communication

The ability to trust is also important in a well-ordered society, and it is a trait that ISJs exemplify. However, trust is largely predicated upon effective communication. If preferences and intentions are not properly understood by others, then the responses of others may be inappropriate due to misinterpretation—even if others respond with altruistic intent. Accordingly, the communicator may not come to trust, or have reason to trust, one who seeks to help him. Miscommunication occasionally occurs with adults who are at the peak of their communication skills. However, children cannot articulate their needs as well as adults can, especially when they cannot speak. Non-verbal communication can be understood, but accurately assessing non-verbal communication of small children can be extremely difficult. This difficulty is compounded because the communication of children, especially babies, must be responded to quickly so that children recognize their attempt at communication was successful. Sometimes a baby may have a series of different cries, where cry_1 means hunger, cry_2 means physical discomfort, etc. The problem is that each child is slightly different, and constant attention is needed to learn the language effectively. Also, daycare workers must not learn one language; they must learn many languages, one for each child in the daycare center. Daycare workers may have an advantage of being professionally trained, in a general sense, in how children communicate. Yet they lack the opportunity that parents have to observe behavior keenly and respond to communication routinely in many different environments. Being sensitively attuned to children helps in communication and in building secure attachment that will likely lead to positive developmental outcomes. However, parents usually do not have to learn as many languages. This may also complicate communication for the children in daycare who have to learn two different languages, that of the parent and that of the daycare worker. This can cause miscommunication if subtle cues are read differently by the daycare worker and the parent. The parent may unknowingly be communicating ineffectively with the baby, and this may be an impediment to securing trust.

5.3 Stability and Permanence

Cooperation and trust also usually require stability and permanence. When children are raised in a neo-nuclear family, clear and consistent care is usually provided. This works in the moral realm where a consistent set of values is articulated by pointing out what is right, what is wrong, and why. Furthermore, this consistency exists with regard to love and the warmth that it provides. For example, whatever his age a child knows that his parents will be there and love him; the time of day does not matter. However, unless they usurp the parenting role altogether, daycare workers cannot provide constant and consistent stability. They simply cannot care for children both day and night. It is also unlikely that a child will be cared for by the same daycare worker for several consecutive years. Consequently, different guidelines and levels of warmth may be provided to the child. Stability also derives from children being able to observe their parents' actions. Not only do children get to see their parents in one particular kind of environment (like daycare workers), but they get to see how their models of behavior—their parents—interact in a loving relationship with each other and in trusting and cooperative activities with their friends, neighbors, and strangers. This consistency across multiple spheres of life is important to develop and affirm a clear, broad, and deep sense of self that ISJs need. It may be objected that daycare simply provides short-term assistance and cannot have quite the effect on children that I have been arguing. But suppose that a single parent uses daycare only when working. Assuming he works eight hours a day and sleeps eight hours a day, the daycare will parent the child just as much as the parent does. Or suppose that the child is older and goes to school. School lasts roughly seven hours a day, so if any daycare at all is had in addition to this then the amount of time that a child will spend with non-parents will be more than with his own parents. As children grow older, they will be able to recognize that though their parents' actions towards them are in accordance with some kind of duty their parents are primarily motivated to act from love.

5.4 The Narrowness of Love

I mentioned above that parents acting from love is important for proper child development. Laurence Thomas has argued something similar,

> [I]t is by virtue of parental love that the child experiences being treated morally not as a duty, but as an act of love. Although every loving parent is deeply motivated to treat her or his child in all the morally right ways, the springs of motivation are most surely not morality itself.[39]

I agree that simply knowing what is just and acting according to the dictates of justice is insufficient for proper parenting; one should also act from love. With this amendment to rule-motivated structures of care, it seems that no distinction can be made between parents and daycare workers. After all, daycare workers can also treat children morally not just as a matter of duty and not just in accordance with what love requires but they can also care for children from love. Yet there seems to be something inappropriate about conceding that daycare workers can care and love children in the same way and with the same motivation as a child's parents. Something else is needed, other than acting from love, to distinguish the relationship that parents have with their children and the relationship that daycare workers have with the children of other people. I think that difference is articulated clearly by Aristotle:

> Socrates is emphatic in his praise of unity in the state, which (as it seems, and as he himself says) is one of the products of affection. In another of Plato's dialogues, one which treats of love, we read that Aristophanes said that lovers because of the warmth of their affection are eager to grow into each other and become one instead of two. In such an event one or the other must perish, if not both. But in a state in which there exists such a mode of association the feelings of affection will inevitably be watery, father hardly ever saying "my son," or son "my father." Just as a small amount of sweetening dissolved in a large amount of water does not reveal its presence to the taste, so the feelings of relationships

are implied in these terms become nothing; and in a state organized like this there is virtually nothing to oblige father to care for their sons, or sons for their fathers, or brothers for each other. There are two impulses which more than all others cause human beings to cherish and feel affection for each other: "this is my own," and "this is my delight." Among people organized in this manner no one would be able to say either.[40]

Before analyzing what this passage from Aristotle adds to understanding the family, I will also note something similar that Huxley wrote. When a group of children is being taught what mothers, fathers, brothers, sisters, monogamy, and romance were—because these no longer exist in their society—the narrator says, "Family, monogamy, romance. Everywhere exclusiveness, a narrow channeling of impulse and energy."[41] In addition to acting from love, parental love should be provided in an *exclusive* and *narrow* way.

That which Aristotle critiqued called for something more radical than the kind of daycare currently under consideration; it called for the complete elimination of families in the guardian class into one large community daycare (presumably akin to the one that Huxley later wrote about but less technologically advanced). Nonetheless, Aristotle's watering-down thesis holds, though to a lesser degree, to the current consideration of daycare to assist parents in raising their children. I already considered the importance of "belonging" for the parent-child relationship, but it is also important to note that this is linked to one's love being focused narrowly and not spread too thinly. Not only do daycare workers have little personal stake or investment in whether the children that they care for develop properly, but they must also spread their love to many children. Daycare centers can have a low daycare worker to child ratio,[42] but practically it cannot be the case that this ratio is ever universally 1:1 or 1:2. Regardless, as Blustein notes from his understanding of the above Aristotle quotation, "Love of children cannot exist as something general but only in particular forms through which individual parents relate to individual children."[43] Here a clear difference emerges between parents and daycare workers. Parents can love their particular child and privilege him with special attention whereas daycare workers can only love the children that they take care of in a general sense. A child can know, for example, that a parent in a neo-nuclear family will take care of him, and his parent will not neglect him in favor of another child.[44] Children in daycare do not have this level of stability because they can observe that daycare workers often take care of the children most in need of care and daycare workers must often leave them to do so. Children can also observe, for example, that their parents are always on twenty-four-hour emergency call, but this is not true of daycare workers. In general, children need to feel valued in a unique way. This requires a special relationship with someone who is consistently there and primarily responsible for them. Narrowing one's love entails a relation of intimacy. In the next section I argue that intimacy requires privacy and, again, the family provides the privacy necessary for children to grow into ISJs better than daycare.

5.5 Intimacy and Privacy

Gerstein notes that intimacy is "an experience of a relationship in which we are deeply engrossed."[45] This seems true, but intimacy also seems to involve engrossment of a particular kind. Part of that, as Schoeman notes, is that "We *share our selves* with those with whom we are intimate and are aware that they do the same with us."[46] Much of what is engrossing in a relationship is a sharing of ourselves. It is tempting to imagine the paradigm case of a deeply engrossing relationship to be some kind of perfect Aristotelian friendship. Such friendship results in profound intimacy because friends: have goodwill for one another, are aware of the other's goodwill, are alike in excellence or virtue, give and receive in a similar form, and are exclusive in the sense that very few, if any, other people are friends of either friend at the same high level.[47] If Aristotelian perfect friendship is the paradigm of intimacy, then it may seem that the parent-child relationship fails because it does not meet any of the five conditions above. In fact, it would appear that the parent-child relationship is friendship of utility. Yet Aristotle is careful to note that the above kinds of friendship are friendships between equals. The parent-child relationship, however, is between unequals. Between unequals, Aristotle notes, "even the friendship of a father for his son is different from that of the son for his father."[48] In thinking about intimacy that requires deep engrossment with the other, it does not seem that the parent-child relationship should be excluded; therefore, it does not seem that the *kind* of reciprocity and sharing exemplified in an Aristotelian perfect friendship is necessary for intimacy to exist.

Reciprocity is not necessary in all intimate relationships. More clearly, *symmetrical* reciprocity is not necessary for an intimate relationship. It is also important to recognize the existence of intimacy where reciprocity is asymmetrical. That is, where the involved intimate individuals are on different planes in many important areas (virtue, power, intelligence, self-control, etc.) but still genuinely reciprocate in the sense that each gives something important back to the other. The paradigm case of an intimate relationship that is asymmetrically reciprocal is the parent-child relationship.[49] Parents in a neo-nuclear family will demonstrate a higher level of power, intelligence, and self-control than their children. In general, parents love their children, and this manifests itself in many caring ways such as protecting and nurturing their children.[50] However, children cannot protect or care for their parents in the same way that their parents protect and care for them. In fact, very young children are likely to have only a primitive concept of love, a concept due to their recognition that they are entirely dependent upon their parents.[51] With regards to *sharing ourselves*, sharing does not need to be symmetrically reciprocal. Parents and children certainly do not give and receive in the same manner. The child's sharing of his self is mainly reactionary to how the parent shares himself with the child. A parent, for example, can share himself by carefully using comforting vocal tones, verbally expressing love for the child, or being physically attentive to the child. As the child grows older, the parent can share a multitude of personal stories, articulate hopes and fears, and open up in a way that cannot be shared with many other people.[52] Children respond accordingly. They primarily share by demonstrating a sense of trust in their parents, which manifests itself in many ways. For example, children are generally more receptive to being held and more interactive with attentive parents. Children demonstrate to their parents some form of recognition of trust. This eventually leads to children becoming more comfortable and trusting of others, first family and friends, and then more trusting of strangers.[53]

Daycare workers simply cannot share at the same level that parents can without being deemed inappropriate. Part of the reason for the intuition that such deep sharing with the children of others is usually inappropriate is that the power of sharing usually derives from the fact that sometimes personal sharing loses its depth when it is shared with many others. This is because that which is being shared is recognized as being special because it is not shared either indiscriminately or with numerous people. As a particular thing is shared more and more, its value often diminishes because it becomes a common commodity. In order to enjoy such intimacy and sharing of oneself, privacy is usually required. This is due to an interesting tendency of human beings: they often act differently in private and public spheres. Some of this may be because people are hypocritical and they modify their behavior in the public sphere. A less cynical hypothesis is that humans are self-conscious creatures. Gerstein captures the ramifications of this beautifully, "Self-consciousness is not in itself a bad thing, it is simply something we must get rid of for a time if we are to lose ourselves in intimacy, and we cannot do that unless we have privacy."[54] This seems correct, but what role self-consciousness plays is still unclear, as is what is meant by "los[ing] ourselves."

As Gerstein notes, being self-conscious need not be a bad thing—though it is usually described as such. I reduce self-consciousness to the recognition that others will observe oneself in many ways and that one is concerned about how he will be perceived by others. This is bad if one is concerned about perceptions pertaining to shallow things or unimportant things. For example, it would be bad if if one is self-conscious about whether he will be accepted into a club because he does not give off an air of being rich and members of that club only care about affluence. However, if one is self-conscious about not being as virtuous as he usually is and is worried about how his more virtuous friend will possibly see him, then this can be healthy. In public, where depth is often rare and shallowness often has importance, it is important for most people to play a certain role, even if this role is not who they are genuinely, for the sake of acceptance. Yet humans usually cannot play roles constantly. Doing so will likely lead to some kind of schizophrenia. For this reason, people need an outlet where they can reveal themselves, including their weaknesses, embarrassments, and deeply personal confidences. However, if one is to do this and it can only be done with one or a few people, then it must be done privately.

Some people are so self-assured and confident that they need not play much of a role in public. This is generally true of ISJs because of their self-respect and strong sense of self-identity. Nonetheless, even ISJs will be self-conscious. Yet their self-consciousness will manifest itself in the more positive way described earlier. Self-consciousness seems ineradicable in humans. As such, ISJs will also need privacy to convey their innermost feelings to one who is trusted. Both ISJs and non-ISJs seem to have a deep need for intimate relationships because such relationships and the sharing that exists in them gives more meaning to life. Perhaps part of this is because self-consciousness implies a comparative or relational state to others. We can only be self-conscious if others exist so that we can make comparisons between ourselves and others.[55] We need various forms of affirmation. In some cases the affirmation of strangers or distant acquaintances might suffice, but at other times we will have a deeper need for the affirmation of either an expert in a certain field or a loved one. These two often overlap in the parent-child relationship. To a young child, parents are often seen as beings with superior knowledge, which is partly why parents are asked so many questions by children. Likewise, and more importantly, a properly raised child develops a loving bond and deep level of trust in his parent. For this reason, it is often of great importance that children receive affirmation out of love. An ethics professor may comment approvingly of a particular act of a child, and this affirmation may mean something important to the child. Yet it is also likely that a parent's affirmation of that same act is more meaningful to the child. The ethics professor may have more expertise than the parent in matters of ethics, but this does not matter much because only the parent is able to provide *intimate* affirmation.

Perhaps part of what makes intimate relationships important is that one enters into a relationship with a particular self-identity but, because self-identity is also connected to being in a relationship, self-identity is occasionally modified by the sharing in a relationship. That is the case with adults in intimate relationships. However, this must be different in the intimate relationship between parents and children. Children gradually develop a self-identity (whereas if and when the identity of an adult changes it is usually more gradual because self-identity can be deep and hard to change quickly once mature). The self-identity of children is largely shaped by the stability and consistency of how they are and were treated by others. Parents can provide a foundation for stable and healthy identity because of their constant presence and guidance. But parents also provide a unique opportunity for intimacy due to the private nature of the family. In particular, a house or apartment literally provides a physical barrier from the public. Having been protected and nurtured for so long by their parents, children are likely to trust parents with things that they deem important, especially if children do not have enough trust in others to broach the subject or are simply too embarrassed to ask others the question. Likewise, especially when older, children will not want to discuss some things with their parents. This can largely be attributed to the asymmetrical relationship between child and adult, which entails that some things cannot be shared. However, if the child develops properly he will have arrived at the second stage of development and will have social relationships with peers that he trusts enough to discuss things with them that he cannot discuss with his parents.

Just as children need privacy to ask embarrassing questions or display emotions that they are uncomfortable displaying in public, parents require privacy too. Earlier I mentioned that intimate space is necessary for things such as telling personal stories. However, this space is also necessary to share life lessons with children. Life is tough, and sometimes it is even cruel. Sometimes parents need to share painful things with children, and this often requires privacy. Yet deeply private sharing is not the only reason a parent needs privacy in relationship to his child. Some parents have positions of respect in public where they must exude seriousness. In these cases, lack of seriousness might demonstrate a weakness. If humor or silliness is to be accepted, then it must be of a certain kind to be accepted. However, one cannot maintain a constant state of seriousness with children. One must be able to play with them, and playing with them often means playing with them at their level; acting as such in public may not be prudent. One must often be serious with children so that they develop from childhood into adulthood, but simply treating them as adults is inappropriate and unhealthy.[56] Daycare workers cannot provide the privacy or the intimacy provided by parents in the above account. The time, resource, and emotional investment is too great.

CONCLUSION

After comparing the traditional nuclear family, the neo-nuclear family, single parents, cohabiting parents, and daycare, I find that the family, especially the neo-nuclear family, uniquely provides the combination of love, stability, privacy, and intimacy needed to develop into an ISJ. This leaves one important question, which will be addressed in the next chapter: how do we best *ensure* that children are likely to be parented well and within a family?

NOTES

1. Francis Shrag, "Justice and the Family," *Inquiry*, 19 (1976), 200.

2. In writing about the family, especially with regards to child development, I must note my deep indebtedness to John Bowlby's attachment theory. It is a powerful explanatory theory, and it yielded much important research. While trying to develop an ISJ account, it has become even more obvious to me how powerful attachment theory is. Of course, other theories, such as social learning, are also needed to understand the complex nature of child development and its relation to society. With respect to this chapter, I have this in mind: "It is because a young child is not an organism capable of independent life that he requires a special social institution to aid him during his period of immaturity. The social institution must aid him in two ways: first, by helping in the satisfaction of immediate animal needs such as nutrition, warmth, and shelter, and protection from danger; secondly, by providing surroundings in which he may develop his physical, mental, and social capacities to the full so that, when grown up, he may be able to deal with his physical and social environment effectively. This demands an atmosphere of affection and security," John Bowlby, *Child Care and the Growth of Love* (Baltimore: Penguin Books, 1957), 82.

3. Schrag, 194.

4. I will not examine marriages that consist of three or more adults.

5. I leave this open for the sake of argument. Discussion about whether ISJs require both a mother and a father, as opposed to two mothers or two fathers, would require extensive discussion and would likely detract from the major purpose of this chapter. There are tensions that both those for and against gay marriage have to face if child maltreatment were taken seriously. For those against gay marriage, I ask whether one would rather have children raised by a heterosexual married couple that abuses their children or by a homosexual married couple who does not maltreat their children. For those who support gay marriage, I ask whether one would still argue that homosexual couples have the same right to rear children as heterosexual couples if it were empirically demonstrated that rates of maltreatment by homosexual couples were significantly higher than that of heterosexual couples.

6. Susan Moller Okin, *Justice, Gender, and the Family* (New York: Basic Books, 1989), 135.

7. For more on the importance of parental love, as opposed to possessing and acting from mere moral knowledge, see Laurence Thomas's *The Family and the Political Self* (New York: Cambridge University Press, 2006).

8. Aristotle, *Politics*, trans. T. A. Sinclair (London: Penguin Books, 1992), Bk. II, Sect. IV, 1262b2,1111.

9. This kind of argument is put forth by Martin Daly and Margo Wilson in "Discriminative Parental Solicitude: A Biological Perspective," *Journal of Marriage and the Family* (May 1980).

10. See Dorothy W. Smith and Laurie Nels Sherwen, *Mothers and Their Adopted Children: The Bonding Process* (New York: Tiresias Press, 1983).

11. Peter L. Benson, Anu R. Sharma, and Eugene L. Roehlkepartain, *Growing Up Adopted: A Portrait of Adolescents and Their Families* (Minneapolis, MN: Search Institute, 1994).

12. Nola L. Passmore, Gerard J. Fogarty, Carolyn J. Bourke, and Sandra F. Baker-Evans, "Parental Bonding and Identity Style as Correlates of Self-Esteem among Adult Adoptees and Nonadoptees," *Family Relations*, 54 (2005).

13. L. DiAnne Borders, Lynda K. Black, and B. Kay Pasley, "Are Adopted Children and Their Parents at Greater Risk for Negative Outcomes?" *Family Relations*, 47 (1998).

14. See LaFollette, 194, n.9. For more recent statistics, in 2004 only 0.6 percent of parental perpetrators of child abuse were adoptive parents. *Child Maltreatment: U.S. Department of Health and Human Resources, Administration on Children, Youth, and Families* (Washington, DC: U.S. Government Printing Office, 2006), 78. However, according to the 2000 U.S. Census, 2.4 percent of children were adopted. United States Census: Adopted Children and Stepchildren—Census 2000 Special Report (U.S. Department of Commerce, 2004), 2. These statistics are from different sources, but it is fairly clear that the rate of abuse is lower in adoptive families.

15. Aristotle, *Nicomachean Ethics*, trans. Martin Ostwald (Englewood Cliffs, NJ: Prentice Hall, 1962), Bk. VIII, Ch. XXII, 1162a27–29, 239–40.

16. They must be bonded in a certain way for this to work. I note this because societies established on the principle that all property is in common or should be shared equally have floundered in the twentieth century. In addition to commonality, a strong sense of responsibility is also needed so that free-riding is not too tempting. And responsibility is often linked to ownership, which naturally provides a sense of "my own." Therefore, the above passage from the *Nicomachean Ethics* needs to be tempered by what Aristotle says in the *Politics*, "the greater the number of owners, the less respect for common property. People are much more careful of their personal possessions than of those owned communally; they exercise care over common property only in so far as they are personally affected. Other reasons apart, the thought that someone else is looking after it tends to make them careless of it. (This is rather like what happens in domestic service: a greater number of servants sometimes does less work than a smaller)," Bk. II, Sect. III, 1261b32–38, 108.

17. The parent left with the child is often at a disadvantage because that parent must now take care of the child alone, and it is also likely that whichever parent is left

with primary childcare responsibilities was, while in the relationship, also predominately involved in caring for the child. As a result, that parent's investment has primarily gone towards one's child, unlike the parent who likely invested in a job outside of the home instead. Consequently, when the parent who was and is primarily
responsible for childcare goes out onto the market, that parent's market value will
likely be lower.

18. Numerous studies have found that children of single parents have two times
the risk of being abused compared to children in two-parent families. See William H.
Sack, Robert Mason, James E. Higgins, "The Single-Parent Family and Abusive
Child Punishment," *American Journal of Orthopsychiatry*, 55 (1983); National Cen-
ter on Child Abuse and Neglect, *Third National Study of Child Abuse and Neglect*
(Washington, DC: US Department of Health and Human Resources, 1996). Patrick F.
Fagan, "The Child Abuse Crisis: The Disintegration of Marriage, Family, and the
American Community," Backgrounder, No. 1115. The Heritage Foundation (March
15, 1997); Jill Goldman and Marsha K. Salus, *A Coordinated Response to Child
Abuse and Neglect: The Foundation for Practice*. U.S. Department of Health and Human Services Administration on Children and Families at www.childwelfare.gov/
pubs/usermanusals/foundation/foundation.pdf (2003); Diane DePanfilies, *Child Neglect: A Guide for Prevention, Assessment, and Intervention* at www.childwelfare.gov
.pubs/usermanuals/neglect/neglect.pdf (2006) (6 Apr. 2008).

19. Okin, 5.

20. It has been suggested to me that perhaps Okin meant something other than the
account provided above. Rather, she meant to argue that more women were willing to
exit marriage in the 1980s than before because they were unwilling to tolerate asymmetrical gender roles and/or society was more tolerant of divorce, and, as a result, the
number of divorces has increased. This argument makes sense, though I find it to be
stretching Okin a bit far from what she actually writes. Regardless, children are
harmed when divorces occur and when women are maltreated in marriage. Therefore,
even if the high divorce rate demonstrates some kind of emancipation of women, it
should be recognized that the emancipation still has harmful effects for children.

21. Morse, 241n.

22. For an excellent review of studies on cohabitation, see Judith A. Seltzer, "Families Forced Outside of Marriage," *Journal of Marriage and the Family*, 62 (2000).

23. Steven L. Nock, "A Comparison of Marriages and Cohabiting Relationships,"
Journal of Family Issues, 16 (1995); R. Forste and K. Tanfer, "Sexual Exclusivity
among Dating, Cohabiting, and Married Women," *Journal of Marriage and the Family*, 58 (1996).

24. Kersti Yllo and Murray A. Straus, "Interpersonal Violence Among Married and
Cohabiting Couples," *Family Relations*, 30 (1981); Murray A. Straus, "The Marriage
License as Hitting License: A Comparison of Assaults in Dating, Cohabiting and Married Couples," *Journal of Family Violence*, 4 (1989); Nicky Ali Jackson, "Observational Experiences of Interpersonal Conflict and Teenage Victimization: A Comparative Study Among Spouses and Cohabitors," *Journal of Family Violence*, 11 (1996);
D. A. Brownridge and S. S. Halli, "'Living in Sin' and Sinful Living: Toward Filling
a Gap in the Explanation of Violence Against Women," *Aggressive and Violent Be-*

havior, 5 (2000). It is also worth noting that cohabiters were about twice as likely to be physically abusive towards their partners compared to those who are simply dating. See Lynn Magdol, Terrie E. Moffitt, Avshalon Caspi, and Phil A. Silva, "Hitting Without a License: Testing Explanations for Differences in Partner Abuse Between Young Adult Daters and Cohabiters," *Journal of Marriage and the Family*, 60 (1998).

25. For example, by the age of five, half of children born to a cohabiting couple will see that couple's relationship end. However, only fifteen percent of children born to married couples will experience the same thing. See Wendy D. Manning, Pamela J. Smock, and Debarum Majumdar, "The Relative Stability of Cohabiting and Marital Unions for Children," *Population Research and Policy Review*, 23 (2004).

26. Susan L. Brown and Alan Booth, "Cohabiting Versus Marriage: A Comparison of Relationship Quality," *Journal of Marriage and the Family*, 58 (1996).

27. See A. Booth and D. R. Johnson, "Premarital Cohabitation and Marital Success," *Journal of Family Issues*, 9 (1988).

28. W. G. Axinn and A. Thornton, "The Relationship between Cohabitation and Divorce: Selectivity or Causal Influence?" *Demography*, 29 (1992).

29. Nock, 67. I have already discussed this somewhat earlier, and I will not do so more here.

30. Nock, 74.

31. Susan L. Brown, "Family Structure and Child Well-Being: The Significance of Parental Contribution," *Journal of Marriage and the Family*, 66 (2004).

32. Patrick F. Fagan, "The Child Abuse Crisis: The Disintegration of Marriage, Family, and the American Family," Backgrounder, No. 1115 (Washington, DC: Heritage Foundation, June 3, 1997). Fagan's account relies upon an important British study: Robert Whelan, *Broken Homes and Battered Children: A Study of the Relationship between Child Abuse and Family Type* (London: Family Education Trust, 1993). See also Michael Gordon and Susan Creighton, "Natal and Non-natal Fathers as Sexual Abusers in the United Kingdom: A Comparative Analysis," *Journal of Marriage and the Family*, 50 (1998); Leslie Margolin, "Child Abuse by Mothers' Boyfriends: Why the Overrepresentation?" *Child Abuse and Neglect*, 16 (1992). Note that British data is largely used here due to a lack of such studies in the U.S. This also occurs because not enough studies differentiate between cohabiting and married parents.

33. Morse, 93.

34. I here refer to daycare in a weak sense, where those who need it are provided with it for their own children. I will refer to a stronger notion, that of mandatory universalized daycare for all children, later. Many of the objections to daycare in the weak sense should still be applicable to the stronger notion.

35. John Locke, *Some Thoughts Concerning Education and of the Conduct of Understanding*, §82, 59.

36. Rousseau, *Emile, or On Education*, trans. Allan Bloom (New York: Basic Books, 1979), Bk. IV, 251.

37. It has been found that constructive conflict management and effective communication of spouses lowers levels of anxiety, anti-social behaviors, withdrawal, and externalizing problems in their children. See L. F. Katz and J. F. Gottman, "Patterns

of Marital Conflict Predict Children's Internalizing and Externalizing Behaviors," *Developmental Psychology*, 29 (1993).

38. *TJ*, 375–76.

39. Thomas, 23.

40. Aristotle, *Politics*, Bk. II, Sect. IV, 1262b8–2,1111. Jeffrey Blustein also gives this passage great weight in understanding the nature of families. Also, this passage nicely continues and expands upon the motivation largely left implicit in his passage on p. 108 (*Politics*) that I referred to earlier.

41. Aldous Huxley, *Brave New World* (New York: Perennial Classics, 1998), 40. In a similar vein, Schoeman writes, "I shall mean by 'family' an intense continuing and intimate organization," 9.

42. Okin makes this objection, and more, nicely: "Even a 'mass society' does not have to provide 'mass' day care. It can provide small-scale, loving day care for all if it cares enough and is prepared enough and is prepared to subsidize the full costs for parents unable to afford it. Good day care, besides being a positive experience for the child, also helps to solve two others problems. Without it, the shared parenting solution is of no help to single parents; and good, subsidized day care can help alleviate the obstacle that the inequality of family circumstances poses for equality of opportunity," 116n.

43. Blustein, 37.

44. Of course, parents are capable of raising multiple children well. However, with regards the narrowness of love, it should also be pointed out that sometimes a large number of children is less than ideal. After all, the risk of child maltreatment increases as the number of children in a family increases. See Samuel S. Wu, Chang-Xing Ma, Randy L. Carter, Mario Ariet, Edward A. Feaver, Michael B. Resnick, and Jeffrey Roth, "Risk Factors for Infant Maltreatment: A Population-Based Study," *Child Abuse and Neglect*, 28 (2004); Edward Zigler and Nancy W. Hall, "Physical Child Abuse in America: Past, Present, and Future," in Cichetti and Carlson (1989).

45. Robert Gerstein, "Intimacy and Privacy," *Ethics*, 89 (1978), 76.

46. Ferdinand Schoeman, "Rights of Children, Rights of Parents, and the Moral Basis of the Family," *Ethics*, 91 (1980), 8. I am extremely indebted to the work of Schrag and Schoeman on the subject of intimacy and privacy. Their work has helped clarify some of my intuitions and helped me see more clearly why the family is such a unique and powerful institution.

47. Aristotle, *Nicomachean Ethics*, Bk. VIII, Ch. II, Sect. II–VI, 217–25. The first and second conditions may be met by older children, but they cannot be met by babies due to a lack of a complex cognitive structure that recognizes things such as intent. Though, of course, they can be aware of how such intent is manifested in action.

48. Aristotle, *Nicomachean Ethics*, Bk. VIII, Ch. VII, Sect. VII, 1158b16, 227.

49. An argument can be made that the man-divine relationship is the most asymmetrical kind of friendship between unequals. This is complicated, though, because Aristotle does not consider this to be a friendship due to the extreme distance between man and the divine. I will not examine this complicated question further. Gerstein does grapple with intimacy and the divine in his essay.

50. Aristotle notes, "In all friendships which involve the superiority of one of the partners, the affection, too, must be proportionate: the better and more useful partner should receive more affection than he gives," *Nicomachean Ethics*, Bk. VIII, Ch. VII, Sect. VII, 1158b24, 227. This may make sense in the case of unequal adults, but it does not seem to be true in the parent-child relationship, especially for babies. Rather, this seems backwards.

51. This changes with time, as Aristotle correctly notes: "parents love their children as soon as they are born, but children their parents only as, with the passage of time, they acquire understanding or perception," *Nicomachean Ethics*, Bk. VIII, Ch. XII, Sect. XII, 237.

52. This does not mean that the parent should open up completely. After all, the relationship is still asymmetrical and that entails, at some points, a wall of sharing to that which would be inappropriate to share with children or, particularly, one's own child.

53. This type of secure attachment is examined nicely in Ainsworth's "Strange Situation" experiments. See Mary D. Salter Ainsworth, Mary C. Blehar, Everett Waters, and Sally Wall, *Patterns of Attachment: A Psychological Study of the Strange Situation* (Hillsdale, NJ: Erlbaum, 1978).

54. Gerstein, 81.

55. For a fascinating account of how social comparison works with humans, see Leon Festinger, "A Theory of Social Comparison Processes," *Human Relations*, 7 (1954). For an argument that affirmation actually gives life meaning, see Laurence Thomas, "Morality and a Meaningful Life, *Philosophical Papers*, 34 (2005).

56. For how children have been treated simply as small adults in large parts of history, see Philippe Aries's *Centuries of Childhood: A Social History of Family Life* (New York: Vintage, 1962).

5

Licensing Parents

The importance of good character, fellow feeling, and trust in society has been recognized throughout history. One of the American Founders, in shaping the mostly well-ordered society that I am now discussing, noted:

> As there is a degree of depravity in mankind which requires a certain degree of circumspection and distrust: So there are other qualities in human nature, which justify a certain portion of esteem and confidence. Republican government presupposes the existence of these qualities in a higher degree than any other form. Were the pictures which have been drawn by the political jealousy of some among us, faithful likenesses of the human character, the inference would be that there is not sufficient virtue among men for self-government.[1]

Government, or at least free government, requires that people have good character, fellow feeling, and trust. Like many other thinkers, Madison presupposes such character in society. Yet what happens when good character, fellow feeling, and trust deteriorate because the family, the most important mechanism for providing such virtues, breaks down? Trust is not always a healthy trait. It is only good when one has sufficient reason to believe that it will be reciprocated and others are likely to fulfill their duties. Trust is fragile.

In the past four chapters I asked how we can move from a mostly well-ordered society toward a completely well-ordered society, create ISJs, prevent child maltreatment, and ensure equality of opportunity. The answer to all of these has been to establish and maintain families with competent parents. However, I have not yet fully answered the question posed by Adeimantus at the beginning of chapter 3: *how* should children be begotten and reared in society if this makes all the difference in a regime? I believe that Adeimantus is correct in that how children are reared directly affects justice in that society, and this does not seem overly controversial. Blustein echoes Adeimantus's concern when he says, "The public has a legitimate concern with the selection of child rearers and with the way in which children are reared, because a society's children are its future citizens and the future contributors to its material, cultural, and moral advancement."[2] Similarly, Archard notes,

> [T]he character of adult society will derive from the ways in which its children are brought up, and that, in turn, the nature of childrearing will reflect the values and priorities of adult society. Yet political and social philosophy seems sometimes to have forgotten this fact, representing as merely natural development what is a choice of upbringing.[3]

In response to Adeimantus, we could argue that children should be reared in neo-nuclear families because only the neo-nuclear family can provide the love, stability, privacy, and intimacy needed to create ISJs. This may be especially tempting after understanding how devastating child maltreatment can be. However, this suggestion still does not answer the implied further question of *how* we can best *ensure* that children will be parented well within the family. It is time to fit this ideal into the real world. The goal is to promote healthy families that provide capabilities to flourish and to prevent unhealthy families that do not provide such capabilities. This chapter offers some solutions about how this can be accomplished. Based upon the substance of the previous chapters, I argue that the best way to ensure healthy families with competent parents for the sake of children and society is to license parents — to allow the state to forbid some potential parents from parenting.

The first section of this chapter outlines the conditions that must be met to implement a system of licensing parents. Section 2 adds to the evidence from previous chapters that the state has a compelling interest in licensing parents. The third section describes why primary prevention is needed based upon child development. It will also show why parenting classes, rehabilitation, and social disapprobation do not sufficiently confront the problem of child maltreatment. The system of licensing parents is outlined is section 4. Section 5 examines alternative licensing and non-licensing solutions.

1. CONDITIONS OF INTERVENTION

If the state were to license parents, it should do so with caution. Prudence should even be exercised in our current system where parents are not licensed but where children are occasionally removed from their parents after being maltreated. The reason for caution is that sometimes the effects of removal, especially if children are placed in foster care, can be worse for their development than staying with the family that maltreats them. Accordingly, some argue that children should almost never be removed from their families, even if maltreated.[4] The motivation behind this is understandable; the continuity and stability of having a loving and caring adult figure is important for child development. Michael Wald proposes a more moderate and widely accepted position about what should be the proper legal response to child maltreatment: only intervene when a child has or is likely to suffer serious harm, only remove if it is not possible to protect the child through less invasive means of intervention, expend great effort to reunite the child with his family if a reunion is unlikely to endanger the child, and terminate parental rights only if the child is under the age of three and cannot be reunited with his family within one year of his removal.[5] Wald also claims,

> In an ideal world, children would not be brought up in "inadequate" homes. However, our less than ideal society lacks the ability to provide better alternatives for most of these children. The best we can do is to expand social welfare services now offered families on voluntary basis.[6]

We cannot live in a completely ideal society, but we can move closer to it than Wald thinks. In fact, the first two conditions that must be met for Wald before intervening and removing a child from his parents are also two conditions that must be met before a system of parental licensing can be established.

Prior to moving toward an ideal society by means of licensing parents, several conditions must be met. After all, licensing parents entails state intervention in the family—the institution that I have argued should now be the center of political philosophy. Part of the reason the family is ideal for child development is that it can provide privacy and intimacy; this should not be forgotten. If parental licensing were to be implemented, it would have to be done in a way that these two virtues provided by the structure of the family were preserved. The *kind* of intimacy and privacy that is important within the family can remain untouched while licensing parents, but this will be discussed more in chapter 8. Five other conditions must be met for parental licensing to be justified: (i) licensing must be a compelling interest of the state, (ii) a test must exist to predict, with reasonable precision, which potential parents will likely maltreat their children, (iii) there must be no less invasive solutions that will yield the similar desired effects of licensing parents, (iv) the policy of licensing parents must be able to be implemented effectively, and (v) it must be demonstrated that prospective parents do not have an indefeasible right to parent. If any of these conditions are not met, then I will concede that licensing parents is unjustified. However, if all of these conditions can be met then it is *permissible*, and *possibly* even *obligatory*, to license parents. I have addressed

(i) and (iii) indirectly, but I will do so directly in this chapter. This chapter addresses (i)–(iv). Condition (v) will be discussed in chapters 6 and 7.

2. COMPELLING INTEREST OF THE STATE

By now it should be recognized that the damage caused by child maltreatment and the resulting negative effects sufficiently demonstrate a compelling interest of the state. Child maltreatment is the surest means of producing non-ISJs, and non-ISJs are prone to be more unjust and violent. In general, they erode trust—a major foundation of a stable and well-ordered society. This is summarized by Alan Sroufe:

> [N]eglected children learn to expect that their caregivers will be unavailable and unresponsive to their emotional needs. This leads to a sense of themselves as isolated, as uncared about, and as unworthy—in essence 'bad.' Other people, in turn, are viewed unrealistically as uncaring and are treated with anger and hostility. . . . Because they feel alienated from other people, neglected children become capable of violent robbery and killing. They have no compunction about taking from the "haves," because they are the "have-nots." They do not feel they are in the wrong because they feel that society has deprived them. Therefore, society should give to them. If society does not, they steal, and murder is incidental. They lead irresponsible lives and coerce or manipulate others to satisfy their own needs without regards for the rights or lives of others.[7]

Not only do we have an environment where trust cannot flourish, we have genuine worries about violence and crime. Not all maltreated children become criminals, but the risk is much higher in those who are maltreated. Of those who commit serious enough crimes to be incarcerated, about 80 percent are maltreated as children. The number incarcerated in the United States is small, but anti-social behavior has a large social and financial cost.

Violence poses a threat to the stability of a nation, but the residual financial costs also pose a considerable threat. Criminal recidivism of habitual criminals (0.2 percent of the population), after the cost of arrests by police, courts, overnight detainment, social worker services, correctional facilities, and loss of federal income taxes amounts to $17.8 billion per year and $1.1 trillion over sixty years. Welfare dependency of those chronically on welfare (0.4 percent of the population), after considering the above costs and AFDC payments, amounts to $12.4 billion per year and $744 billion over sixty years of life. Child abuse and neglect services cost $8.4 billion per year and $504 billion over sixty years of life. When totaled, 0.9 percent of the population costs the government $2.7 trillion dollars over sixty years, and this does not include the tens of trillions lost in decline of national productivity due to un-qualified workers.[8] It may later be objected that a system of licensing parents would be prohibitive due to the large bureaucracy and financial costs in-volved. The above should be kept in mind when such objections are made. Li-censing parents would require some bureaucracy, but it would mostly replace the current bureaucracy that exists to deal with the negative effects of child maltreatment. If a bureaucracy must exist and if money must be spent, then the better investment is to ensure that children are not maltreated rather than to deal with the negative effects of permitting them to be maltreated.

3. JUSTIFIED COERCION

This chapter will provide an implementation scheme to promote healthy fam-ilies, produce ISJs, and prevent potentially unhealthy families from maltreat-ing children and producing non-ISJs. Earlier, I put forth the neo-nuclear fam-ily as the ideal, but this ideal cannot pragmatically be secured universally and effectively. We can, however, provide all children with a minimal level of de-cent parenting. This entails a need to prevent those who *will* maltreat their children from parenting, but this cannot be done due to lack of omniscience. However, as will be clear later, we can prevent those who *will likely* maltreat their children from parenting. Licensing parents seeks only to forbid the very worst potential parents from parenting; it does not require that parents be prospectively good or excellent. Most prospective parents will be permitted to parent, as most prospective drivers are permitted to drive. However, a few will not be permitted to parent. I offer a conservative top-down model of pri-mary prevention to address the problem of child maltreatment.

3.1 Primary Prevention

If we seek to reduce the number of non-ISJs and the best way to do this is by reducing the number of potentially incompetent parents, what is the best means to reduce the number of potentially incompetent parents? To borrow from Caplan's *Principles of Preventative Psychiatry*, *primary* prevention re-duces the rate of new cases of disorder in a society by counteracting negative influences *before* they can produce dysfunction.[9] *Secondary* and *tertiary* pre-vention identify problems *early* and intervene before problems yield serious mental illness, or they *rehabilitate* individuals *already suffering* from mental, emotional, or behavioral problems. Only primary prevention will counter the problem of maltreatment and individuals not becoming ISJs. In the Rawlsian model of development, children develop gradually and cannot bypass stages of moral development. By citing empirical data, I have shown that child mal-treatment often thwarts development. The special developmental psychology of children requires maltreatment to be prevented *before* it happens. If abuse or neglect occurs, then development is at risk of being stunted, decreasing the likelihood that children become ISJs. Primary prevention may seem to be overly protective and to go beyond current legal precedent, and this is true to some degree. However, current laws tend to be adult-centered. Adults are usually as psychologically mature as they ever will be—whether they are ISJs or not. An adult who is maltreated will still feel pain, and the pain may be in-tense and prolonged. Nonetheless, maltreatment of an adult will not have the same impact as maltreatment of a child, which is more harmful. Child mal-treatment carries not only intense and prolonged pain, but, as I have shown, it often thwarts moral and psychological development.

3.2 Aristotle and Locke

One who is not as impressed by Rawls's developmental moral psychology as I am may not be convinced that secondary and tertiary prevention are insuf-ficient. Secondary and tertiary prevention are currently used to confront child maltreatment. They are minimally invasive; they require that children be re-moved from their parents or that some sort of rehabilitation be provided only *after* children have been maltreated. One of my objectives is to show what follows from a Rawlsian model of development, so I could simply assume that his model is true. However, there are other ways to reach the same con-clusion as Rawls without appealing to his theory. The first is that the keenest observers of human nature have argued something similar to Rawls, that it is not truly possible to rehabilitate fully those not nurtured properly as children, a sentiment that Aristotle is clear about several times, especially when he says: "it is no small matter whether one habit or another is inculcated in us from early childhood; on the contrary, it makes a considerable difference, or, rather all the difference," and "Argument and teaching, I'm afraid, are not ef-fective in all cases: the soul of the listener must first have been conditioned by habits of the right kind of likes and dislikes, just as land must be cultivated before it is able to foster the seed."[10] Similarly, Locke observes, "Virtue is harder to be got than a knowledge of the world, and if lost in a young man is seldom recovered."[11]

3.3 Sociobiological Harm

If unconvinced by Rawlsian developmental moral psychology or that es-poused by Aristotle and Locke, then there may still be reason to embrace primary prevention. Recent studies show that child maltreatment may have a negative affect on human biology.[12] In particular, child maltreatment has been associated with adverse influences on brain development.[13] This manifests in different ways. For example, a decreased hippocampal size is common in adults who have experienced post-traumatic stress syndrome due to severe childhood maltreatment; this helps explain the memory loss experienced by many victims.[14] Increased electrophysiological abnormalities, especially in the left side of the frontal, temporal, and anterior regions of the brain, have also been found in maltreated children. This helps support the thesis that early childhood maltreatment can alter brain development, especially the limbic structures. Improper development can lead to affective instability and poor control over anger, impulse, and stress.[15] Lastly, and important to my forthcoming proposal that children may require an increased level of protection than adults, childhood trauma may be more harmful than trauma experienced as an adult due to the combination of trauma, psychology, and neurodevelopment.[16]

3.4 Rehabilitation and Recidivism

In the context of child maltreatment, there are two major kinds of secondary or tertiary means of prevention—education and rehabilitation. There are also two groups of people—adults and children. Therefore, I will examine education programs for adults, rehabilitation programs for adults, and rehabilitation programs for children.[17]

3.4.1 Parenting Classes

Parenting classes for adults may seem like a good idea because parents who abuse their children often overestimate their children's abilities.[18] Part of this is due to ignorance, perhaps because parents never had proper models themselves, and part of this may result from parents not observing how other children develop and are raised. Also, those who maltreat children tend not to regulate their emotions properly and lose control easily. For children, who often learn by making mistakes, this provides an environment where maltreatment occurs simply because they do not act like adults.

In another sense, parenting classes inadequately address this problem. Most child maltreatment is not due to a lack of education. If a parent does not *know* that it is wrong to abuse or neglect his child before taking a parenting class, then we should pause to consider how effective such a class would be. Most parents know that abusing and neglecting children is wrong, though they may not fully understand how detrimental maltreatment is to child development. Sometimes parents do not care enough, as much as we may not want to believe this about any parent, or their affections are constituted in a way that can be overcome by lack of self-control or anger, which are passions that override knowing what they do is wrong. Chasteen is also skeptical about trying to teach high-risk parents how to parent, "Those of us who teach are continually disheartened at the difficulties encountered in trying to teach what people do not want to learn."[19] Lastly, those most at risk to maltreat children are least likely to attend parenting classes. Apathy, social isolation, and lack of responsibility are atop a list of reasons for this. Thus, it is nearly impossible to attain data about how successful parenting classes can be for *truly* high-risk parents. For example, group sessions for one study involving home-visitation and parent group sessions had to be cancelled because so few of the parents actually attended.[20]

3.4.2 Rehabilitation and Social Disapprobation

If parenting classes do not work well, then perhaps it will help to provide adults with rehabilitation after maltreating children.[21] Many different treatments with wide-ranging successes have been employed for those who have maltreated their children. In an analysis of these programs, David P. H. Jones notes that 20 percent to 87 percent of families were unchanged or worse at the end of treatment and the recidivism rate was between 16 percent and 60 percent.[22] It is good that *some* parents can be helped with their parenting deficiencies. However, most of those who are at the highest risk to maltreat their children and who also usually maltreat their children most severely are not included in such studies. Such parents are often too socially isolated, apathetic, or irresponsible to take part or participate consistently. Consequently, these tests probably measure best the effects of treatment on moderate-risk parents or those who maltreat moderately. We should try to help moderate-risk parents, but the highest-risk parents are much more dangerous because severe maltreatment damages children more than moderate maltreatment. Severity and frequency are important in the developmental effects of maltreatment. The children in frequently and severely abusing families have little chance to develop properly in any theory of child development. In egalitarian considerations of equal opportunity, they are nowhere near the starting gate.

Suppose that treatment programs become more effective, which is possible, and treatment consistently yields a 75 percent rate of success without recidivism. This is excellent from an adult-centered standpoint, but it is less so from a child-centered standpoint. Parents who are at highest risk are unlikely to be treated. If treated, treatment will unlikely be successful. Even if 100 percent of moderate-risk parents could be treated successfully, this would not benefit the highest-risk parents or their children. More importantly, while these parents would no longer *continue* to maltreat their children, they would have *already* maltreated their children. Consequently, devastating developmental harm would probably have *already* occurred in their children. The harm that children suffer before their parents are successfully treated can prevent them from becoming ISJs. Only a primary means of prevention to ensure that they are not maltreated in the first place will actually allow children to more likely become ISJs. Many oppose primary prevention because of the coercion that is required for implementation, but coercion will eventually be necessary. For example, some argue that we should force high-risk parents to take parenting classes for the sake of equality and protecting children. Blustein says,

> [I]f society is committed to having children raised in the family, then equal opportunity for children requires some transfer of resources to partially equalize the environments of children. Parents, in turn, have a duty to avail themselves of needed support services so that they can provide their children with an environment that affords them access to a full range of future opportunities.[23]

Unfortunately, having a duty does not necessarily entail that fulfilling such a duty will occur. If we wish to protect children, then it seems that we would have to coerce families to take parenting classes. If coercion is the objectionable feature of licensing parents, then a mandatory parenting-class solution does not advance the cause as one might initially think.

It may be objected that coercive intervention in the family is not necessary to strengthen and maintain families or prevent child maltreatment. Rather, non-coercive social disapprobation will suffice. Social disapprobation can be incredibly powerful. I concede that if one already lived in a completely well-ordered society then social disapprobation *should* generally be the primary means of regulating manners, mores, and behavior. However, the issue of child maltreatment is an exception to this rule.

The power of social disapprobation derives largely from the shame of not living up to the standards of others in society and being reminded of this frequently by many in society or by a few who are important enough to cause a sufficient amount of shame or guilt. However, the worst cases of child maltreatment often occur where the family is largely isolated from society. If society does not play a central role in these families, then it is difficult to understand how social disapprobation, which derives its force from society being meaningful to individuals or groups, will successfully change behavior. Social disapprobation also requires, to some degree, that people care about how they are perceived by others or how their actions correspond with a particular normative system. In families where maltreatment is worst, the likelihood of apathy is high. Sometimes social disapprobation is insufficient to address a problem entirely. This is evident because even in the best societies police are needed to apprehend and punish criminals who are apathetic to the disapprobation that follows from perpetuating a crime, do not recognize anything morally wrong with criminal activity, recognize it as wrong but otherwise justify their actions, or think that they will not be caught. Social disapprobation can be extremely powerful, but it can only work effectively in certain environments.

The worst cases of maltreatment seem to involve parents who were, themselves, maltreated. Consequently, these parents are probably not developmentally mature or psychologically stable. Not all maltreatment is passed down this way, but investigations into the most severe cases of maltreatment often reveal an intergenerational link. It is thus unlikely that social disapprobation will be sufficient to change behavior. Those who maltreat severely are also likely to lead lives that are disapproved of by many in society. For social disapprobation to work most effectively, one must already accept, or at least largely act according with, the values accepted by society. It is unclear that this is the case with many who maltreat severely, where, even if the same values are shared, social disapprobation seems insufficient to overcome the damaged affectational structures of high-risk potential parents.

A similar objection states that reviving the family would be sufficient to combat child maltreatment. This objection is often employed in tandem with an argument for social disapprobation. Yet social disapprobation is not as powerful as it might seem after the nature of child maltreatment is carefully considered. The heart of this objection, that what we need to do to combat child maltreatment is to revitalize the family, *is* correct. After all, a major premise of this book is that ISJs are needed in society; ISJs tend to come from healthy families, and non-ISJs tend to come from unhealthy families. We need to discover how best to reverse the trend of unhealthy families and child maltreatment. However, *simply* saying that we need to revitalize the family is uninformative as a solution. It is rhetorically powerful, but it amounts to saying that we need healthy families in order to have healthy families. More substance is needed to elude this circularity. If character development largely takes place within the family, then what happens if the character of citizens deteriorates due to the deterioration of the family? The self-reinforcing mechanism of the family is needed to produce the requisite character for individuals, but the mechanism to fix it is broken. Simply saying, "We need healthy families" is as unhelpful as saying "We need an unbroken hammer" when the only thing that could fix the hammer would be the unbroken hammer or that which could be produced by the unbroken hammer. This problem can be avoided by denying the positive power that families have, denying the negative power that maltreatment has on children, or denying the difficulty of rehabilitation. Those who advocate the family as a solution because of its positive effects and because of the negative effects of unhealthy families cannot consistently deny any of these three things. Therefore, the problem remains.

3.4.3 Rehabilitating Children

The third option, after education for parents and rehabilitation of parents, concerns the effectiveness of rehabilitating children after they have been maltreated. Unfortunately, there are few studies on this, especially compared to the number of studies on the effectiveness of adult rehabilitation programs. Studies on the effectiveness of programs for adults are residually beneficial to children in an obvious way, but it is revealing that comparatively little has been studied about how successfully the effects of harm on children can be ameliorated. Despite a lack of data, we do know two things. First, children who are maltreated with greater frequency and intensity are, *ceteris paribus*, harmed more and are less likely to be helped by rehabilitation. Secondly, children who are maltreated are generally at higher risk than those who are not maltreated, even when help is provided to the former. Aristotle's and Locke's observations on how difficult it is to develop the habits of virtue if they are not instilled properly in childhood support this. It is sufficient for the purposes of this book that Rawls's developmental moral psychology entails that rehabilitation is unlikely to be as successful as we want it to be. However, I believe that this theory has independent support.

3.5. Top-Down vs. Bottom-Up

Earlier I mentioned that I advocate a conservative top-down approach of primary prevention. Primary prevention need not necessarily be coercive. However, in the case of child maltreatment and the family I hope to have shown that some state intervention is necessary as the substance of primary prevention. I appeal to Carl Hedman's distinction between a "liberal top-down" and "conservative bottom-up" approach to the problem of child maltreatment.[24] In the liberal top-down approach, the state intervenes by licensing parents. In the conservative bottom-up approach, state intervention is rejected due to the belief that the only effective means of preventing child maltreatment is a revitalization of the two-parent family. Hedman's reasoning for a bottom-up approach is generally correct, "in the long run state intervention only makes things worse because it short circuits bottom-up mechanisms for promoting virtue."[25] In dealing with people choosing unwisely, making bad decisions, or leading immoral or unhealthy lifestyles that do not affect others, the state generally should not intervene. However, child maltreatment cases do not deal with individuals making bad decisions for themselves only; rather, they are actively harming defenseless human beings—children. Providing a chance for a likely abusive parent to refrain from being abusive is not noble if his failure to be virtuous entails irreparable harm to a child. It is also unclear what force implementing only informal measures such as social disapprobation or education would have. The targets of disapprobation would be individuals who are at high risk to maltreat their children. Child maltreatment is not a mere intellectual mistake. The cause of abuse likely stems from something deeper within a person's psychology, and this largely depends upon whether he is an ISJ. If not an ISJ, it is unclear how education or disapprobation will affect a person; not being moved by such things is one of the vices that follow from being a non-ISJ.

Trying to pit the liberal top-down and conservative bottom-up approaches against each other exposes a false dichotomy. Hedman exposes part of the false dichotomy when he advocates his radical bottom-up approach. I reconcile part of the conservative bottom-up framework with the liberal top-down framework. I import the two-parent family requirement from the conservative bottom-up approach into the top-down model for licensing parents, yielding a conservative top-down model for licensing parents. As can be inferred from my defense of the neo-nuclear family in chapter 4, an age requirement of eighteen years old might be ideal. Requiring parents to be over the age of eighteen and married would, based upon the thesis defended so far, help to reduce child maltreatment and revitalize healthy families. This may be a step towards progress, but a family headed by two married adults is not necessarily sufficient to yield a healthy environment for the adults or children in that family. Parents must also have the requisite level of character and not be non-ISJs. In an ideal world, we might allow only ISJs in neo-nuclear families to parent, but this would cause too much state intervention in the family. For the sake of protecting children from maltreatment (especially severe maltreatment), promoting healthy families, moving from a formally well-ordered society towards a completely well-ordered society, and responding to the egalitarian concern of a meaningful equality of opportunity, the best plan is to forbid only those who are obviously likely to be the worst of the worst parents, obvious cases of non-ISJs, from parenting. There is ample reason to give ISJs and those whose status is unclear the opportunity to parent. Such parents may maltreat their children, but the risk is low. It is also a risk that must be taken if families are to be permitted in society. There is less reason to provide an opportunity for those obviously likely non-ISJs who are likely to maltreat their children. This has been defended implicitly until now, and it will explicitly be defended in chapters 6 through 8. However, it may be objected that none of this matters because we do not have a means of accurately predicting which parents are non-ISJs or which parents will almost surely maltreat their children.[26] I mentioned that we must have the means to predict accurately which adults will maltreat their children before we are justified in licensing parents, and I will now show that this objection can be met.

4. THE LICENSING PROCEDURE

The purpose of a licensing test is *not* to predict which potential parents will be "moderate" or "excellent" parents. A licensing test should be designed to identify the prospectively very worst parents, those extremely likely to abuse or neglect their children. I follow LaFollette in this respect.[27] When LaFollette published his essay in 1980, tests to predict the likelihood of child maltreatment were just beginning to be developed. He cited a test where researchers identified 20 percent of participants as "at risk." After one year they found, "The incidence of major breakdown in parent-child interaction in the risk group was approximately four to five times as great as in the low risk group."[28] More research has been done since then, and we can now better predict which prospective parents will maltreat their children.

Several tests have since emerged, but the two most prominent are the Child Abuse Potential (CAP) Inventory and the Family Stress Checklist.[29] Parenting tests can be remarkably accurate. In one of the earliest studies that predicted risk of maltreatment, the sensitivity rate (ability to identify abusers correctly) was 85 percent with only 15 percent false negatives.[30] The specificity rate (ability to identify non-abusers correctly) was 89 percent with only 11 percent false positives. In "Licensing Parents: How Feasible?," Claudia Pap Mangel makes a good case that the CAP-Inventory and Family Stress Checklist would fulfill LaFollette's condition, and thus mine, of an accurately predictive test for licensing parents. I concur, but I have some reservations and would like to examine these tests in depth. The CAP-Inventory is the most researched test for predicting risk.[31] It consists of 160 questions posed by a professional with answers of "agree" or "disagree." The test is unable to locate fine-grained distinctions about *positive* parental competence; it cannot accurately differentiate between moderate and excellent parents. However, it does accurately predict which test takers are likely to be extremely bad parents. Consequently, it can be a useful tool in a system of licensing parents.

The Family Stress checklist seems even more useful than the CAP-Inventory because it takes into account whether the prospective parent has a history of criminal activity, has a mental illness, or was maltreated as a child, in addition to questions similar to those in the CAP-Inventory.[32] The Family Stress checklist has also produced impressive results. The sensitivity rate (ability to identify abuse correctly) was 80 percent with only 20 percent false positives. The specificity rate (ability to identify non-abusers correctly) was 90 percent with only 10 percent false positives. These statistics were attained by later examining the children of these parents, parents who were tested before their children were born. The children were examined between the ages of one and two, and records were referenced to examine whether they had been maltreated.

I now consider objections to these tests. First, the prospective mothers had nothing to lose by telling the truth when they were given the tests. Even if identified as high-risk, a prospective mother knew she would be allowed to parent. However, the stakes would be higher and many might be inclined to lie in a society where failing a parental licensing test meant not being able to rear children. Fortunately, these tests can largely account for lies; a lie scale has been developed for the CAP-Inventory.[33] A second objection is that some, though few, of the questions on such tests relate to how prospective parents treat children that they already have. Because this information will often be unavailable in a system that licensed parents, this is likely to decrease predictive accuracy. A third objection is that the test is not 100 percent accurate and that both false positives and false negatives will exist. This is true, but false positives and negatives could be controlled by rescaling or cutting scores in different places.[34] For example, in the Family Stress Checklist data listed above, a total of 17.6 percent of adults were predicted to abuse. However, in my program which seeks only to forbid the worst prospective parents from parenting, I assume that roughly only three percent of parents would be forbidden from parenting.[35] If this were the case, the scores would be cut higher and thus likely increase the accuracy of the sensitivity rate and lower the accuracy of the specificity rate, thus giving prospective parents the benefit of the doubt. The results of cutting scores higher may not be the best utility-maximizing measure, but erring in this way is likely to be the best way to initiate a program of licensing parents. Prospective parents would be able to re-take the test, increasing the *overall* accuracy of the test. Lastly, it may be objected that misclassifications would be too high even if sensitivity and specificity ratings were 95 percent while utilizing a base prevalence rate of 5 percent. Kaufman and Zigler object:

> Because the 5 percent abuse rate implies that 95 out of every 100 parents will not become abusers, accuracy could be assured 95 percent of the time by always predicting that parents will not abuse their children. This hit rate is considerably higher than any rate achieved with existing screening methods. In order for a screening device to be considered efficient, it must increase the number of correct predictions that are possible using the base rates alone.[36]

Only identifying *that* five percent of children will be abused is unhelpful for public policy to confront child maltreatment; it is also necessary to know *which* parents are likely to maltreat. If efficiency were all that mattered, then this objection would be more powerful. However, efficiency is only *a* factor.

The utility and harm involved in child maltreatment must also be considered. As has been shown, the harm done to maltreated children ranks high as a disutility. I will argue later that if that we can accurately identify abusers with a 90 percent rate and non-abusers with a 95 percent rate, then it would be better to forbid 5 percent of prospective parents from parenting even though some would have otherwise not maltreated for the sake of preventing 5 percent of children from being maltreated.

The CAP-Inventory and Family Stress Checklists are not perfect, but they can be improved through additional testing. Yet even if refined and improved, no test will be perfect. In my system of licensing, these tests would be *components of* a comprehensive testing process. Interviews are important, so versions of the CAP-Inventory and Family Stress Checklist would be given, along with other yet to be created exams.[37] Knowledge of basic proper parenting would be tested. Because measuring only knowledge does not suffice to gauge how likely a prospective parent is to maltreat a child, it will also be necessary to conduct a background check to see what environmental factors a person has experienced. Two requirements would have to be met without exception. The first would be that one not have any past convictions of rape, molestation, murder, or sexual assault. The second would be that prospective parents cannot have an illness or disability that would reasonably endanger a child.[38] It *may* also be prudent to implement *temporary but automatically disqualifying* conditions for licensure. One such condition might be age; a person could not have a license to parent until the age of eighteen. Fourteen-year-olds might *later* qualify for a license, but they would have to wait four years to attain it. A second condition might be to issue licenses only to married persons. Unmarried persons would have the *potential* to attain a license, but a license would not be given until they marry, and both parents would have to be licensed before parenting. If age and marriage conditions are not judged to be temporary automatic disqualifying conditions, then perhaps they could be part of a list of conditions to be considered but would not automatically disqualify a potential parent from being licensed. A psychological examination would also be given. Perhaps it might also be helpful to see how potential parents interact with children under the observation of childcare professionals. If a person were not given a license to parent, he will be disallowed to parent. He will be legally forbidden from parenting; if a child is born to an unlicensed parent, the child will be placed for adoption.

The problem of not having an accurate test to identify likely maltreating parents has largely been overcome. However, another obstacle exists—how to implement this policy effectively. It is unclear how many people would not bear children simply because they did not possess a license. Some might be deterred by the illegality of it, but if some other kind of deterrence did not exist then many people might evade the law and rear children without licenses. Penalizing such parents would negatively affect their children, the children that need help in the first place. Imprisoning parents would be counterproductive because children would then be separated from their parents. However, if this was done immediately after birth and the child was placed with an adoptive family, this would be less of a problem. Another solution might be to penalize unlicensed parents with a fine. However, especially for lower-income families, this could take away the opportunity for families to provide even minimal resources for their children. Ultimately, some prospective parents might seek to evade the system by having their child outside a hospital. This not only poses a danger to the health of women who give birth in such situations, but it also poses a health risk to children. These families would thereafter have to evade detection of the state. For these reasons, implementation seems problematic. A system of universal reversible sterilization, however, overcomes the implementation problem.

Current technology does not permit a means whereby a workable full-scale system of licensing parents *and* sterilization is feasible. However, it is only a matter of time before a long-term procedure for reversible sterilization is possible. That is, a procedure or drug that renders one sterile until a counter-procedure or drug renders one fertile.[39] The closest that we have now are things such as Depo-Provera or IUDs. Discussion of this is important, minimally, because we will eventually have this technology and be confronted with whether and how it should be used. With such technology, though not available yet, all children (male and female) would be sterilized at birth. When such children grow up and wish to have children, if they received a license to parent, they would be provided with the reverse sterilization procedure.

5. ALTERNATIVE APPROACHES

Perhaps the above approach to licensing is unnecessary and the outcomes desired could be secured by other means. I will now examine some alternatives. One possibility is to continue the practice of allowing everyone to rear children, but children would be randomly assigned and given to different families in society. This solution addresses an egalitarian desire to have equal opportunity, but it is unclear how it provides equal opportunity and how it successfully addresses the question of preventing child maltreatment and promoting ISJs. Genetics do play a role in child development, but this is usually outweighed by how parents nurture their children. Non-biological children of parents who would have otherwise maltreated their biological children will likely be maltreated. Likewise, the children of parents who are likely to nurture properly will probably be nurtured properly regardless of their biological relationship to their parents. This process need not be random. To try to secure an egalitarian society, both parents and newborns could be screened extensively. Children with poor health can be assigned to the most psychologically secure and financially stable parents while newborns with the best genetic features can be assigned to the potentially worst parents.[40] This would likely yield a *slightly* more egalitarian outcome, but such an outcome would come at too high of a price. Even genetically healthy children who receive the best prenatal care would be at risk of being maltreated by high-risk parents. They would perhaps be maltreated slightly less because the attributes of children do play a role in child maltreatment, but personal characteristics of children are unlikely to be a sufficient condition to make an otherwise abusive parent non-abusive.

The above systems also provide a large disincentive for proper prenatal care at the societal level. If one knows that he will not parent his biological child, there is less motivation to eat, drink, and exercise properly, and seek neo-natal care. Most people would continue to be careful with their prenatal health because they would recognize the importance of prenatal care and not wish to harm a child/potential child, even if that child will not be reared by them. However, many people do not care, even in that situation. For example, crack babies and babies with fetal alcohol syndrome continue to exist. If such parents do care about their child, this is often trumped by lack of self-regulation or shortsightedness. They can justify partaking of pleasures that are bad for their baby *at that time* because these pleasures trump future events that do not seem real or seem only like a potentiality. These alternative programs may not even yield any net improvement with regards to the egalitarian condition.

Less invasive means of licensing do exist. LaFollette writes,

> It may well be that there are alternative ways of regulating parents which would achieve the desired results—the protection of children—without strictly prohibiting nonlicensed people from rearing children. For example, a system of tax incentives for licensed parents, and protective services scrutiny of non-licensed parents, might adequately protect children. If it would, I would endorse the less drastic measure.[41]

While putting forth alternatives to and variations of licensing parents, Westman also suggests this possibility. However, I think prudently, he rejects the suggestion:

> Tax incentives for voluntarily licensed parents and supportive services for unlicensed parents might be seen as adequately protecting children. Compromises of this nature, however, would not affect incompetent parents, who necessitate a licensing process in the first place because they are irresponsible and do not seek supportive services.[42]

The most effective alternative method of licensing to the one put forth by me in this chapter is Westman's. He lists three conditions.[43] The first is that a prospective parent would have to be eighteen years old to be licensed to parent. If under eighteen, a minor could obtain a provisional license if the minor's parents take explicit responsibility for the minor and the minor's child. The second condition is that an applicant for a parental license would agree to nurture properly and not maltreat his child. If this agreement is broken and the child is maltreated, then intervention in the parent's right to rear would not be based on criminal action; it would be based on breach of contract. The third option, which Westman leaves optional, requires a potential parent to take a parenting course. If a parental license is not obtained, the state could remove the child and transfer him to an adoptive family.

Westman's plan is the best alternative, and it would help to protect children from maltreatment. However, I doubt that it goes far enough. He allows teenagers to parent via a provisional license. As he acknowledges, raising a child when one is not yet an adult is likely bad for the child and the parent. I am also skeptical about the environment where a minor's parents are responsible for taking care of the minor and the minor's child, even if the minor's parents agree to care for the minor and his child. The minor's parents could be incompetent and should not parent at all. They might not have a license themselves, especially in the first generation of implementation of this plan. This is pertinent because many teenagers who bear children are reared in unhealthy families, often from families where sexual abuse occurs. Explicitly taking responsibility for another human being *may* help to awaken a sense of duty to a child. Yet if this is seen as a mere bureaucratic step, high-risk parents might agree without taking it very seriously. It is also unclear that removal based on breach of contract would be easier than removal based upon criminal activity. Both require proof of child maltreatment, and this proof is often difficult to obtain. Westman's third condition, mandatory parenting classes, would likely yield some positive benefits. However, child maltreatment is usually not an intellectual mistake. If one does not have an idea about how to care even basically for a child, then we should be skeptical that a parenting class would be able to impress upon him the fundamental things about human beings that most people know simply by virtue of observation and being nurtured oneself. Likewise, the highest-risk parents would likely be unaffected.

If in a society where reverse sterilization were not used, as mentioned before, there is a problem when non-ISJ women become pregnant. I have suggested forced adoption in these instances, but that may seem too callous to do to a woman who has carried the child for nine months. Perhaps instead a mother could choose to enter a parenting facility or give up her child for adoption. If she chooses the former, she would be under constant supervision and take parenting classes and/or other rehabilitation efforts. This is a noble attempt to reward pregnant women who give birth, but it falls short in many important aspects. To ensure that her child is not endangered, the mother would have to be kept under constant surveillance (as well as her husband, if married). Such surveillance would likely preclude the aforementioned intimacy and privacy that can be powerful within families. I have also already shown that parenting classes and rehabilitation have limited effect on non-ISJs. It is unclear what effects observing one's mother under constant surveillance, as if her mother were a child, would have upon a child. Most importantly, if the parenting test is accurate, then those who cannot pass it are highly likely to maltreat their children. These tests can be re-taken, and if one believes parenting classes might help then she can take them before testing again. Therefore, this plan fails to take seriously the predictive powers and implications of this licensing test. That is, allowing the option to be in such a facility will simply allow the mother to (likely) maltreat her child and eventually require officials to transfer the child to adoptive parents. This outcome benefits neither the child nor the mother.

6. NON-LICENSING ALTERNATIVES

The above are major variations of parental licensing. However, it may be asked why non-licensing solutions will not work. This should be clear from previous chapters and this chapter, but I will briefly consider some alternate solutions here.

Westman suggests a better system of child support where *both* parents' social security numbers are listed on every newborn's birth certificate.[44] This enables the government to track and withhold wages from absent parents. Why such a plan is unlikely to succeed was already discussed earlier in the context of evolutionary biology. In addition to concerns expressed there, mothers might be unaware who the biological father is due to numerous or unknown sexual partners. A biological parent might have little money and would not be able to provide childcare, even if forced. Likewise, the other biological parent might have abandoned multiple children. If so, this is likely to drain his resources considerably. This program may instead serve as an incentive to foster and maintain welfare dependency, or cause one to seek a sufficiently low-income job so as to avoid legal and social pressure to be responsible for and provide support to his children. Even if child support is guaranteed when a biological parent abandons the family, the child will likely be raised by a single parent, which has been shown to be a suboptimal environment for producing ISJs.

Another suggestion is that universal daycare should be provided by the government. This was dismissed in chapter 3 because it was a less than ideal environment for ISJs to be produced. Yet this was not an objection to universal daycare on the grounds of child maltreatment. However, unless children are to be in daycare for twenty-four hours a day, children will ultimately have to return to their own families. If parents will maltreat their children, then daycare will only provide an opportunity for parents to benefit financially and a brief respite for the child. Thus daycare does not resolve the problem of abuse.

A similar, but more plausible, solution is put forth by Duncan and Magnuson: "Prudent policy should ensure that all parents are given a genuine choice about working when their children are very young."[45] Their policy is based upon child development research that demonstrates that the first five years of a child's development are of the utmost importance for their long-term development. Their policy suggests:

> [E]xemption from all welfare-related work requirements for mothers of children younger than six months and exemption from full-time (more than thirty hours a week) work requirements for mothers of children between six months and one year of age. Work requirements imposed on mothers with children older than twelve months not to be affected. At the same time, working parents (one per family) would be entitled to six months of parental leave.

and

> [A] child allowance for children under the age of five living in families with incomes under $60,000. The (taxable) allowance would be $300 per month during the child's first year and $200 per month between ages one and five, with no benefits for older children. Families with two children under age five would receive allowances for both children. No additional allowances would be extended to families with more than two age-qualifying children.[46]

Duncan and Magnuson's suggestions are an improvement upon solutions that only provide those who are financially poor with more money in order to provide necessary resources for their children. This is evident from their effort to find a way for children to be parented by their families when extremely young. Yet this is only applicable for the first year of a child's life. The family thereafter only receives an economic allowance for children, and children then only have more access to educational and mental health programs. If, as seems to motivate their policy at the beginning of their essay, the first five years of development are key (and I believe that this is true), then why not extend long-term exemption from all welfare-related work requirements? Under their system, children can essentially be raised by the state after age one in various social programs, and it is fairly clear that they do not want such an outcome (though they may find such an outcome preferable to such children being raised in abusive homes).

There are other worries. What about the children of poor parents who have more than two children and will not benefit from such a program? Their disincentive measure has good intentions, but good intentions do not help the children of poor parents with more than two children. In addition, what is going to ensure that this money will be spent on helping children develop properly and not on buying things for the parents? If the necessity of a disincentive is valued, why not provide no assistance? That would be the best means of forcing parents to take responsibility for their actions. Lastly, Duncan and Mugnuson's model seems to presume that a major roadblock to proper child development in society is an economic one. Economics does play a role, but I have argued that it plays a small role compared to the role of a healthy family, and it would play even less of a role in a society where more people were ISJs.

It may be asked why we do not construct a policy that takes my first objection to Duncan and Magnuson's plan into account. That is, provide an exemption from all welfare-related work requirements for all mothers (or fathers) up to the age of five (or if we were *really* serious about development, until the age of eighteen). In addition to being economically unfeasible, this vitiates an important disincentive for potential parents not to parent until they are ready to parent responsibly. It is also likely to perpetuate, in most cases, an unhealthy and non-ideal environment: the single parent family. We could narrow this policy to be applicable only to those with true financial need. However, this is tantamount to providing only to single-parent families. This should be clear from previous discussion about income and wealth differentials between single- and two-parent families. This would also likely perpetuate a structure where much abuse takes place. Child maltreatment may take place slightly less often because being both a single parent and poor is presumably more stressful than being a single parent and not poor, but it would still not provide children with the proper modeling that was discussed in chapter 4. Government should not encourage actions and choices via incentives that lead to environments which are harmful to society.

CONCLUSION

To protect children from maltreatment, to help progress towards a stable and well-ordered society, and to ensure a meaningful equality of opportunity, it is necessary to forbid some people from parenting. In addition to being necessary, parental licensing is justified. Licensing is a compelling interest of the state, an accurate test to predict maltreatment exists (or at least is likely to be possible in the future), no other less invasive solution yields the similar desired effects of licensing parents, and licensing parents can be implemented effectively (or is likely to be possible in the near future). This may seem overly protective, but methods such as social disapprobation are unable to stop the cycle of child maltreatment effectively. Moreover, the state is ultimately going to intervene when a child has or is likely to suffer harm. If the harm to children from child maltreatment is as bad as I have claimed, rehabilitation is unlikely, and we can accurately predict which parents will likely maltreat their children, then licensing parents makes the process much more just and efficient. Adults who would have otherwise maltreated, children, and society will benefit.

Three considerations have yet to be dealt with. It has not been shown that the right to parent is defeasible; this will be discussed in chapter 6. In chapter 7 I will first consider some common objections to licensing parents and show that it has legal precedent. In particular, I will address a particular worry that people have about licensing parents—the violation of prior restraint. It has also yet to be considered whether a formal system of parental licensing is detrimental to the informal realm of social warmth and might erode trust, thus undermining a goal of licensing parents to establish more societal trust. Along with determining whether licensing parents is a case of protecting ourselves into oblivion, this will be discussed in chapter 8.

NOTES

1. Alexander Hamilton, James Madison, and John Jay, *The Federalist*, ed. Jacob E. Cooke (Hanover, NH: Wesleyan University Press, 1961), *The Federalist* No. 55, 378.
2. "Childrearing and Family Interests," in Onora O'Neill and William Ruddick, eds. *Having Children: Philosophical and Legal Reflections on Parenthood* (New York: Oxford University Press, 1979), 119.
3. David Archard, *Children: Rights and Childhood* (London: Routledge, 2004), 209.
4. For an extreme case of this, see Anna Freud, Joseph Goldstein, and Albert Solnit, *Before the Best Interests of the Child* (New York: The Free Press, 1979).
5. Michael S. Wald, "State Intervention on Behalf of Endangered Children—A Proposed Legal Response," *Child Abuse and Neglect*, 6 (1982), 9.
6. Wald, 16.
7. Alan Sroufe, "Relationships, Self, and Individual Adaptation," in Arnold J. Sameroff and Robert N. Emde, eds. *Relationship Disturbances in Early Childhood*

(New York: Basic Books, 1989), cited in Westman, 65. I take much of what Sroufe mentions to be applicable to abused children as well.

8. The above statistics were compiled by Westman, 87–96. AFDC (Aid to Families with Dependent Children) has since been replaced by TANF (Temporary Assistance for Needy Families) as a system of welfare; it is not yet clear how this change affects the above statistics. For another analysis, which finds that child maltreatment costs over $94 billion per year, see Jill Goldman and Marsha K. Salus, A Coordinated Response to Child Abuse and Neglect: The Foundation for Practice. U.S. Department of Health and Human Services. Administration on Children and Families. www.child welfare.gov/pubs/usermanuals/foundation/foundation.pdf, 39 (6 Apr. 2008).

9. Gerald Caplan, *Principles of Preventative Psychiatry* (New York: Basic Books, 1964). Secondary and tertiary prevention are also his concepts.

10. Aristole, *Nicomachean Ethics*, Bk. II, Ch. II, Sect. I, 1103b24–25, 34–35 (note the parallel structure to Adeimantus's statement about the role of childrearing) and *Nicomachean Ethics*, Bk. X, Sect. IX, 1179b24–26, 296.

11. John Locke, *Some Thoughts Concerning Education and of the Conduct of Understanding*, §70, 46. Note also a contemporary account: Justin Aaronfreed argues, "moral education must build upon the strong affective dispositions acquired in early experience—that affective values are, as it were, the ultimate axiomatic base upon which moral principles can engage the child's conduct among and toward others. If the wrong emotions (by whatever criteria) have been attached to certain actions during childhood, then affective reeducation and not just moral reeducation will be required," "Moral Development from the Standpoint of a General Psychological Theory," in Bill Puka, ed. *Moral Development: Defining Perspectives in Moral Development*, Vol. 1, ed. (New York: Garland Publishing, 1994), 180.

12. In general, see Charles A. Nelson and Floyd E. Bloom, "Child Development and Neuroscience," *Child Development*, 68 (1997) and Sandra J. Kaplan, David Pelcovitz, and Victor Labruna, "Child and Adolescent Abuse and Neglect Research: A Review of the Past 10 Years. Part I: Physical and Emotional Abuse and Neglect," *Journal of the American Academy of Child and Adolescent Psychiatry*, 38 (1999).

13. See M. D. De Bellis, M. Keshavan, D. B. Clark, B. J. Casey, J. Giedd, A. M. Boring, K. Frustaci, and N. D. Ryan, "A.E. Bennett Research Award. Developmental Traumatology Part II: Brain Development," *Biological Psychiatry*, 45 (1999); M. D. De Bellis, A. S. Baum, B. Birmaher, M. S. Keshavan, C. H. Eccard, A. M. Boring, F. J. Jenkins, and N. D. Ryan, "Developmental Traumatology Part I: Biological Stress Systems," *Biological Psychiatry*, 45 (1999). In general, "the psychobiological sequelae of child maltreatment may be regarded as an *environmentally induced complex developmental disorder*," Michael D. De Bellis, "Developmental Traumatology: The Psychobiological Development of Maltreated Children and Its Implications for Research," *Development and Psychopathology*, 13 (2001), 539. For an excellent review of the contemporary literature on how affection affects brain development and the nervous system, see Sue Gerhardt's *Why Love Matters: How Affection Shapes a Baby's Brain* (New York: Brunner-Routledge, 2004).

14. See J. D. Bremer, P. Randall, T. M. Scott, S. Capelli, R. Delaney, G. McCarthy, and D. S. Charney, "Deficits in Short-Term Memory in Adult Survivors of Childhood

Abuse," *Psychiatry Research*, 59 (1995); J. D. Bremer, P. Randall, E. Vermetten, L. Staib, R. A. Bronen, C. Mazure, S. Capelli, G. McCarthy, R. B. Innis, and D. S. Charney, "Magnetic Resonance Imaging-Based Measurement of Hippocampal Volume in Posttraumatic Stress Disorder Related to Childhood Physical and Sexual Abuse: A Preliminary Report," *Biological Psychiatry*, 41 (1999).

15. See Yutaka Ito, Martin H. Teicher, Carol A. Glod, David Harper, Eleanor Magnus, and Harris A. Gelbard, "Increased Prevalence of Electrophysiological Abnormalities in Children with Psychological, Physical, and Sexual Abuse," *Journal of Neuropsychiatry and Clinical Neurosciences*, 5 (1993); Yutaka Ito, Carol A. Glod, and Erika Ackerman, "Preliminary Evidence for Aberrant Cortical Development in Abused Children: A Qualitative EEG Study," *The Journal of Neuropsychiatry and Clinical Neurosciences*, 10 (1998).

16. M. D. De Bellis and F. W. Putnam, "The Psychobiology of Childhood Maltreatment," *Child and Adolescent Psychiatric Clinics of North America*, 3 (1994); M. D. De Bellis, M. Keshavan, D. B. Clark, B. J. Casey, J. Giedd, A. M. Boring, K. Frustaci, and N. D. Ryan (1999).

17. I omit the fourth possibility, education for children, because it is unclear that teaching children in an academic setting how they should be raised will protect them from being maltreated in the first place. It may help children identify when they or others have been maltreated and better enable them to turn in perpetrators. According to my model, however, this is likely too late for the well-being of children.

18. See J. Spinetta and D. Rigler, "The Child-Abusing Parent: A Psychological Review," *Psychological Bulletin*, 77 (1972).

19. Edgar R. Chasteen, *The Case for Compulsory Birth Control* (Englewood Cliffs, NJ: 1972), 91.

20. W. J. van Doornick, P. Dawson, P. M. Butterfield, and H. I. Alexander, "Parent-Infant Support Through Lay Health Visitors," Final Report Submitted to the Bureau of Community Health Service, National Institute of Health, Department of Health, Education, and Welfare, 1980.

21. Perhaps "rehabilitate" is not the proper word, but I am unaware of any better for what I am trying to capture. By "rehabilitate," I mean to provide treatment for parents that will cause them to no longer maltreat their children. This presumably means also reshaping their affectional structure. Of course, if their affectional structure was never properly formed, then the "re" part of rehabilitation is misleading.

22. David P. H. Jones, "The Untreatable Family," *Child Abuse and Neglect*, 11 (1987). For an evaluation of eleven federally funded child maltreatment projects with only 40–50 percent success rates, see Gertrude J. Williams, "Management and Treatment of Parental Abuse and Neglect of Children: An Overview," in Gertrude J. Williams and John Money, eds. *Traumatic Abuse and Neglect of Children at Home*, (Baltimore: The Johns Hopkins University Press, 1982); Gertrude J. Williams, "Toward the Eradication of Child Abuse and Neglect in the Home," in Williams and Money (1982).

23. Blustein, 128. Blustein does not here further argue that the duty of persons to avail themselves of support services further entails the right or obligation of the state to coerce fulfillment of this duty. However, the kind of argument cited in this passage often serves as the foundation for such a stronger argument.

24. Carl Hedman, "Three Approaches to the Problem of Child Abuse and Neglect," *Journal of Social Philosophy*, 31 (2000). Hedman does not support either of the above approaches. Rather, he supports a "radical bottom-up" approach. Hedman pursues the establishment of a "post-nuclear" family because he believes that the traditional family is immoral because it biases against women and perpetuates patriarchal attitudes. Although Hedman successfully locates an important topic and makes excellent distinctions, his account is unconvincing to me and I will not consider it here further.

25. Hedman, 70.

26. I assume that the set of non-ISJs and those likely to maltreat their children generally overlap. If one maltreats a child, then one is likely a non-ISJ.

27. LaFollette says, "It is highly improbable that we can formulate criteria that would distinguish precisely between good and less good parents. There is too much we do not know about child development and adult psychology. My proposal, however, does not demand that we make these fine distinctions. It does not demand that we license only the best parents; rather it is designed to exclude only the bad ones," 190.

28. LaFollette, 191. LaFollette was referring to the research of Altemeir, which was reported by Ray Helferin, "Review of the Concepts and a Sampling of the Research Relating to Screening for the Potential to Abuse and/or Neglect One's Child." Helferin presented this paper at a workshop sponsored by the National Committee for the Prevention of Child Abuse, 3–6 December 1978.

29. For other tests, see M. A. Disbrow, H. Doerr, and C. Caulfield, "Measuring the Components of Parents' Potential for Child Abuse and Neglect," *Child Abuse and Neglect*, 1 (1977); William A. Altemeir, Susan O'Connor, Peter Vietze, Howard Sandler, and Kathryn Sherrod, "Prediction of Child Abuse: A Prospective Study of Feasibility," *Child Abuse and Neglect*, 8 (1984); Mary I. Benedict, Roger B. White, Donald A. Cornley, "Maternal Perinatal Risk Factors and Child Abuse," *Child Abuse and Neglect*, 9 (1985); Raymond M. Bergner, Leslie K. Delgado, and Daniel Graybill, "Finkelhor's Risk Factor Checklist: A Cross-Validation Study," *Child Abuse and Neglect*, 18 (1994).

30. Disbrow, et al. (1977).

31. For more on the CAP-Inventory, see Joel S. Milner and Ronald C. Wimberly, "Prediction and Explanation of Child Abuse," *Journal of Clinical Psychology*, 35 (1980); Joel S. Milner and Catherine Ayoub, "Evaluation of 'At-Risk' Parents Using the Child Abuse Potential Inventory," *Journal of Clinical Psychology*, 36 (1980); Catherine Ayoub, Marion M. Jacewitz, Ruth G. Gold, and Joel S. Milner, "Assessment of a Program's Effectiveness in Selecting Individuals 'At Risk' for Problems in Parenting," *Journal of Clinical Psychology*, 39 (1983); Joel S. Milner, Ruth G. Gold, Catherine Ayoub, and Marion M. Jacewitz, "Predictive Validity of the Child Abuse Potential Inventory," *Journal of Consulting and Clinical Psychology*, 52 (1984); Joel S. Milner and Kevin R. Robertson, "Development of a Random Response Scale for the Child Abuse Potential Inventory," *Journal of Clinical Psychology*, 41 (1985); Doyle L. Pruitt and Marilyn T. Erickson, "The Child Abuse Potential Inventory: A Study of Concurrent Validity," *Journal of Clinical Psychology*, 41 (1985); Joanne Ro-

bitaille, Eleanor Jones, Ruth G. Gold, Kevin R. Robertson, and Joel S. Milner, "Child Abuse Potential and Authoritarianism," *Journal of Clinical Psychology*, 41 (1985); Mary E. Haskett, Susan Smith Scott, and Kellie D. Fann, "Child Abuse Potential Inventory and Parenting Behavior: Relationships with High-Risk Correlates," *Child Abuse and Neglect*, 19 (1995); Scot McNary and Maureen M. Black, "Use of the Child Abuse Potential Inventory as a Measure of Treatment Outcome," *Child Abuse and Neglect*, 27 (2003); Mark Chaffin and Linda Anne Valle, "Dynamic Prediction Characteristics of the Child Abuse Potential Inventory," *Child Abuse and Neglect*, 27 (2003).

32. See Solbritt Murphy, Bonnie Orkow, and Ray M. Nicola, "Prenatal Prediction of Child Abuse and Neglect: A Prospective Study," *Child Abuse and Neglect*, 9 (1985); Bonnie Orkow, "Implementation of a Family Stress Checklist," *Child Abuse and Neglect*, 9 (1985).

33. Joel S. Milner, "Development of a Lie Scale for the Child Abuse Potential Inventory," *Psychological Reports*, 50 (1982).

34. See Richard N. Tsujimoto and Dale E. Berger, "Predicting Child Abuse: Value of Utility Maximizing Cutting Scores," *Child Abuse and Neglect*, 12 (1988).

35. I use this number because it is approximately the current number of parents who maltreat their children. This is an estimate. Furthermore, this number can change. Supposing that my system were implemented and the percentage of parents who maltreated their children dropped to one percent, then it would perhaps only be necessary to prevent only about one percent of prospective parents from parenting. Eventually, if licensing parents worked, it would eliminate the need for parents to be licensed.

36. Kaufman and Zigler, in Cicchetti and Carlson (1989), 145. Michael J. Saudmire and Michael S. Wald have similar concerns in "Licensing Parents—A Response to Claudia Mangel's Proposal," *Family Law Quarterly*, 24 (1990). I think that they unfairly exploit statistical interpretation of data that shifts with small base rates. For example, they consider a hypothetical model of 1000 people with a 10 percent prevalence rate of abuse with a test that has 90 percent sensitivity and 95 percent specificity. This sample yields 90 true positives, 10 false negatives, 45 false positives, and 855 true negatives. They worry about the "Percentage misclassified as abusive," 33 percent [false positives / (true positives + false positives)]. They make this 33 percent sound as if 33 percent of the 1,000 would be misclassified as abusive; however, the number of false positives remains only 45, or 4.5 percent of the population. For similar worries, see Milton Kotelchuck, "Child Abuse and Neglect: Prediction and Misclassification" and Raymond H. Starr, Jr., "A Research-Based Approach to the Prediction of Child Abuse" in Raymond H. Starr, Jr., ed. *Child Abuse Prediction: Policy Implications* (Cambridge, MA: Ballinger Publishing, 1982). See also Jessica H. Daniel, Eli H. Newberger, Robert B. Reed, and Milton Kotelchuck, "Child Abuse Screening: Implications of the Limited Predictive Power of Abuse Discriminants from a Controlled Family Study of Pediatric Social Illness," *Child Abuse and Neglect*, 2 (1978). Saudmire and Wald are correct that the CAP-Inventory does have some methodological problems, but I believe that tests such as the Family Stress Index take

account of these. In any case, much more research would need to be done before these tests are used in the way that I suggest that they might be used.

37. For example, another test has been recently designed, though it will require more testing. See Kym L. Kilpatrick, "The Parental Empathy Measure: A New Approach to Assessing Child Maltreatment Risk," *American Journal of Orthopsychiatry*, 75 (2005).

38. This will be discussed in more depth in chapter 6.

39. In an essay confronting neo-Malthusian overpopulation concerns and concerns about the quality of children, Margaret P. Battin writes about something similar. See her "Sex and Consequences: World Population Growth vs. Reproductive Rights," *Philosophic Exchange*, 27 (1997). Roger W. McIntire introduced, via a hypothetical scenario, a society in which a dose of "Lock" will prevent the possibility of ovulation until "Unlock," the antidote, is given. These drugs are first sold privately, but the government quickly uses them in conjunction with a screening process, whereby prospective parents can only receive a prescription for Unlock after passing parenting exams. See McIntire's "Parenthood Training or Mandatory Birth Control: Take Your Choice," *Psychology Today*, 34 (Oct. 1973). The idea of possibly needing reversible sterilization was discussed even earlier by Carl Djerassi in considering what was perceived to be a problem of overpopulation, especially in developing countries. He considers such an approach "Orwellian" and thus, presumably, an extreme measure only to be used in extreme situations. See his "Prognosis for the Development of New Chemical Birth-Control Agents," *Science*, 166 (Oct. 1969), 469–70 and "Birth Control After 1984," *Science*, 169 (Sept. 1970), 948–49.

40. These two possibilities are mentioned by Blustein, 208–09.

41. LaFollette, 195.

42. Westman, 244.

43. Westman, 240.

44. Westman, 244.

45. Greg J. Duncan and Katherine Magnuson, "Promoting the Healthy Development of Young Children," in Isabell Sawhill, ed. *One Percent for the Kids*, 23.

46. Duncan and Magnuson, 18.

6

Rights and Duties

The foremost objection to licensing parents is that it violates the parental right to bear and raise children freely. To address this objection, I will examine where parental rights come from, which leads to understanding how, when, and why parental rights are defeasible. I also ask why the parent-child relationship is discussed predominately in terms of rights instead of duties. Because discussing the parent-child relationship in terms of rights or duties has problems, I will identify these problems and demonstrate what this means concerning the justification of licensing parents. I do not seek to *prove* that such rights or duties exist. For the most part, I appeal to common intuitions that people hold concerning such things and show that taking these intuitions seriously commits us to accepting licensing parents as morally and legally justifiable. The relationship between the state and the family in relation to children will be explored, and it will be revealed that much resistance to licensing parents often manifests from an unhealthy fetish with liberty and rights for adults. Ultimately, I wish to show that our acceptance of the current practice of adoption commits us to embracing a scheme whereby children reared by their biological parents should receive more protection than they currently do for their sake and for the sake of society.

1. ADOPTION AND LICENSES

Hugh LaFollette notes that we *already* license parents insofar as we license adoptive parents.[1] Furthermore, the practice of licensing adoptive parents is widely accepted as morally and legally justifiable; we do not take licensing to be an infringement of the rights of prospective adoptive parents. More importantly, most people would find it morally repugnant if a licensing process were not used to determine who could be an adoptive parent. That is, we would be morally outraged if just any person off the street, especially if that person were a known (or suspected) child abuser or drug abuser, could adopt and raise a child. Yet most of us do not think twice about allowing just anyone, regardless of the threat posed to children, to bear and rear children freely. What seems to motivate the acceptance of licensing adoptive parents is that most people believe that children deserve at least some minimal level of parenting, and children should not be raised below a certain threshold. It is unclear why this sentiment and the according practice do not also apply to non-adoptive parents and their biological children. It does not seem that we accord less worth to the biological children of non-adoptive parents; we believe that they possess the same basic moral and legal rights as adopted children. We may accept licensing of adoptive parents simply as a response to supply and demand when there exist more people willing to adopt than there are children who need to be adopted. However, even if the number of children who needed to be adopted were fewer than the number of those willing to adopt them, I doubt that we would accept a policy that permitted just anybody off the street to walk up to an adoption agency counter and take a child home with no questions asked. However, that is what we allow with prospective non-adoptive parents insofar as all that they need to do to rear children is have sex. Consequently, it seems that many people accord to non-adoptive prospective parents biologically based ownership or rights to raise children, rights that prospective adoptive parents lack. However, this conflicts with another strong belief that children are not our property and that we cannot do as we please with them.

Some oppose licensing parents based on horror stories in the news about child services failing to protect children or some adoptive parents maltreating their children. Opposing licensing parents on this ground is unjustified because the rate of maltreatment is higher in non-adoptive families than in adoptive families.[2] If one opposes licensing parents based on accounts of maltreatment in adoptive families, then one should be more opposed to the practice of allowing people to bear and rear their biological children freely because the latter practice is more dangerous for children than the system of licensing adoptive parents. Licensing adoptive parents is often justified by the argument that adopted children may be more difficult to raise and require a special kind of parent due to possible attachment disorders and because adopted children sometimes experience maltreatment prior to adoption. Though true, it is also true that many biological parents maltreat their children largely because they believe that they are their property or because they did not want (and sometimes never want) their children. As such, especially when considering rates of abuse, setting a higher standard for biological parents may be justified. As Peg Tittle notes, "the fact that adoptive parents have *consciously chosen* parenthood would seem more than enough to compensate for any difficulties that might be inherent in adoptive parenting."[3]

LaFollette observes that we sometimes license activities that require a certain competence for safe performance when we have a procedure that can reasonably measure competence. Furthermore, we often find this licensing justified and not an infringement of our rights. We prefer a world in which doctors, lawyers, psychologists, and drivers are licensed to one in which no licensing takes place. Parenting requires a certain competence, and parenting below a certain competence can cause serious harm to children. As shown in chapter 5, we also have at least the beginnings of a procedure that can measure parental competence insofar as it measures who is likely to maltreat children. It may be objected that many of the aforementioned things are licensed by independent licensing agencies but that licensing parents would be implemented by the state. If that is the concern, then perhaps an independent agency could regulate licensing parents if one accepts independent agencies as appropriate for licensing elsewhere. Of course, we do accept the state licensing drivers. It may be objected that the original intent of licensing drivers was to, for example, increase tax revenue. However, it is unclear why we should believe that our current justification for a practice must accord with the original intent of the practice. If we did, for example, we would be committed to believing that parental rights are founded on an economic basis, as that is arguably upon which our common law justification for parental rights is founded.[4] It may also be objected that there is an asymmetry between licensing parents and licensing drivers because it is still possible for individuals to drive (illegally) if unlicensed, whereas licensing parents would preclude some people from parenting if they did not pass a test in the sense that they could not parent (even illegally) if they wanted to do so. It is unclear that is a virtue that unlicensed drivers are able to drive, albeit illegally, especially if they are at an extremely high risk to harm themselves and others, as is true of those who fail a parental licensing test. I also suspect that if there were a practical and cheap way to ensure that only licensed drivers could drive then most people would support this measure. Imagine if all cars were equipped with a fingerprint and retina scanner that had to be activated by the driver before the engine could start and this were linked to a database that recognized all licensed drivers. In any case, unlicensed drivers driving are far less dangerous than unlicensed parents rearing children.

2. PARENTAL RIGHTS IN HISTORY

Part of the belief that parents have something akin to property rights in children may be a vestige of our historical treatment of children. Under Roman law, *patria potestas* gave the father the power of life and death over his children.[5] Furthermore, the Bible provides explicit instructions for children to obey their parents, but it is less clear what, if any, duties parents have to children. In fact, paralleling Roman law, the Bible gives parents the right of life and death over their children.[6] Locke was one of the first to break in a new direction in natural rights theory by arguing explicitly for parental duties to children. Addressing Filmer's justification of monarchy from combining the Fifth Commandment with natural rights doctrine, Locke writes, "Adam and Eve, and after them all *Parents* were, by Law of Nature, under an obligation to preserve, nourish, and educate Children, they had begotten, not as their own Workmanship, but the Workmanship of their own Maker, the Almighty, to whom they were to be accountable for them."[7] This is an important break in thinking about children, but parental duties to children for Locke are still only indirect insofar as they are performed to accord with God's will and not for the sake of children themselves. Yet the consequence of this is revolutionary when Locke says of parental rights,

> Nay, this *power* so little belongs to the *Father* by any peculiar right of Nature, but only as he is Guardian of his Children, that when he quits his Care of them, he loses his power over them, which goes along with their Nourishment and Education, to which it is inseparably annexed, and it belongs as much to the *Foster-Father* of an exposed Child, as to the Natural Father of another: So little power does the bare *act of begetting* give a Man over his Issue, if all his Care ends there, and this be all the Title he hath to the Name and Authority of a Father.[8]

Locke puts forth three important things about parental rights. They derive from a duty, are defeasible, and do not necessarily follow from a biological relation to children.

Parental rights in Anglo-American common law differ considerably from the *patria potestas* of Roman law. In early America, for example, remnants of the Elizabethan poor laws forced many parents to forfeit their children to the community in return for poor relief, and "overseers of the poor were appointed by communities to visit families to determine whether parents were able to maintain their children.[9] Such practices, in various structures, existed in the United States through the end of the nineteenth century. We used to believe that we owned children (or perhaps that they were simply on loan from God), but we have mostly rejected the belief that children are our property and that they may be treated as we please; we no longer find child maltreatment acceptable. We still use the possessive idiom "my child," but this is usually meant to express a special relationship to the child, not property ownership. This is good because we often treat best that which we think our own. However, we often think that the utterance "my children" warrants rights even when we are unable to fulfill our duty to children. This is odd because people generally hold that children deserve to be treated in a minimally decent way, and if unable to treat children in a minimally decent way then parents lose their right to parent. The communitarianism of early America was far from ideal because it allowed children to be taken away from their parents merely for the sake of the well-being of the community with little regard for the interests or well-being of children or parents. Acceptance of the *patria potestas* power is also repugnant, but society's ever increasing valuing of privacy, adult liberty, and adult autonomy is causing our society to move closer to respecting *patria potestas*. We do little to prevent even convicted rapists, murderers, or child abusers from parenting after they have served their sentences. Likewise, most people would rather allow parents to raise children, knowing that they will maltreat their children, which will later require state intervention, than to prevent maltreatment in the first place. As child maltreatment is sometimes arguably as bad as death, it is unclear how substantially different we are from the Romans.

3. RIGHTS AND DUTIES

3.1 Rights or Duties?

There is debate about whether to frame the parent-child relationship in terms of rights or duties. Philip Montague argues, "since parental rights to care for their children are incompatible with parental obligations to do so, there are no parental rights."[10] Less controversially, Onora O'Neill claims, "We can perhaps go *further* to secure the ethical basis of children's positive rights if we do *not* try to base them on claims about fundamental rights" because "when we take rights as fundamental in looking at ethical issues in children's lives we also get an indirect, partial and blurred picture."[11] Likewise, Laura Purdy believes that rights talk often leads to equal rights talk at all levels, which is dangerous because it leads to positions embraced by child liberationists who do not recognize that it is not in the best interests of children to be treated as full-fledged rights bearers in all aspects of their lives.[12] Others, however, believe that rights talk does a better job of protecting children.[13] I wish to evade the debate about language because almost all interlocutors in the rights/duty

debate concede that rights *and* duties exist, and much of the debate is motivated by trying to capture the entire parent-child relationship with one word
or concept. This fails because rights and duties exist in the parent-child relationship. Furthermore, this mixture of rights and duties accords with the common intuition that children have certain rights and duties and parents have
certain rights and duties. This was captured beautifully by Locke in his discussion of parental rights, but it is captured most clearly by James Kent when
he writes, "The rights of parents result from their duties."[14] While conceding
that rights and duties exist, I emphasize the duties of parents because society
is becoming predominately interested only in rights, and duties are falling to
the wayside. Rights are often insufficient to provide the requisite protection
that children need because parents also have rights. Furthermore, the rights of
parents easily trump whatever rights children have when the two come into
conflict because children cannot defend themselves because of the vastly
asymmetrical power relationship.

Elizabeth Anderson describes parents' rights over their children as "trusts,"
and Brennan and Noggle describe parental rights as "stewardship rights."[15]
Stewards do not own those whom they are entrusted to care for. Concerning
children, stewards derive their right from the fact that children are unable to
care for themselves and exercise and protect their rights without assistance.
Most people find a trust or stewardship conception of the parent-child relationship to be reasonable, and this seems to be the reason why we believe that
a parent's ability to exercise great power over his children is justified. This
also lends support to the thesis that many biological parents have presumptive rights over their children because it is presumed that they will have affection and love for their children. Biological parents are generally best suited
to care for their children because, due to the nature of human pregnancy, they
often invest considerable love, time, energy, and money in seeing to it that
their child is born. Furthermore, biology equips most mothers with the ability to feed and nurture their biological children in a way that cannot be fully
duplicated. Biological parents are often remarkably suited to taking care of
their children adequately. For these reasons and others, most parents ought to
have a presumptive right to bear and rear their biological children. However,
our belief that most parents have a presumptive right should not trump our
other belief that parents have duties to children. Echoing Locke, O'Neill
writes, "the right to beget or bear is not unrestricted, but contingent upon
begetters and bearers having or making some feasible plan for their child to
be adequately reared by themselves or by willing others. Persons who beget
or bear without making any such plans cannot claim that they are exercising
a right."[16] I agree, but what is doing the work here is not *having a plan* to rear
children adequately. Rather, it is the *feasibility of being able to implement a*

plan. If unfeasible, then the children will not be protected and no right is maintained. Likewise, David Archard notes, "would-be parents are entitled to exercise their rights to bear so long as they do not harm any future child," which Brennan and Noggle echo, "parents do have rights, but because those rights have thresholds, they can be infringed if this is necessary for preserving the rights of the child or for making sure that her needs are met."[17]

The above presupposes that children have certain basic rights which must be protected if they are to exercise their rights as adults. However, the injustice of children's rights being violated simply as children should not be overlooked. Archard notes, "the right to bear is constrained by a duty to ensure that any child born has the reasonable prospect of enjoying a minimally decent life."[18] I agree with Archard, but the meaning of minimally decent is problematic because the conditions that must be met are controversial. Some believe that it requires a certain level of income, education, or physical health. However, my previous chapters identified an uncontroversial threshold—child maltreatment. The minimum is to ensure that children are not abused or neglected by their parents because maltreating them violates their most basic rights and is likely to disrupt their developmental psychology, possibly precluding them from becoming ISJs. Not being an ISJ increases the likelihood that they are threats to themselves and others leading decent lives. As such, I agree, "The satisfaction of one person's rights and interests cannot be at the expense of another's. Hence it is wrong to bring about a life whose prospects you can be reasonably sure will fall below a minimal threshold of decency."[19]

Rawls never considers child abuse or neglect behind his veil of ignorance, but in a variant of this hypothetical contract, which also holds some force about what we should take to be fair and inform our beliefs about rights and duties, David Gauthier writes, "We may, I think, safely assume that, faced with a hypothetical agreement on conditions of interaction, persons would not be willing to risk being raised in emotionally or materially impoverished conditions simply in order to gain the freedom to raise children themselves, or to produce children whom they would abandon to be raised in such circumstances."[20] Consequently,

> The reproductive familial arrangements of a contractarian society will, I believe, aim at affording each child an upbringing undertaken primarily by the joint efforts of its natural parents, and the justification for the constraints on individual life-plans of both mothers and fathers needed to meet this aim may be found in the unwillingness of the parties to the social contract to risk being raised in emotionally or materially impoverished conditions.[21]

Tim Mulgan offers two objections. First, he writes, "People disagree strongly about what is best for children" and asks, "do the parties to the social contract know in advance which arrangements would actually be in the best interests of children?"[22] Secondly, he states, "Few people will deliberately reproduce if they believe themselves unable to provide a decent life for their children."[23] The first objection is also applicable to licensing parents, but it misses the point. What is *best* for children is controversial, but that is importantly different from knowing what is uncontroversially *bad* for children. It is uncontroversial that child abuse and neglect are bad. Mulgan's second objection is overly optimistic. I hope that nobody would deliberately reproduce if he believed himself unable to provide a decent life for his children. However, one of the foremost objections to licensing parents is, "It may be nice in theory, but most people who are denied licenses will procreate and rear anyhow; therefore, licensing parents is useless because it is unenforceable." This common reaction reveals a deep suspicion of Mulgan's assumption. If Mulgan qualified his claim to "rational and moral people will not deliberately reproduce if they believe themselves unable to provide a decent life for their children," then he would clearly be correct. However, irrational and immoral people exist. As such, to repeat an earlier observation, it is empirically false that people do not deliberately reproduce if they believe themselves unfit to parent (on the assumption that at least some are not simply delusional). For example, crack babies continue to exist. In any case, one cannot have it both ways. One cannot believe both (i) the non-sterilization version of licensing parents would be ineffective because unlicensed people would proceed to bear and rear children while knowing that their chance of maltreating their children is extremely high and (ii) human beings are decent insofar as they will not procreate and rear if they know that they are likely to maltreat their children. An ISJ would want to know the result of a test that would reveal whether he would likely maltreat his children, and he would voluntarily refrain from rearing children if he failed the test. No coercion would be necessary in a society of ISJs because all citizens would seek to be tested and would refrain from having children if they failed. However, we do not live in a society of ISJs, and because many people today would not want to know the results of this test or would continue to bear and rear children if they failed the test, it is clear that our society has many non-ISJs who care more about their own desires than the well-being of their children and society.

3.2 Duty to Whom?

Supposing that parents have a duty to children, and it is generally agreed that they do, from where does this duty arise? For Locke, it is primarily a duty to be fulfilled to God. Locke also implicitly recognizes that this duty is necessary for the sake of children to be able to develop properly. If we love children, we should fulfill this duty for their sake. That is, we know that we love them, want to take care of them, and have an idea about how to care for them, so our love binds us to caring for them. We can also fulfill our duty in the sense that we are fulfilling some abstract moral principle that we should take care of any vulnerable creature in need, but this is slightly different. Because Gauthier's contractarian model was mentioned, it is important to note an additional source of duty—the state. Mark Vopat observes, "obligations parents have to their children derives [sic] from an implicit contract, not between parent and child, but between parents and the state."[24] He explains,

> [T]he intuitions regarding children make them fundamentally equal to adult members of society, thus deserving of the respect and protection of the state. Consequently, the state is justified in acting in the best interests of the child to insure that his or her intrinsic value and interests are met. In this capacity as protector, the state is justified in dispensing with its duties to children by contracting with parents.[25]

I take Vopat to be correct, but I wish to make an important distinction. Having an obligation to the state does not mean that parents must be *motivated* to fulfill their duty to their children from their duty to the state. Parents should be motivated by their love and desire to care for their children. While that is commonly believed, the state also has a duty to protect children insofar as it serves to protect citizens and children are citizens. As long as parents fulfill their duties to their children, the state does not need to intervene. However, if a threat is posed to children by their parents or prospective parents, the state has a right to intervene for their protection. We do not often think of the state in this way because parents usually protect and nurture their children adequately. But when they do not, the *parens patrie* power of the state becomes evident. This also becomes evident, for example, in debates about the ontological status of the fetus in pro-life/choice debates. Pro-life advocates often seek to establish that the fetus is a person not simply to establish a moral claim but to establish a legal claim, which yields protection by the state by virtue of the fetus as a person, thus a citizen who is guaranteed protection. The question of licensing parents is less complicated than the question of abortion in that there are no controversial ontological disputes; the disagreement is simply about who should be able to bear and rear children.

One may still be skeptical about whether the state may intervene in cases when parents are unable to fulfill their duty, and Mill addresses this skepticism when he writes, "It still remains unrecognized that to bring a child into existence without a fair prospect of being able, not only to provide food for its body, but instruction and training for its mind is a moral crime, both against the unfortunate offspring and against society; and that if the parent does not fulfill this obligation, the State ought to see it fulfilled at the charge, as far as possible, of the parent."[26] Some may accept this while rejecting licensing parents because Mill implies that the charge is up to the parent. However, if developmental psychology is as I have put forth and children are as fragile as I have claimed, then the charge required of some potential parents is to not parent at all, and the state is obligated to ensure this.

The above paragraphs are strengthened when we acknowledge that children cannot claim rights for themselves, unlike most other minority or oppressed groups. This is pertinent when recognizing that we only recently allowed the state to intervene in the family to protect women from abusive husbands. However, the case is more severe for children, especially very young ones, who cannot seek the police or flee from the family to evade abuse, as adult women can do. Children can be severely maltreated for years without anybody outside the family knowing. Some women may choose not to report their abuse to the police, but young children do not even have this choice. Furthermore, unlike the case of the battered or raped wife, children do not consent to who their parents are. Consenting to marry does not justify spousal abuse, but children do not have *any* power concerning who their families will be. Discussing married couples is particularly relevant if we imagine treating adult women as we treat children. Suppose that women could be claimed as wives by men who capture them (this captures the analogy of entering a relationship with no consent), and suppose that the state respects this practice as legal. Suppose further that a small subpopulation of men could be identified, with 90 percent accuracy, as likely to be highly abusive to their wives.[27] Overlooking the injustice of women having to marry whomever they are captured by, assuming it is just for the sake of argument (as it is a fact that children never give consent to the families into which they are born), our society would find it morally repugnant if the men identified as 90 percent likely to maltreat their spouses were able to marry women. Furthermore, our society would likely forbid such men from marrying in the first place (assuming that they only marry non-consensually by capturing women). That is, we would not argue, "Well, marriage is important to people and a right that all people have. Besides, there is no guarantee that all such men will abuse the wives with whom they entered into a non-consensual relationship because there is a 10 percent chance that everything will work out just fine. It is best to let the men abuse the women and then try to remedy things after the abuse. That is, if such maltreated women came forward. And if such men allowed them to leave the house. And if. . . ."

The situation of children is worse than that of women in this counterfactual scenario. Adult women can survive without spouses, but young children cannot survive without parents. Adult women do not need spouses to develop psychologically (at least not for the most basic stages of development), but parents are essential for child development. Adult women are psychologically developed, they have some belief system of right and wrong, and spousal abuse need not entirely form their moral psychology (although sometimes they may come to accept the abuse as a coping mechanism if they do not escape). However, children are largely formed by their early experiences in life, both physically and psychologically, and being abused as young children is likely to cause them to develop in an unhealthy way, which will likely cause them to be at high risk of maltreating their own children.

Citizens entered into relationships where consent is *completely* absent, when such citizens are *completely* vulnerable, deserve extra protection from the state—a kind of protection that is not and should not be given to those who are not *completely* vulnerable and do not *completely* lack consent. This should be clear from the counterfactual case of adult women provided above, and such women were not even completely vulnerable and did not completely lack consent (they did not completely lack consent because they could have emigrated, committed suicide, killed their spouse, etc. to avoid their almost inevitable maltreatment). At the very least, if we had no idea what kind of life we would have but could be guaranteed only one thing by the state, I imagine that most people would choose to ensure that their parents would not maltreat them. That is not to say that parental rights do not exist. Yet if we could only choose to be ensured that we would not be maltreated by our parents (which would also largely ensure that we would not maltreat our own children if we were to parent later) or to be ensured that we would be completely free to parent later (while accepting that we could be maltreated by our parents and, furthermore, if such maltreatment occurred then we would be at high risk to maltreat our own children) then I take it that we would choose the former. In any case, this would be the choice of an ISJ. This lends credence to the former being a more basic right, if merely comparing rights.

4. A DUTY TO LOVE[28]

I have already mentioned some problems concerning speaking about the rights of children, as opposed to parental duties to them. Rights talk often leads to liberationist positions that do not protect children adequately, and talking about trusts, at a certain level, makes it appear that we value children

only as future adults and do not value them *as children*. Also, rights talk often settles little because we believe that parents have rights, and these are usually deemed to trump the rights of children. While recognizing the importance
of children's rights, I have tried to emphasize the duties that parents have.
However, speaking of the parent-child relationship in terms of duties also has
problems. In this section I will reveal some of these problems, demonstrate
how they are surmountable, and show how they can help to understand the
parent-child relationship better in my licensing scheme.

In chapter 2, I detailed the importance of parental love in gaining self-
respect and becoming an ISJ. I also argued that, despite the importance of
parental love in child development, love is a necessary but insufficient condition for proper parenting. Likewise, being competent in the sense of knowing how to parent well is a necessary but insufficient condition for proper parenting. I cited various reasons why love is necessary, but there are more
tangible and empirically verifiable reasons. That is, studies of children in various institutional (non-family) environments and studies of primates demonstrate that adequate care without love can cause physical and psychological
failure to thrive and can even cause death.[29] The claim that parents must love
their children for their children to develop properly is a strong one, and many
might object that all that we can demand of parents as a duty is to act *as if*
they loved their children because that is all that children need. The studies
mentioned above demonstrate that merely acting as if one loves another is insufficient. However, there are other reasons to believe that parents have a
duty to love their children and not simply act as if they did. It is questionable
whether a parent can exude the subtle tone and non-verbal behavior that
would naturally manifest from love if he did not love his children. It is logi-
cally possible, but it seems highly unlikely. I also doubt that it is psychologically possible for an adult to maintain a charade of love for a child without
genuinely feeling the emotion of love. In any case, this is unlikely to be sus-
tainable over the span of a child's life, especially if the parent were to remain
psychologically healthy. Likewise, even extremely young children are often
incredibly perceptive. They would be likely to recognize that the parent is acting and that his love is not genuine. This kind of discovery would be devastating to children at multiple deep levels.

A more basic problem is whether a duty to love can exist. Liao and Solheim
note that love is generally not considered a duty because love is an emotion,
emotions cannot be rationally controlled by the will, and we cannot have duties to things beyond our control if ought implies can. For a few people it will
be the case that their inability to love will entail a lack of duty, in some sense,
to their children; however, this will be discussed later. Here I simply wish to
show that it is possible for most people to have a duty to love, at least a duty

to love their children. This should not be too controversial if we take Aristotle seriously about cultivation not being simply a matter of reflection but also a matter of habituation.[30] We sometimes claim that people are responsible for their emotions insofar as they demonstrate either the wrong emotion or an excess or deficiency of an emotion in certain situations. We often recognize that certain emotions (or range of emotions) are appropriate in certain situations or relationships. Furthermore, we believe that people ought to regulate themselves, often by means of habituating the proper emotion. This can involve giving ourselves reasons to have emotions or making states of affairs such that we are more inclined to exude the proper emotions naturally. If a parent wanted to love his child consistently, he should not engage in behavior or place himself in situations where the sentiment would likely be precluded. For example, he would not consume illegal drugs or vast quantities of alcohol, which are likely to give him less control over his emotions. Likewise, a parent who wanted to love consistently would be advised to have some basic knowledge of what children are developmentally capable of so that the parent would not attribute childhood mistakes to malice or lack of love towards the parent.

Establishing that most parents may have a duty to love their children, however, does not entail that a parent's love should be motivated by duty. A parent's duty to love his child need not be solely for the sake of fulfilling that duty. In fact, most would find it repugnant if a parent were to love his child only for the sake of duty. Furthermore, loving one's children only for the sake of duty is as psychologically implausible as a parent consistently acting as if he loved his child consistently without actually loving the child. The existence of a duty is compatible with being able to fulfill that duty without being motivated by that duty. That said, it is not necessarily repugnant to act in a loving manner without being motivated only by love (and instead being motivated by duty). Ideally, parents always act from love of their children. However, this seems supererogatory. Certain events in life, such as tragedies, may preoccupy a parent and the space for love becomes temporarily filled with sadness or another emotion. For example, suppose that a parent's close friend died on the day of his young daughter's birthday. Knowing that giving a gift is an important means of affirmation to her, the parent may buy and give her a gift. But because of his sadness, his action may be motivated from knowing what he should do, as a generally loving father, despite the fact that his heart is not quite in it. This does not mean that his act betrays a lack of love for his daughter. It demonstrates that sometimes our knowledge of our duties enables us to maintain healthy loving relationships, even when we do not act from love directly. After all, it would be better that the father gives his daughter a gift to affirm her, in accordance with his duty, than to allow his other emotions engulf him and cause him not to affirm her at all.[31] Of course, acting this way is justifiable only in certain situations and could not be done frequently in a healthy relationship.

I am willing to concede that parents should be motivated to love their children out of duty, on the assumption that we can be motivated by multiple things at the same time. That is, "We can be motivated to do something for the sake of duty, and, at the same time, for the person's sake," or "Sometimes, being motivated to do the right thing is being motivated to do it for the other person's sake. The content of the duty is just to be motivated for the other person's sake. For example, in the case of loving a child, being motivated to do the right thing is just being motivated to give the child love for the child's sake."[32] In fact, it is difficult to imagine how love would be effective in yielding healthy child development if it were not also paired with the motivation to do what is good for the child while understanding the child's needs to express love effectively. I take it that most people love their children most of the time. However, love is a necessary but insufficient condition for proper parenting. Parents must often understand and be motivated by a knowledge of their duty to love (more precisely, knowledge about what this duty requires) for their affection to be expressed properly. This way of thinking about duties does not commit one to loving children only from duty because one can (and should) still do things for one's child for the sake of that child. At the very least, in my birthday-present scenario, it is important for parents to sometimes be motivated by their duty.

Most potential parents will have little problem fulfilling their most basic duties to any children that they might have because the natural affection of love will motivate them to know how their children should be treated and to behave accordingly. Part of understanding what children need is understanding their various vulnerabilities. For most parents bearing a child entails an implicit contract to fulfill certain duties to that child, or at least ensure that these duties are fulfilled by others. This is at least true when the parental role is undertaken voluntarily, as it is in our society where contraception is readily available, abortion is legal, and adoption is a socially acceptable practice. Yet some parents (or potential parents) are unable to love or care for children and are thus unable to have a duty to love or care for them. I agree with Solheim, "that we cannot plausibly hold *a* duty-bound to love *b* because *a* may not have control over all of the variables of her developing love for *b*—still holds in the case of parents and children."[33] That is, parents who are unable to fulfill duties to children cannot have duties to children if ought implies can. Some severely mentally retarded people, for example, cannot have a duty to love or care for any children that they bear because they cannot love or care for children in a way necessary for children to develop properly. They should not be allowed to rear children if the nature of children creates a duty for others to love them. Likewise, some otherwise normally functioning people (in the sense that they are not severely mentally retarded) are unable to love, or at least love children in a healthy way. Such people cannot have a duty to love any potential children that they might bear. An inability to love may result from being abused or neglected as a child or perhaps originates from experiencing a serious psychological problem. The vulnerability of children, as well as their moral and legal rights as citizens, should entail that they only be raised by individuals who have a duty to love and care for them.

The state's entrusting those *without a duty* to children *to fulfill a duty* to children is negligence. One may object that the state has no duty to protect children because that is the job of the family, but any such objection ignores the commonly held belief that the state has a *parens patrie* power. It may be further objected that the state ought to intervene *after* child abuse has taken place (this objection will be explored in the next chapter), but it remains true that most people believe that the state is justified to intervene earlier in the family to protect children in at least some instances. Such objections are often motivated by the belief that it is *ideal* that the state not intervene in the family and raising children *should* be the responsibility of families. I agree that this is ideal. Pretending that this ideal is met, however, is dangerously naïve because it enables many parents, who do not have their children's interests in mind, to maltreat children. Montague correctly notes, "while parents have broad discretion regarding *how* to fulfill their obligations, they do not have discretion *whether* to fulfill them."[34] Licensing parents allows those who will fulfill their duties broad discretion in how their duties will be fulfilled and precludes those without duties or obligations to children from rearing any children. An overarching objection to this thesis is that licensing parents is repugnant because it is paternalistic. The charge is thought to be devastating because it implicitly refers to being paternalistic to *adults*, and in this sense 'paternalism' is usually and justifiably a pejorative term.[35] However, this is not limited to adults; it is also about children, and paternalism (and maternalism) is needed for children to develop properly. In our *laissez-faire* system of parenting, the state, in most cases, will eventually "protect" the children of those individuals who disregard (or lack) the most basic duties to children. Unfortunately, state intervention *after* children have been maltreated does not protect them in any meaningful way, as the harm is often irreparable.

5. LIFE PROJECTS, AUTONOMY, AND RISK

John Robertson writes, "The moral right to reproduce is respected because of the centrality of reproduction to personal identity, meaning and dignity,"[36] and many are convinced that this is why the state lacks the right to forbid some adults from parenting. Bearing and rearing are often central to one's identity and meaning, but it is unclear why it follows that the state cannot forbid some from bearing or rearing. I take it that many people deeply desire to rear children, and this desire is often not fleeting. Rather, it is a carefully considered matter, and rearing children constitutes an important part of leading a meaningful or enjoyable life. I also agree, for the most part, with Elizabeth Anderson, "To respect a person is to treat her in accordance with principles she rationally accepts—principles consistent with the protection of her autonomy and her rational interests."[37] Accepting the above, presume that a couple wishes to bear a physically healthy child. The couple consults with a doctor, who informs them that if they bear a child there is a 90 percent chance that the child will have a serious disability with little chance to function as a healthy human being. If the parents take physical health to be an important condition for their child, then it would be irrational for them to bear a child with the knowledge that they are unlikely to have a healthy child. Now suppose that a couple wishes to rear a child, but only if they have good reason to believe that they will raise their child in at least a minimally decent way. Suppose also that the couple makes clear their belief that abusing or neglecting a child is not minimally decent. Suppose further that this couple consults with an expert who informs them that there is a 90 percent chance that they will abuse or neglect their child.[38] Of the things that we might say about this couple if they choose to rear a child, they are no longer acting in their rational interests (or in that of their potential child's welfare interest). If we preclude them from raising children, then we are not disrespecting them or violating their autonomy according to Anderson's abovementioned passage. It is one thing to desire to rear children, but it is another thing entirely to actualize this desire with the knowledge that one is almost certain to abuse or neglect a child. The decision to raise a child despite knowing one's likelihood to abuse or neglect that child illustrates my point: conceding that the desire to raise a child trumps the desire to raise a child in the manner that a child deserves fails to recognize or protect the child's interest or welfare in any meaningful way.

It is a commonly held belief that people in the above cases should not bear or rear children. One way to justify this is to argue, as David Velleman does, "people should not deliberately create children who they already know will be disadvantaged."[39] However, this position is too extreme. I take it that most children, in some way or another, will be disadvantaged. Some children will have more than their share of advantages, and some will have more than their share of disadvantages. However, it is unacceptable to procreate deliberately when the resulting children will be disadvantaged below the threshold of decency—being abused or neglected as a child. Most people accept this for themselves. When asked if they would rear a child knowing with 90 percent accuracy that they would maltreat their child, very few would maintain that they would. At a very minimum, to do so would be indecent. Some object, "But *I* know that the test is wrong because *I* know that *I* would parent decently." This simply denies the predictive power that has already been assumed, and many people would make the same claim. But when asked if we should tolerate others parenting in such a situation, considerably more are accepting. What changes? We might think that some *other* people's desires, unlike ours, do not change after knowing that they are likely to maltreat their child. As such, it is wrong to prevent the desire of adults to be fulfilled, especially if this hinders them from coming closer to fulfilling their life plan. Ignoring the fact that rearing in such cases will, nine times out of ten, not fulfill their life plan and make life worse for themselves and their children, it remains the case that "human beings do not simply accept passively a set of aims or a life plan. Rather, values, aims and plans are all subjects for deliberation and choice."[40] People are able to control their desires with varying degrees of success, but what are we to say of the person who *still* wishes to rear while knowing that he will likely maltreat his children? The person who chooses to rear in such a scenario, I think, reveals that the 90 percent probability that he will maltreat his child is probably too low for him in the sense that his lack of adequately weighing his potential child's well-being demonstrates that he will almost surely maltreat his child.

To limit the discussion of autonomy and life plans to adults would be incomplete. Children also have interests, and they will mature to have autonomy and life plans. As demonstrated in the first half of this book, life plans and autonomy often depend on how people were raised. Minimally, children who experience abuse and neglect often experience a serious reduction in their autonomy. Experiencing maltreatment is often a great impediment to developing self-respect and becoming ISJs, which will negatively affect their aspirations and life plans. It may be objected that things, such as being economically disadvantaged, also limit autonomy, but such an impediment can be overcome if one has loving and competent parents. Those who are maltreated, regardless of socioeconomic status, are unlikely to develop properly and become fully autonomous individuals. Someone who chooses to raise a child despite knowing he is likely to maltreat that child greatly limits the autonomy and constrains the life plans of that child. If we take life plans and autonomy seriously, then these considerations also need to be weighed carefully. The selfishness of the individual who seeks to rear a child while knowing that he will likely maltreat the child is made clear by David Benatar when he writes about the distinction between grief and regret concerning the existence of children,

Bringing people into existence as well as failing to bring people into existence can be regretted. However, only bringing people into existence can be regretted *for the sake of* the person whose existence was contingent on our decision. One might grieve about not having children, but not because the children which one could not have had been deprived of existence. Remorse about not having children is remorse for ourselves, sorrow about having missed child-bearing and child-rearing experiences. However, we do regret having brought into existence a child with an unhappy life, and we regret it for the child's sake, even if also for our own sakes.[41]

Besides weighing the interests of the parent and child, it is also important to consider the interests of society. When that is done, it is better to have a small set of upset adults who would have otherwise maltreated their children than a set of abused and neglected children who are likely to become non-ISJs.

6. SEX, BIOLOGY, AND LIBERTY

As noted earlier from Locke, the act of begetting does not necessarily yield parental rights. We may hold it as an ideal for the sex act to lead to parental rights, but that is contingent upon prospective parents being able to fulfill duties to children. For this important fact, we should recognize that the acts of sex and childrearing can be separable. Sexual capability (or fertility) does not entail parental capability. People should be more responsible when having sex, but they sometimes are not. Until we no longer presuppose that biology grants rights, our idealism will acquiesce to the maltreatment of children.

Many reject licensing parents based on the idea that, although child maltreatment is distressing, criminal, and unjust, state intervention in the family is nonetheless unjustified. Yet we already accept and support the state's integral role in protecting children. Both the adoption screening process and child protective services (the legal process that removes children from abusive or neglectful or potentially abusive or neglectful parents) embrace state protection of children. We recognize that children are different from adults. As citizens they have the same basic rights as adults, but they are not capable of securing and exercising those rights on their own behalves. Moreover, they are extremely vulnerable and incapable of adequately caring for themselves. For these reasons, the kind of potential harm that children face demands that society address child maltreatment with more than only moral repugnance. What is telling, however, is *how* we today justify why many parents have a presumptive right, as opposed to how it has historically been justified. Classical and modern thinkers often write that the natural affection of parents ensures that the duty to children will be fulfilled by parents. This is an overly optimistic claim about all parents because some have no such affection, but these thinkers at least seek to ensure that duties to children are fulfilled. The natural affection thesis still exists, but it is overshadowed by another kind of justification. Arguments today tend to focus on the autonomy of adults to such a degree that anything needed to fulfill one's life plan becomes tantamount to a right. Justification of parental authority is increasingly founded on arguments for adult liberty and rights, though a perverse form of both. Consequently, many objections to licensing parents are founded on an unhealthy fetish with adult liberty and rights. Mill noted this emerging trend as early as the late nineteenth century,

> Yet the current ideas of liberty, which bend so easily to real infringements of the individual in things which concern only himself, would repel the attempt to put any restraint upon his inclinations when the consequences of their indulgence is a life or lives of wretchedness and depravity to the offspring, with manifold evils to those sufficiently within reach to be in any way affected by their actions. When we compare the strange respect of mankind for liberty with their strange want of respect for it, we might imagine that a man had an indispensable right to do harm to others, and no right at all to please himself without giving pain to anyone.[42]

Rearing children when maltreatment is 90 percent likely is a paradigm case of indulgence whereby the result is an evil likely to spawn depravity and wretchedness.

CONCLUSION

Most people should have presumptive parental rights because they are able and likely to fulfill basic duties to children. Biological parents are usually in an optimal situation to parent their children well because of their prenatal investment, stable postnatal structure, and their natural bond of love. In a world in which we cannot accurately predict who will maltreat children, our current system of allowing those who bear children to rear them is a decent one, for the most part. Such a world has historically been the only world available. However, in a world in which we can accurately predict who will maltreat children, we have other options—and a genuine opportunity to reduce the perpetuation of child maltreatment. Our common and deeply held intuitions and actions commit us to accepting that not all people should parent and that the state is justified in enforcing this. We accept government regulation of some activities when a lack of competence is likely to cause considerable harm to others, if competence can be measured. Parenting is a paradigm case of where incompetence can severely harm others, and a reasonable test has been put forth to measure the likelihood of maltreatment. We also believe that children deserve some minimal standard from which to begin life, that they should not be parented below a certain threshold, and we can regulate parents so that children are not likely to be raised by those who are unable to be minimally decent parents. This is clear from how we accept our adoption system.

Parental love is necessary for children to develop properly, and parental love towards children is a duty. Some people are unable to love or care for children in a minimally decent way. If ought implies can, then some people cannot have a duty to rear children. If parental rights result from duties, then some people do not have rights to rear children. State enforcement of this may be paternalistic, but children need paternalism. All this is particularly evident in a contractarian system in which we would ultimately prefer to have the government ensure that we not have parents who maltreat than to have a *laissez-faire* system of parenting. In addition to having a duty to children, parents have a duty to the state.

The uniqueness of the biological parent-child relationship makes it difficult to show that our categorical acceptance of biology entailing a right to rear is unjust because no direct analogy can be made. However, in attempting to make an analogy (by asking what we would think of a system where we treated adult women like children in my wife-capturing scenario), it should be clear that what largely holds us back from accepting more protection of children is a deeply engrained ageism. After all, few would find it unjust for the state to forbid the men in that scenario from marrying. To allow the men to marry would be impermissible. We have come to see the injustice of sexism only relatively recently. Unfortunately, we have yet to realize fully the injustice of ageism. As it stands, our preoccupation with adult liberty, adult rights, and adult life plans, with little regard to the corresponding things for children, is unjust and socially destructive.

State enforcement of licensing parents may ultimately be deemed *imprudent*, but this is separable from the claim that the state cannot *justifiably enforce* such a policy. At the very least, I am unaware of any persuasive argument for why the state would not be justified to enforce this policy. We initially resist this conclusion, but resistance becomes extremely difficult after it is clear that parental rights are defeasible. Some may concede that parental rights are defeasible, but by "defeasible" they mean only "can be taken away after harm has occurred." Such usage is odd and too narrow because a defeasible right is simply a right that is subject to forfeiture—nothing about defeasibility requires forfeiture *after some act*. Nonetheless, the argument goes something like this: "parental rights are defeasible, but the state cannot take that right away before one has been shown to be unfit to exercise that right." However, that presumes that the *state takes away* the right. Yet that does not accurately describe what mostly happens in licensing parents. Rather, the state merely acts in accordance with the recognition that some individuals are incapable of fulfilling a duty and because they are incapable of fulfilling a duty then they cannot have parental rights. The state does not cause this right to be lost or take it away; it simply recognizes that some parents do not have the right in the first place, and the state ensures that those without such rights do not parent. It may be objected that an extremely few people who have not maltreated children or who would not maltreat children were they given the opportunity to parent will be prevented from parenting. However, this objection will be considered in the next chapter, along with other concerns about prior restraint.

NOTES

1. Hugh LaFollette, "Licensing Parents," *Philosophy and Public Affairs*, 9 (1980), 193–95. Most communities require adoptive parents to be eighteen years or older, be in good health, meet the state's home safety standards, have sufficient income for family needs, be emotionally stable and have character references, have no criminal record, be willing to work with social workers, agree to discipline without physical contact, and agree to attend a parenting workshop.

2. See LaFollette, 194n9. For more recent statistics, in 2004 only 0.6 percent of parental perpetrators of child abuse were adoptive parents. *Child Maltreatment: U.S. Department of Health and Human Resources, Administration on Children, Youth, and Families* (Washington, DC: U.S. Government Printing Office, 2006), 78. However, according to the 2000 U.S. Census 2.4 percent of children were adopted. United States Census: Adopted Children and Stepchildren—Census 2000 Special Report (U.S. Department of Commerce, 2004), 2. These statistics are from different sources, but it is fairly clear that the rate of abuse is lower in adoptive families.

3. Peg Tittle, "Introduction," in Peg Tittle, ed. *Should Parents Be Licensed? Debating the Issues* (Amherst, NY: Prometheus Books, 2004), 15.

4. Sanford N. Katz, *When Parents Fail: The Law's Response to Family Breakdown* (Boston: Beacon Press, 1971), 4.

5. It is less widely known that the Persians, Greeks, Egyptians, and Gauls also granted nearly absolute power to the father over his children through much of their history. See James Kent, *Commentaries on American Law* (New York: O. Halstead, 1832), Vol. II, Part IV, Lecture XXIX, Section II, "Of the Rights of Parents," 203.

6. For example, see Exodus 21:15, 17; Leviticus 20:9; Deuteronomy 21:18–24; Zechariah 13:3.

7. John Locke, *Two Treatises of Government* (Cambridge: Cambridge University Press, 1996), 305.

8. Locke, 310. Locke also writes, "*Paternal* or *Parental Power* is nothing but that, which Parents have over their Children, to govern them for the Children's good," and

"The *Power*, then *that Parents have* over their Children, arises from that Duty which is incumbent on them, to take care of their Off-spring, during the imperfect state of Childhood," 381 and 306.

9, See Jeanne M. Giovannoni and Rosina M. Becerra, *Defining Child Abuse* (New York: The Free Press, 1979), 36.

10. Philip Montague, "The Myth of Parental Rights," *Social Theory and Practice*, 26 (2000), 57–58.

11. Onora O'Neill, "Children's Rights and Children's Lives" in Philip Alston, Stephen Parker, and John Seymour, eds. *Children and the Law* (Oxford: Oxford University Press, 1992), 54 and 52.

12. Laura Purdy, *In Their Best Interest? The Case Against Equal Rights for Children* (Ithaca, NY: Cornell University Press, 1992). For child liberationist views, see John Holt, *Escape From Childhood: The Needs and Rights of Children* (New York: Ballantine Books, 1974) and Richard Farson, *Birthrights* (New York: Macmillan, 1974).

13. See Tom D. Cambell, "The Rights of the Minor: as Person, as Child, as Juvenile, as Future Adult," John Ekelaar, "The Importance of Thinking that Children Have Rights," and Michael D. A. Freeman, "Taking Rights More Seriously," in Alston, Parker, and Seymour, eds. Joel Feinburg puts forth an account whereby there exist adult only rights (A-rights), child only rights (C-rights), and rights common to adults and children (A-C rights). See his "The Child's Rights to an Open Future," in William Aiken and Hugh LaFollette, eds. *Whose Child? Children's Rights, Parental Authority, and State Power* (Totowa, NJ: Rowman and Littlefield, 1980).

14. Kent, Vol. II, Part IV, Lecture XXIX, Section II, "Of the Rights of Parents," 203.

15. Elizabeth Anderson, "Is Women's Labor a Commodity?" *Philosophy and Public Affairs*, 19 (1990), 75–76 and Samantha Brennan and Robert Noggle, "The Moral Status of Children: Children's Rights, Parents' Rights, and Family Justice," *Social Theory and Practice*, 23 (1997), 11–13. William B. Irvine also develops a stewardship model of parenting in *Doing Right by Children: Reflections on the Nature of Childhood and the Obligations of Parenthood* (St. Paul, MN: Paragon House, 2001). See also Irvine's *The Politics of Parenting* (St. Paul, MN: Paragon House, 2003).

16. Onora O'Neill, "Begetting, Bearing, and Rearing" in Onora O'Neill and William Ruddick, eds. *Having Children: Philosophical and Legal Reflections on Parenthood* (New York: Oxford University Press, 1979), 25.

17. David Archard, *Children: Rights and Childhood* (London: Routledge, 2004), 140–41 and Brennan and Noggle, 10.

18. Archard, 149.

19. Archard, 140–41. However, Archard rejects parental licensing because he finds it pragmatically unfeasible.

20. David Gauthier, "Political Contractarianism," *The Journal of Political Philosophy*, 5 (1997), 146.

21. Gauthier, 147.

22. Tim Mulgan, "Debate: Reproducing the Contractarian Debate," *The Journal of Political Philosophy*, 10 (2002), 474–75.

23. Mulgan, 474–75.

24. Mark Vopat, "Contractarianism and Children," *Public Affairs Quarterly*, 17 (2003), 49. I think that this duty exists, but I also believe that most parents also have a duty to their children independent of the existence of the state.

25. Vopat, 58.

26. John Stuart Mill, *On Liberty* (London: Penguin Books, 1985), 176.

27. I use 90 percent to parallel how accurately we can identify prospective parents who will maltreat their children.

28. In this section, I am deeply indebted to Barbara P. Solheim's "The Possibility of a Duty to Love," *Journal of Social Philosophy*, 30 (1999). I am also indebted to S. Matthew Liao's "The Right of Children to Be Loved," *The Journal of Political Philosophy*, 14 (2006) and "The Idea of a Duty to Love," *Journal of Value Inquiry*, 40 (2006).

29. Some early and classic studies in the psychoanalytic tradition are: René Spitz, "Hospitalism: An Inquiry Into the Genesis of Psychiatric Conditions in Early Childhood," *The Psychoanalytic Study of the Child*, 1 (1945); R. Spitz and K. M. Wolf, "Anaclitic Depression: An Inquiry Into the Genesis of Psychiatric Conditions in Early Childhood," *The Psychoanalytic Study of the Child*, 2 (1946); H. F. Harlow, R. O. Dodsworth, and M. K. Harlow, "Total Social Isolation in Monkeys," *Proceedings of the National Academy of Sciences*, 54 (1965). For more studies, including recent neuroscientific studies, see Liao, "The Right of Children to Be Loved," n10–n20. For a review of the contemporary literature on how affection affects brain development and the nervous system, see Sue Gerhardt's *Why Love Matters: How Affection Shapes a Baby's Brain* (New York: Brunner-Routledge, 2004).

30. Aristotle, *Nicomachean Ethics*, trans. Martin Ostwald (Englewood Cliffs, NJ: Prentice Hall, 1962), Bk. I, Ch. I, 1102a33–b29.

31. Another example might be a parent who has to care for his sick infant, which may require several straight days without sleep. At some point, it seems that a sense of duty may help to motivate the proper action of caring for the sick infant.

32. Liao, "The Idea of a Duty to Love," 18–19.

33. Solheim, 13.

34. Montague, 62.

35. The paternalism objection against licensing parents has more force from either libertarian or conservative non-egalitarians, as much of liberal egalitarianism can be justifiably described as paternalistic.

36. John A. Robertson, *Children of Choice: Freedom and the New Reproductive Technologies* (Princeton: Princeton University Press, 1994), 30.

37. Anderson, "Is Women's Labor a Commodity?" 81. I write "for the most part" because I also believe it important to consider the autonomy and rational interests of *other* people.

38. Presume also that education or rehabilitation is unlikely for the couple.

39. J. David Velleman, "Family History," *Philosophical Papers*, 34 (2005), 364.

40. Gauthier, 138. It is for this reason that Gauthier also writes, "If, as seems psychologically plausible, the social growth of a child is significantly enhanced by being raised in an emotionally warm and stable environment in which the child develops

strong affective ties with an adult of each sex, and especially its natural parents, then persons who want children will need to commit themselves, so far as possible, to create and maintain such an environment. That some will not want, or even be able, to do this is in no way to condemn them, but rather to indicate the sort of constraints imposed on acceptable life-plans, insofar as these plans involve children, by the demand for effective upbringing, which must be part of any set of interaction acceptable to all," 147.

41. David Benatar, "Why It Is Better Never to Come Into Existence," *American Philosophical Quarterly*, 34 (1997) 346.

42. Mill, 179–80.

7

The Constitution, Due Process, and Prior Restraint

In chapter 6 I discussed parental rights in the context of licensing parents, but I did so primarily by asking what would be required in the kind of completely well-ordered society towards which I strive. I am working from our current society because I assume that it is formally well-ordered, and I seek consistency with the fundamental principles of the United States as much as possible. This chapter begins by asking if licensing parents is compatible with the ideals put forth in the Founding, if it is compatible with American jurisprudence, and if it is compatible with the historic relationship between the family and the state. I then examine what standard of due process or burden of proof is necessary to implement a system of licensing parents. I argue that two major trends have formed regarding legislative and judicial treatment of the family. The first trend began in colonial America and lasted, roughly, until the 1920s. The second has existed since then, and it has been strengthened since the 1960s when the Supreme Court discovered a substantive constitutional right to privacy. I find both trends unjust. However, I believe that several arguments by conservative justices[1] in the latter half of the twentieth century properly discern the role of the federal government in domestic matters, the relationship between the state and the family, and the burden of proof that must be met before the state can intervene in the family.[2] Finally, discussion of due process leads to the question that was left at the end of chapter 6: is prior restraint justifiable?

1. TRANSITION FROM RIGHTS

Consider the preamble to the U.S. Constitution, "We the People of the United States, in Order to form a more perfect Union, establish Justice, insure domestic

159

Tranquillity, provide for the common defense, promote the general Welfare, and secure the Blessings of Liberty to ourselves and our Posterity, do ordain and establish this Constitution for the United States of America."[3] The argument for licensing parents as a means to prevent child maltreatment is justified on two grounds: a police power to maintain political stability and order and a *parens patriae* power to protect the welfare of those unable to act in their own best interests (such as children or the mentally incompetent). The police power is justified to insure domestic tranquility, establish justice, and secure the blessings of liberty to our posterity. The *parens patriae* power is justified to promote the general welfare and secure the blessings of liberty to our posterity. The Constitution does not limit these powers to protecting "ourselves"; it extends to "our Posterity." Licensing parents seeks to promote that which is sought in the preamble of the Constitution. Yet the preamble is vague, and it may be argued that licensing parents, while having a noble goal, remains antithetical to American ideals in fundamental ways. In fact, one objection lodged against licensing parents is that it is contrary to the Constitution and the beliefs of the Founders, even if it is otherwise morally justified. However, because "family," "children," and "parents" are not mentioned in the Constitution, Declaration of Independence, or the *Federalist Papers*, this objection does not have quite the force that those who lodge it might think. This is particularly true when considering that the practice of vast state intervention in families was accepted throughout most of United States history and has only changed recently.

I do not make the strong claim that licensing parents and the state intervention needed to implement it is necessarily entailed by the *Federalist Papers*, Founding Fathers, or the Constitution. I do not think that a clear case can be made either for or against licensing parents on those grounds due to a lack of attention given to the role of children, parents, and families in relation to the state in early America. I make a weaker claim: licensing parents is *compatible* with American ideals, as articulated in the preamble, and it is not clearly antithetical to the Constitution; therefore, it is a policy that states are *permitted* to enact. This may seem trivial, but because many people believe that there is something unconstitutional or "un-American" about licensing parents, it merits treatment. This compatibility claim recognizes that many court cases have been, or appear to have been, decided in a way that would preclude justification of licensing parents or contain principles or arguments that would preclude such. For example, *Stanley v. Illinois* (1972) appealed to *Meyer v. Nebraska* (1923), which held that the rights to conceive and raise one's children has been established as "essential,"[4] appealed to *Skinner v. Oklahoma* (1942), which held that parental rights are "basic civil rights of man,"[5] appealed to *May v. Anderson* (1953), which held parental rights as "far more precious . . . than property rights,"[6] and appealed to *Prince v. Com. of Mass-achusetts* (1944), which argued, "It is cardinal with us that the custody, care and nurture of the child include preparation for obligations the state can neither supply nor hinder."[7] Likewise, in *Santosky v. Kramer* (1982) it was written that the "Court's historical recognition that freedom of personal choice in matters of family life is a fundamental liberty interest protected by the Fourteenth Amendment."[8] Similarly, *Roe v. Wade* (1973) ruled, "Several decisions of this Court make it clear that freedom of personal choice in matters of marriage and family life is one of the liberties protected by the Due Process Clause of the Fourteenth Amendment."[9] Also, in *Eisenstadt v. Baird* (1972), "If the right to privacy means anything, it is the right of the individual, married or single, to be free from unwarranted governmental intrusion into matters so fundamentally affecting a person as the decision whether to bear and beget a child,"[10] and in *Hodgson v. Minnesota* (1990), "parents have a liberty interest, protected by the Constitution, in having a reasonable opportunity to develop close relations with their children."[11] Finally, in *Parham v. J.R.* (1979), "The statist notion that governmental power should supersede parental authority in all cases because some parents abuse and neglect children is repugnant to the American tradition."[12] These cases seem to provide justification against licensing parents, but other cases and justifications with different conclusions are abundant. Moreover, the careful reader will note that most of the above cases do not attack my parental licensing plan. For example, I concede that parental rights are more precious than property rights, the family (not the state or federal government) should care for and nurture children, and personal choice in family matters is extremely important and deserves respect. Likewise, individuals have a right to be free from *unwarranted* governmental intrusion; I simply believe that the intrusion of licensing parents is *warranted*. Individuals should have a *reasonable* opportunity to develop close relationships with their children, but I believe that some opportunities are *unreasonable*. Finally, *Parham v. J.R.* only attacks an uncharitable caricature of licensing parents because licensing parents does not require governmental power to supersede parental authority in all cases because some parents abuse and neglect children. Only an extremely few people will be permanently precluded from parenting, and those who are permitted to parent will have as much liberty to parent as parents currently have.

2. HISTORY AND AUTHORITY

Reviewing judicial decisions about the family is difficult because, until the twentieth century, most domestic matters were left to the states, not the federal government, per the Tenth Amendment.[13] In most of those, the standard state rulings followed a similar line of reasoning:

> The father is the natural guardian and is *prima facie* entitled to the custody of his minor child. This right springs from two sources: one is, that he who brings a child, a helpless being, into life, ought to take care of that child until it is able to take care of itself; and because of this obligation to take care and support this helpless being arises a reciprocal right to the custody and care of the offspring whom he must support; and the other reason is, that it is a law of nature that the affection which springs from such a relation as that is stronger and more potent than any which springs from any other human relation.[14]

and

> A parent's right to the custody of a child is not like the right of property [which may be asserted by any man, no matter how bad, immoral, or unworthy he may be], an absolute and uncontrollable right. It will never be enforced where its enforcement will obviously destroy the happiness and well-being of the child.[15]

Similarly, "The state has a right to thus interfere for the protection of neglected children, and its action in such a matter is not to be set aside upon the mere demand of a parent asserting his natural rights."[16] Raymond O'Brien notes, "In the nineteenth century and early twentieth century, the courts imposed few limitations on the state's ability to intervene in the family relationship. . . . Since the parent's rights derived from the state, which delegated control over children to their parents as a trust, failure to discharge faithfully the trust justified state intervention."[17] It has also been observed that "Most late nineteenth century courts thus acknowledged that the *child's* welfare, not the parent's legal right, was the determinative factor in private custody decisions under the *parens patriae* power."[18] Douglas Rendleman notes, "Involuntary apprenticeship of the children of undeserving parents was an integral part of the poor law in colonial North America."[19] As mentioned in chapter 6, overseers of the poor existed for much of America's history and they visited families to determine whether parents were able to care for their children adequately. Furthermore, they often terminated parental rights without trial if parents were deemed incapable. Parental rights were once believed to be tied to obligations and duties, parental rights were once believed to derive largely from the state as a trust, parental rights did not simply follow from natural rights doctrine (even in a time when natural rights doctrine was pervasive), children were once treated significantly different from mere property by the courts, and the welfare and well-being of children was once weighed nearly the same as parental interest and liberty. Until the twentieth century, vast power to intervene in the family was left largely to the states. I note this to remind those who embrace a history that did not exist in the United States until recently. Parental rights may be more than that which is yielded from an obligation to children or the responsibility to care for children in the role of a trustee, but these justifications for parental authority did not seem to become dominant in courts and legislatures until the twentieth century.

In citing pre-twentieth century court cases and traditions, however, I wish to be clear that I also oppose much of that tradition. I oppose the all-too-common removal of children without due process, especially in colonial America. I also oppose the major justification for intervening for the well-being of children because it seems that the well-being of children was sought only for the good of society. Securing the basic well-being of children is a compelling interest of the state, but per my conditions in chapter 5 this is a necessary but insufficient condition for state intervention in the family via the state's police powers. I take a more demanding stance by also requiring that the state intervene for the well-being of children and for the sake of children via its *parens patriae* powers.

State intervention in the family, tying rights to responsibility and duty, and denying a categorical right from biology has also been recognized in the twentieth century. Yet such are anomalous judgments of the Court, usually written by conservative justices. In *Hodgson v. Minnesota* (1990) it was argued, "Parental authority is not limitless. Certainly where parental investment *threatens* to harm the child, the parent's authority must yield," and "A natural parent who has demonstrated sufficient commitment to his or her children is thereafter entitled to raise the children from undue state interference."[20] Here, limits to parental authority are shaped by the *threat* of harm to children. This also structures parental rights in a conditional manner. *If* a parent demonstrates sufficient commitment to children, *then* he has a right to raise children from undue state interference. Similarly, in *Lehr v. Robertson* (1983), it was argued, "the Court has emphasized the paramount interest in the welfare of children and has noted that the rights of the parents are a counterpart of the responsibilities they have assumed," and

> The significance of the biological connection is that it offers the natural father an opportunity that no other male possesses to develop a relationship with his offspring. If he grasps that opportunity and accepts some measure of responsibility for the child's future, he may enjoy the blessings of the parent-child relationship and make uniquely valuable contributions to the child's development. If he fails to do so, the Federal Constitution will not automatically compel a State to listen to his opinion of where the child's best interests lie.[21]

This recognizes rights as a counterpart to responsibilities, and it emphasizes the unimportance of mere biological claims to parental rights. It also establishes a conditional relation: *if* one accepts responsibility for children, *then* one may enjoy the blessings of that relationship.

Most twentieth century jurisprudence concerning the family is vastly different from that of the eighteenth and nineteenth centuries. In 1923, with its decision in *Meyer v. Nebraska*, the Court embraced the position that parental rights are embodied in the Constitution itself. This, along with *Pierce v. Society of Sisters*, was decided according to the trend of substantive due process of the *Lochner* era.[22] This yielded widespread judicial review of state law, which I deem a usurpation of legislative powers. A right to privacy also gained constitutional protection, especially with *Griswold v. Connecticut* (1965), though sometimes *Meyer* and *Pierce* are read to have been privacy cases. Even though a right to privacy has been protected, it is still not *categorically* protected, as evident by the majority in *Roe v. Wade*, "it is not clear to us that the claim asserted by some amici that one has an unlimited right to do with one's body as one pleases bears a close relationship to the right of privacy previously articulated in the Court's decisions. The Court has refused to recognize an unlimited right of this kind in the past."[23] Justice Rehnquist argues even more strongly in his dissent, "I have difficulty in concluding, as the Court does, that the right of 'privacy' is involved in this case . . . the 'privacy' that the Court finds here [is not] even a distant relative of the freedom from searches and seizures protected by the Fourth Amendment to the Constitution, which the Court has referred to as embodying a right to privacy."[24]

I find pre-twentieth century jurisprudence to be lacking, but I also find much of twentieth century jurisprudence lacking. Not only has the danger of judicial activism via appeals to substantive due process usurped legislative powers, but this is even more worrisome when applied to privacy.[25] Once something such as privacy is embodied as something akin to an inviolable right, it leads to privacy and the requisite liberty needed to provide space for that privacy for adults but not for children. The result has been a tendency for the Supreme Court to hear and decide matters of family law, rather than state courts, despite the fact that state courts ought to have jurisdiction. Supreme Court decisions have evolved to show a bias towards adults, as will be made clear in sections 3 and 4 of this chapter. Pre-twentieth century laws and court decisions helped children and balanced their interests with adults better than those in the twentieth century, but this was done primarily as a means to ensure political stability. This changed in the twentieth century when the rights and interests of adults predominately trumped all other relevant factors. I seek a position between these extremes that promotes the stability of the state while balancing the rights and well-being of adults *and* children. Licensing parents is that moderate position.

3. A POSITIVE CASE FOR STATE INTERVENTION IN THE FAMILY

Childbearing and childrearing are often considered sacred or inviolable rights. Marriage is often believed to have a similar status. Consequently, an examination of marriage and family law is helpful. These cases are relatively few because, like the parent-child relationship, the marriage relationship has traditionally been addressed by the states, not the Supreme Court. In the latter half of the twentieth century the status of the family in the Supreme Court is largely split based on the political positions of judges, as I will show is also the case with what constitutes a sufficient burden of proof for state intervention in the family in section 4. I will show that my position largely falls into the conservative camp in recent important decisions on the status of marriage, family, and the state.

In *Santosky v. Kramer*, which determined that a fair preponderance of evidence standard for neglect proceedings in New York violated the Due Process Clause of the Fourteenth Amendment, the liberal majority (Black, Brennan, Marshall, Powell, and Stevens) wrote, "The fundamental liberty interest of natural parents in the care, custody, and management of their child is protected by the Fourteenth Amendment."[26] The conservative dissent written by Rehnquist, joined by Burger, White, and O'Connor, was troubled by the majority's due process analysis, but they had a more fundamental concern:

> By parsing the New York scheme and holding one narrow provision unconstitutional, the majority invites further federal-court intrusion into every facet of state family law. If ever there were an area in which federal courts should heed the admonition of Justice Holmes that 'a page of history is worth a volume of logic,' it is in the area of domestic relations. This area has been left to the States from time immemorial, and not without good reason.[27]

I take this, largely, to be the conservative position of the late twentieth century. This position respects federalism by granting states autonomy to promulgate policies in domestic matters, so long as they are reasonable. In this sense, the conservative position of the late twentieth century largely overlaps most pre-twentieth century cases on domestic matters, including marriage. For example, in *Reynolds v. U.S.* (1878), it was written,

> Marriage, while from its very nature a sacred obligation, is nevertheless, in most civilized nations, a civil contract, and usually regulated by law. Upon it society

may be said to be built, and out of its fruits spring social relations and social obligations and duties, with which government is necessarily required to deal.[28]

Likewise, in *Maynard v. Hill* (1888),

> Marriage, as creating the most important relation in life, as having more to do with the morals and civilization of a people than any other institution, has always been subject to the control of the legislature. That body proscribes the age at which parties may contract to marry, the procedure or form essential to constitute marriage, the duties and obligations it creates, its effects upon the property rights of both, present and prospective, and the acts which many constitute grounds for its dissolution.[29]

These cases demonstrate profound respect for marriage and its important role in society. The court recognized that marriage has a profound societal importance and needs to be regulated accordingly. Consequently, it respected the tradition of marriage as a civil contract, a contract subject to control of the legislature. In *Zablocki v. Redhail* (1978), the liberal Court majority ruled that, contrary to state law, there is a constitutional right to marry even if one owes child support elsewhere. While Justice Stewart joined the majority opinion, he did not hold that the Wisconsin law violated the Equal Protection Clause. Rather, he found it unconstitutional because it invades the sphere of liberty protected by the Due Process Clause of the Fourteenth Amendment. He wrote,

> I do not agree with the Court that there is a "right to marry" in the constitutional sense. That right, or more accurately that privilege, is under our federal system peculiarly one to be defined and limited by state law. *Sosna v. Iowa*, 419 U.S. 393, 404. A state may not only "significantly interfere with decisions to enter into the marital relationship," but may in many circumstances absolutely prohibit it. Surely, for example, a State may legitimately say that no one can marry his or her sibling, that no one can marry who is not at least 14 years old, that no one can marry without first passing an examination for venereal disease, or that no one can marry who has a living husband or wife. But, just as surely, in regulating the intimate human relationship of marriage, there is a limit beyond which a State may not constitutionally go.[30]

Going further, in the conservative dissent, Rehnquist wrote, "I substantially agree with my Brother POWELL's reasons for rejecting the Court's conclusion that marriage is the sort of 'fundamental right' which must invariably trigger the strictest judicial scrutiny."[31] I cite these cases to show that the utmost respect and importance may be given to an informal and pre-political institution while maintaining that it is just for states to set boundaries for the relationship. This is not a radical position; in fact, it is quite conservative. It may be argued that some of these boundaries (age limits, disallowing family members to marry, disallowing polygamy, etc.) are for the benefit of children. If true, this lends credence to the position that the state can set certain limitations on families to protect children. Perhaps this is doubly necessary because, unlike the adults in the marriage relationship, children do not enter into any civil contract and are, thereby, particularly vulnerable to harm.

In general, I take the following from *Prince v. Com. of Massachusetts* to be correct, "the family itself is not beyond regulation in the public interest. . . . And neither rights of religion nor parenthood are beyond limitation."[32] This is apparent in the aforementioned cases where the state is justified in regulating marriages, and it is clear in cases where the state can regulate vaccination of children, school attendance, child labor laws, and termination of parental rights. The real question, then, is under what circumstances the state may justifiably intervene in the family (and there must be some limits, following the end of the section quoted from Justice Stewart's concurring opinion in *Zablocki v. Redhail*). Perhaps the best guide for when the state should intervene is articulated in *Lehr v. Robertson*, which makes a distinction between cases such as *Stanley v. Illinois* and *Caban v. Mohammed* 441 U.S. 380 (1979) and similar but importantly different cases such as *Quilloin v. Walcott* (1978):

> The difference between the developed parent-child relationship was implicated in *Stanley* and *Caban*, and the potential relationship involved in *Quilloin* and this case, is both clear and significant. When an unwed father demonstrates a full commitment to the responsibilities of parenthood by "com[ing] forward to participate in the rearing of his child," *Caban*, 441 U.S., at 392, his interest in personal contact with his child acquires substantial protection under the Due Process Clause. At that point it may be said that he "act[s] as a father toward his children." *Id.*, at 389, n. 7. But the mere existence of a biological link does not merit equivalent constitutional protection.[33]

Not all families and parents are equal, and mere biological relation does not necessarily yield parental rights. Rather, akin to what was put forth in chapter 6, parental rights derive from a commitment to and responsibility for children. However, one can only be committed toward and responsible toward children if one is able to care for them in a minimally decent way. If a parent is unable to treat children in a minimally decent way and only a biological relationship exists, then a parental right need not exist nor be recognized by the state.

4. DUE PROCESS AND A SUFFICIENT BURDEN OF PROOF

Another objection to licensing parents is that if parental rights are to be revoked then their revocation is only justified after the most demanding standard of proof has been met to show that potential parents will harm their children. This is because, it is argued, parenting is incredibly valuable, perhaps even a fundamental right. Parenting *is* extremely important, it is valued highly by many people, and we should be extremely careful when preventing people from parenting. However, holding the above extreme (though commonly held) position is dangerous and unjust. To explain why, I will examine an important case for determining what standard of proof is necessary to terminate parental rights, *Santosky v. Kramer*, and then examine a civil commitment case where the standard of proof was given great attention, *Addington v. Texas* (1979).

The liberal majority in *Santosky v. Kramer* ruled that a New York law, holding that a 'fair preponderance of the evidence' standard is sufficient to terminate parental rights upon a finding that the child is permanently neglected, was unconstitutional. It ruled, "Before a State may sever completely and irrevocably the rights of parents in their natural child, due process requires that the State support its allegations by at least clear and convincing evidence,"[34] a standard which is more demanding than the mere preponderance standard but less demanding than a beyond a reasonable doubt standard. In short, at least an intermediary standard of clear and convincing evidence is necessary to meet the Due Process Clause.

In *Addington v. Texas* a clear and convincing standard was also ruled necessary to meet the requirements of the Fourteenth Amendment in a civil commitment proceeding to commit an individual involuntarily to a mental hospital. The Court explained that the function of a standard of proof is "to allocate the risk of error between the litigants and to indicate the relative importance attached to the ultimate decision."[35] *Addington* nicely summarizes the distinction and justification between the three major standards of proof:

> At one end of the spectrum is the typical civil case involving a monetary dispute between private parties. Since society has a minimal concern with the outcome of such private suits, plantiff's burden of proof is a mere preponderance of the evidence. The litigants thus share the risk of error in roughly equal fashion.
>
> In a criminal case, on the other hand, the interests of the defendant are of such magnitude that historically and without any explicit constitutional requirement they have been protected by standards of proof designed to exclude as nearly as possible the likelihood of an erroneous judgment. In the administration of criminal justice, our society imposes almost the entire risk of error upon itself. This is accomplished by requiring under the Due Process Clause that the state prove the guilt of an accused beyond a reasonable doubt. . . .

The intermediate standard, which usually employs some combination of the words "clear," "cogent," "unequivocal," and "convincing," is less commonly used, but nonetheless "is no stranger to the civil law." *Woodby v. INS*, 385 U.S. 276, 285 (1966). . . . One typical use of the standard is in civil cases involving allegations of fraud or some other quasi-criminal wrongdoing by the defendant. The interests at stake in those cases are deemed to be more substantial than mere loss of money and some jurisdictions accordingly reduce the risk to the defendant of having his reputation tarnished erroneously by increasing the plantiff's burden of proof.[36]

I am swayed by Rehnquist's conservative dissent in *Santosky* (which Burger, White, and O'Connor joined),

When, in the context of a permanent neglect termination proceeding, the interests of the child and the State in a stable, nurturing homelife are balanced against the interests of the parents in the rearing of their child, it cannot be said that either set of interests is so clearly paramount as to require that the risk of error be allocated to one side or the other. Accordingly, a State constitutionally may conclude that the risk of error should be borne in a roughly equal fashion by use of the preponderance-of-the-evidence standard of proof.[37]

In addition to granting states autonomy in domestic issues, Rehnquist also differed significantly from the majority in how to employ the three *Eldridge* factors, which are considered the definitive conditions in determining due process: the private interests affected by the case, the risk of error created by the State's choice of procedure, and the government's interest in using such a procedure.[38] Rehnquist recognized *two* private interests in the case; therefore, the preponderance of the evidence standard would respect the due process of both the adult and the child. However, the majority focused on the liberty interest of the parents and made it clear that the case was a matter between the parents and the state. I challenge this reasoning because people often demand an extremely high burden of proof in a termination case because the loss to a parent or potential parent is extremely significant. I concede that the loss to a parent or potential parent is extremely significant. However, concurring with the dissent, I believe that in weighing these issues we should *also* weigh the interests and well-being of children by considering them private parties and not simply weighing the interests of adults and the state. A similar position is put forth by Raymond O'Brien in "An Analysis of Realistic Due Process Rights of Children Versus Parents,"

[T]he clear and convincing standard adopted by the Court deprives the child of his of her due process rights. The minimum standard should be reduced to at least one of preponderance of the evidence. Such a standard would recognize the

so-called parental presumption, i.e. the historical preference given to parents,
but give greater recognition to the rights of the child.[39]

I also agree with Rehnquist's partial justification of considering the interests
of children in such cases when he writes,

> Few could doubt that the most valuable resource of a self-governing society is
> its population of children, who will one day become adults and themselves as-
> sume the responsibility of self-governance. "A democratic society rests, for its
> continuance, upon the healthy, well-rounded growth of young people into full
> maturity as citizens, with all that implies." *Prince v. Massachusetts*, 321 U.S.
> 158, 168 (1944). Thus, "the whole community" has an interest "that children be
> both safeguarded from abuses and given opportunities for growth into free and
> independent well-developed . . . citizens." *Id.*, at 165.[40]

This beautifully captures the fact that children are fundamentally different
from adults. If not safeguarded properly, then they are at risk of improper
maturation. A self-governing society needs responsible and mature citizens.
Consequently, children must be safeguarded for their own sake and for the
sake of society. I am not arguing that the well-being interests of children
should always trump the liberty interests of parents; that would be as unjust
as the current system where the liberty interests of parents always trump the
well-being interests of children (insofar as all people are allowed to procreate). Rather, I am arguing that we should take the well-being and interests of
children into account by respecting the notion that parents have certain obligations to children and that *some* people are unable to meet these obligations
and should not parent.

Santosky and *Addington* are also instructive in other ways relating to this
book and concerning what constitutes a sufficient burden of proof for state intervention in the family. For example, in *Addington*,

> The reasonable-doubt standard is inappropriate in civil commitment proceed-
> ings because, given the uncertainties of psychiatric diagnosis, it may impose a
> burden the state cannot meet and thereby erect an unreasonable barrier to needed
> medical treatment. The state should not be required to employ a standard of
> proof that may completely undercut its efforts to further the legitimate interests
> of both the state and the patient.[41]

This is important for licensing parents because there is a large psychiatric
component to the test, a component that is subjective and fallible. However,
so long as the test yields highly accurate results, while not perfect (and I take
90 percent to be reasonable), then the legitimate interests of the state and children require intervention. Demanding certainty or not recognizing the impor-

tance of psychological health, as opposed to physical illnesses that are more objectively identifiable, harms both children and society by requiring a standard of proof that will undermine the interests of children, adults, and society.

Many laws and courts have been reluctant to allow the state to intervene in families because of the irreparability condition. It has historically been the case that if a person is sterilized then sterilization cannot be reversed and that if a child is removed due to serious abuse or neglect then one's parental rights, at least to those children, are permanently forfeited. This makes sense because removal from one's parents is likely to cause attachment problems for children, even if they have been abused or neglected by the parents who are denied custody after maltreatment. In *Santosky*, for example, it was written,

> The balance of private interests affected weighs heavily against use of such a standard [preponderance of evidence] in parental rights termination proceedings, since the private interest affected is commanding and the threatened loss is *permanent*. Once affirmed on appeal, a New York decision terminating parental rights is *final* and *irrevocable*.[42]

In Blackmun's liberal dissent (in which Brennan and Marshall joined) to *Lassiter v. Department of Social Services* (1981), a case ruling that the Constitution does not require counsel to be appointed for indigent parents in all parental status termination proceedings, it was written, "In this case, the State's aim is not simply to influence the parent-child relationship but to *extinguish* it. A termination of parental rights is both *total* and *irrevocable*."[43] Finally, in *Skinner v. Oklahoma*, a case about sterilization, "There is no redemption for the individual whom the law touches. Any experiment which the State conducts is to his *irreparable* injury. He is *forever* deprived of a basic liberty."[44] The irreparability condition, however, does not have the same force in the context of licensing parents because most will be permitted to parent, and those who fail the test will be able to re-take the test. It is not as if the sterilization were permanent or that a potential parent could not later become licensed after failing a test. Some may re-take the test and fail, but those are the people who should not be parenting. Also, because they are unable to fulfill the requisite duties to children, no right is being violated in preventing them from parenting. The Court has often valued the irreparability condition for parents, but it is rarely applied to children. However, as some children are irreparably harmed by child abuse and neglect, this would seem appropriate.[45]

Licensing parents is not a punitive system, and criminality is not at issue. If a person is unable to pass a parenting test, he is not being punished by being forbidden to parent nor is he deemed a criminal. Such descriptions would be inappropriate. I have advocated a licensing procedure, akin to many other licensing procedures. If one is denied a driver's license and not allowed to drive, then we do not claim that he has been denied due process, that he has been punished, or that he is a criminal. Nonetheless, such a misunderstanding about punishment is common. Chief Justice Burger, for example, wrote a separate concurring brief in *Lassiter* simply to emphasize this, "I join the Court's opinion and add only a few words to emphasize a factor I believe is misconceived by the dissenters. The purpose of the [parental] termination proceeding at issue here was not 'punitive.' *Post*, at 48. On the contrary, its purpose was *protective* of the child's best interests."[46] On this note, it is perhaps better to think of the parental licensing process in terms of a dependency action rather than a neglect or abuse proceeding, as practiced today. This would allow a more appropriate weighing of the interests and well-being of children. In *In re East* (1972), a case which involved parental termination of an incorrigible sixteen-year-old mother to her two-day-old child when the child had not been abused or neglected but whose environment was unlikely to meet the threshold of decency, the court opined,

> The law does not require the court to experiment with the child's welfare to see if it will suffer great detriment or harm. Succinctly stated, in a dependency action, where the child's condition or environment warrant it, the child may be removed from the custody of the mother and it is not necessary that she first be given the opportunity to prove that she can properly care for the child.[47]

The focus should be the environment of the child, as determined by parental capability and ability to provide decent parenting.

5. MILL'S BRIDGE AND PRIOR RESTRAINT

A seemingly important objection is that licensing parents will inevitably forbid some potential parents from parenting even though they would not maltreat their children if they were given a chance to parent. Some see this as a devastating objection to licensing parents, even when it is conceded that such errors will be extremely rare. To these individuals, the injustice of this error—that an individual could fail the test despite the fact that he would actually be a competent parent—is a sufficient reason to oppose licensing parents. Putting aside the fact that we do not demand certainty in other licensing procedures, this objection is usually disingenuous. This is because many who object to licensing parents when the licensing test is 90 percent accurate would also oppose licensing parents if it were 100 percent accurate. Because no potential parent would be unfairly treated in a scenario where a licensing test is infallible (where *only* those who would maltreat would be forbidden from parenting and *all* who will parent decently would be able to parent), the major justification for objecting to licensing parents seems to lie elsewhere. Part of this may be due to pragmatic concerns over whether such tests are possible, slippery slope concerns about the licensing process becoming corrupt, etc. However, the foremost legal objection is that licensing parents employs prior restraint.

It may be conceded that the state is sometimes justified in intervening in the family but that the truly troublesome part of licensing parents is that it employs prior restraint: it prohibits some actions from taking place due to highly probabilistic harm. I concede that this would generally be an unjust way to run a criminal justice system, and it is also repugnant as a general rule for all people because it is paternalistic. However, licensing parents does not charge people as criminals or punish them. To the contrary, it is for the benefit of a certain set of citizens, children, who are completely vulnerable, and no less invasive system yields an outcome that helps children akin to how licensing parents helps them. The kind of paternalism involved is not obviously repugnant. I have also shown that we accept prior restraint in the licensing of drivers, doctors, lawyers, etc. More importantly, we employ prior restraint when we license adoptive parents. Consistency entails that the prior restraint involved in licensing parents is compatible with our other accepted uses of prior restraint.[48] Yet some may still be unconvinced, so I will offer one more consideration that helps to demonstrate why, in the case of licensing parents, prior restraint is justified.

I take Mill to value liberty, for the most part, in the correct way. He understands the importance of liberty and that it should be valued accordingly, but he also understands its limitations. I have been arguing that the thesis that the desires and liberties of adults should always trump the well-being of children demonstrates an unhealthy fetish with adult liberty and freedom. Mill saw this abuse clearly,

> A person should be free to do as he likes in his own concerns, but he ought not to be free to do as he likes in acting for another, under the pretext that the affairs of the other are his own affairs. The State, while it respects the liberty of each in what specifically regards himself, is bound to maintain a vigilant control over his exercise of any power which it allows him to possess over others. This obligation is almost entirely disregarded in the case of family relations, a case in its direct influence on human happiness, more important than all other taken together.[49]

Many cite this passage because of its relevance to women, but it is also relevant to children:

> It is in the case of children that misapplied notions of liberty are a real obstacle to the fulfillment by the State of its duties. One would almost think that a man's children were supposed to be literally, and not metaphorically, a part of himself, so jealous is opinion of the smallest interference of law with his absolute and exclusive control over them.[50]

Finally, Mill writes about prior restraint and liberty explicitly,

> If either a public officer or anyone else saw a person attempting to cross a bridge which had been ascertained to be unsafe, and there were no time to warn him of his danger, they might seize him and turn him back, without any real infringement of his liberty. . . . Nonetheless, when there is not a certainty, but only a danger of mischief, no one but the person himself can judge of the sufficiency of the motive which may prompt him to incur the risk; in this case, therefore (unless he is a child, or delirious, or in some state of excitement or absorption incompatible with the full use of the reflecting faculty), he ought I conceive, to be only warned of the danger; not forcibly prevented from exposing himself to it.[51]

Prima facie, this example seems to argue that the prior restraint of licensing parents is unjustified because there is no certainty of harm, only a danger of it; therefore, prospectively bad parents should only be warned that they pose a danger to any children that they might rear. However, I believe that Mill would reject that conclusion: he is clear that the harm posed is to the bridge-walker "himself." If the bridge-walker only poses harm to himself, then I am willing to allow him to cross the bridge, even if it will almost certainly entail his death.

To capture accurately the prior restraint involved in licensing parents, consider a modified bridge case. A man approaches a bridge that authorities have estimated has a 90 percent chance of collapsing and killing those who walk on it. This man, unlike the man in Mill's example, seeks to cross the bridge with two of his extremely young children in his arms. His actions now affect his two children, in addition to himself. Because his children are extremely young, they cannot act for themselves; their father must act for them. Considering what Mill says about one's actions when they harm others, the state is justified in restraining the father from crossing the bridge and almost surely killing himself and his children. *Certainty* no longer matters; the *potential* for danger gains importance. It does not suffice merely to warn the man that he will be killing his children if he crosses a bridge. His epistemic foundation does not matter; he may believe that there really is not a 90 percent chance that the bridge will collapse, despite what the experts say. Or he may believe that a risk does exist but that the risk does not apply to him. It does not matter that he believes himself to be on a religious quest in which he must cross the bridge.[52] The modified bridge case captures something importantly different from the unmodified bridge case. The modified bridge case largely captures the issue of prior restraint involved in licensing parents. Many may object to the prior restraint involved in licensing parents, but I suspect that most people accept prior restraint in the modified bridge case.

Perhaps one can accept that the modified bridge example helps to show that the prior restraint involved in licensing parents is justified while objecting to licensing parents on other grounds. In citing Mill, it may be assumed that licensing parents is part of some major utilitarian scheme but that even a utilitarian should not come to the conclusion that I do in accepting licensing parents. The reason for this, the argument goes, is that procreating is a fundamental right and this right is sacrificed for 100 percent of the population in an attempt to preempt injury. It would thus be just only to confine the injury of not being able to procreate to the small set of people who are likely to abuse or neglect, as opposed to infringing upon the rights of everyone and thus putting the whole of society in danger. To put forth this objection is to misunderstand licensing parents. First, the objection implies that procreative rights will be completely denied, but almost all (97 percent) eligible people who seek to procreate will be able to procreate. To bar completely all persons from procreating permanently to preempt harm is absurd, but that is not what is being done. Second, it is unclear why sterilization unquestionably constitutes a harm any more than, say, forced vaccination (which will be discussed more in section 6). One may argue that we have a fundamental right to our bodies and may do as we please with our bodies (and refuse to have things done to our bodies), but that is clearly false, per the vaccination case just mentioned. Besides, even *Roe v. Wade* rejects the thesis that we may do whatever we please with our bodies. This is true even if procreation is a fundamental right because other parties are involved. Recall that the only people (with very few exceptions) who will be permanently forbidden from procreating will be those who will abuse or neglect children, and it is clear that they do not have a fundamental right to abuse or neglect children. Thirdly, it is unfeasible to forbid only those who will abuse or neglect their children from being able to procreate. That would require sterilization to be performed only on adults because it could not be determined whether one would abuse or neglect before such persons are born. That would not only require the state to sterilize forcibly individuals as adults, it would require the state to find and force all adults to take a licensing test. However, because many would seek to evade this system (and presumably many of those most likely to abuse or neglect their children), this would make licensing parents pragmatically unfeasible. What is most troubling about this objection, though, is that it speaks only to the rights of parents without addressing the rights, interests, or well-being of children.

A similar objection states that prior restraint precludes a state of affairs where the potential for virtue is maximized. I agree with the underlying premise of this argument: actions can only be virtuous if they are done freely and not from coercion. Therefore, licensing parents does limit the potential for virtue to some degree. However, it is important to consider several other things. First, most people who seek to become parents will be permitted to parent. So long as they parent, they will frequently be confronted with situations where they may either be good or bad parents, thus virtuous or not virtuous. Parenting can be extremely difficult, and simply passing a test does not mean that parenting decently will be easy or guaranteed. Secondly, those who will be forbidden from parenting will not have the freedom to be virtuous in this particular aspect of their lives. I concede that such a small chance exists, but the 90 percent risk that they will not be virtuous is too high of a risk for children and society. It helps to not simply discuss *virtue*. After all, in the case just mentioned, in 90 percent of the cases there will be actual *vice*. Our current *laissez-faire* system provides the maximum amount of *potential* virtue, as it gives all a chance to parent. However, it also yields an unacceptable amount of *actual* vice. Licensing parents seeks to strike a balance—a balance that allows as much potential virtue as possible while lowering the actualization of vice by precluding from parenting those who will almost surely perpetuate vice.

If I were writing a book about prior restraint, criminal law, and punishment, I would be forced to examine two extremes.[53] The first is articulated by Beccaria, "It is better to prevent crimes than to punish them. This is the fundamental principle of good legislation."[54] The other extreme is articulated by Kant, "Judicial punishment can never be used merely as a means to promote some other good for the criminal himself or for civil society, but instead it must in all cases be imposed on him only on the ground that he has committed a crime."[55] It may seem that licensing parents appeals only to Beccaria's theory and that it is completely at odds with Kant's, but things are not that simple. It is better to prevent crimes than to punish them, and this sometimes requires prior restraint. However, in most cases, per my earlier discussion on social disapprobation, we can prevent crimes without employing prior restraint. Licensing parents is also compatible with Kant, as articulated above, at least concerning one of the two justifications given for state intervention. The police power argument for the general welfare and stability of the state likely fails on Kant's position. Although, Kant does write that punishment can never be used *merely* to promote some other good for the criminal himself or for civil society, but licensing parents does not *merely* seek to do this. However, the *parens patriae* justification seems compatible with Kant because the state does not seek to promote some other good for the criminal himself or for civil society on that account; rather, it seeks to provide protection for a child who will be harmed by a parent. It may then be objected that Kant requires an actual crime to have been committed (or so it seems here), but this is in the context of judicial punishment, to which licensing parents is unrelated. It is unclear what Kant, or a Kantian, would have to say about the moral or legal status of licensing, which by its very nature requires some form of prior restraint. I am not advocating prior restraint as the foundation of our criminal justice system, nor am I arguing that it should be the foundation of our civil justice system. Rather, I have put forth a minimal claim: sometimes prior restraint can be justified, particularly when social disapprobation is unlikely to deter the objectionable activity when the risk is too high to the completely vulnerable. The case of licensing parents fits these conditions.

Alan Dershowitz notes, "The issue therefore is not whether prevention should play any role in a system of criminal justice—virtually all commentators (with the exception of strict Kantians) would agree that it should—but how much and what kind of role it should play."[56] I agree, but this raises an important objection: if the law is generally accepted as a preventive mechanism, why not simply punish those who perpetuate child maltreatment? Moreover, because it is commonly accepted that if one seeks to reduce the incidence of something then punishment for that thing should be increased, why not only punish those who maltreat children after they maltreat children? It should be clear why this is unlikely to work, at least in my system. All punishments seem to also harm the children of abusive parents. For example, suppose that large fines are imposed upon child abusers. This punishment would residually punish children, especially children in poor families. A more likely punishment, because people generally accept removing parents from their children after harm has occurred, is either revocation of parental rights or sentences to prison. However, in such cases children are harmed by losing their parents and needing to adapt to a new family. Nonetheless, because we are considering a forward-looking approach, let us consider increasing disincentives by using the death penalty for child abusers. Again, children are harmed in the same way as the previous cases because they would lose their parents and need to adapt to a new family. But that point would be moot if the threat of the death penalty were to lead to a significant decrease in child maltreatment. Yet it seems unlikely that even the death penalty would greatly decrease the incidence of child maltreatment. Child maltreatment is usually not something that people plan or seek to do. Child maltreatment is not usually premeditated, though cases of premeditated maltreatment do exist. Rather, it is the lack of any parental meditation at all that seems to pose the greatest threat to most children. People often perpetuate child abuse from a lack of knowing how to care for children properly or because they are unable to regulate themselves properly to provide the appropriate care. A severe threat is unlikely to eliminate these problems. Most importantly, the severe punishment thesis does not adequately consider the fact that if the law only intervenes after the harm to children has taken place then irreparable harm and the foundation for long-term harm has already taken place.

6. STERILIZATION

It may have seemed as though I discussed sterilization too quickly, especially as it relates to court rulings. Two major Supreme Court cases speak to the law as it relates to sterilization: *Buck v. Bell* (1927) and *Skinner v. Oklahoma* (1942). In *Buck v. Bell*, the plaintiff, Carrie Buck, was described as a "feeble-minded white woman who was committed to the State Colony [for Epileptics and the Feeble Minded]. . . . She is the daughter of a feeble-minded mother in the same institution, and the mother of an illegitimate feeble-minded child."[57] Oliver Wendell Holmes (in)famously delivered the opinion of the Court,

> It is better for all the world, if instead of waiting to execute degenerate offspring for a crime, or to let them starve for their imbecility, society can prevent those who are manifestly unfit for continuing their kind. The principle that sustains compulsory vaccination is broad enough to cover cutting the Fallopian tubes. Three generations of imbeciles are enough.[58]

Buck v. Bell was based on bad science at the height of the eugenics movement in the United States. The ruling permitted the sterilization of thousands of people, many of which were unjustified and would be unjustified in my licensing parents program. For this reason alone, we should take pause and be extremely careful before implementing a licensing scheme which includes sterilization. If the sterilization is based on bad science and many people are permanently sterilized needlessly (or, more accurately, permanently not desterilized), then the program would be unjust. The political process may even yield legislation that, in order to gain public acceptance, may eventually turn out to be ineffective. Nonetheless, I wish to emphasize one part of the justification in *Buck v. Bell* because I believe that it helps to show why sterilization in my licensing program is justified.

In *Buck v. Bell*, Holmes appeals to *Jacobson v. Com. of Massachusetts* (1905), which ruled that coerced vaccinations to help prevent the spread of smallpox are constitutionally permissible. It was ruled that, "a community has the right to protect itself against an epidemic of disease which threatens the safety of its members," and "The authority of the state to enact this statute is to be referred to what is commonly called the police power,—a power which the state did not surrender when becoming a member of the Union under the Constitution."[59] As smallpox was a threat, I recognize child maltreatment as a similar threat. Perhaps child maltreatment is a greater threat because it involves more than mere physical harm and death of citizens. As with licensing parents, there are risks to universal coerced vaccination. In any large population, some people will die from adverse reactions to vaccinations. Likewise, some people will naturally be immune to smallpox, and vaccination would be unnecessary for them. As with sterilization, forced vaccination requires the state to compel action to one's body, and it is generally accepted that the individual usually has a right over his body. Furthermore, for those worried about a system of licensing parents being corrupted in the hands of the government, the government could also ensure that many other things, other than what is necessary for inoculation, is contained in mandatory vaccinations. The *Jacobson* court recognized what I believe to be the proper appreciation of the role of liberty,

> [T]he liberty secured by the Constitution of the United States to every person within its jurisdiction does not import an absolute right in each person to be, at all times and in all circumstances, wholly freed from restraint. There are manifold restraints to which every person is necessarily subject for the common good. On any other basis organized society could not exist with safety to its members. Society based on the rule that each one is a law unto himself would soon be confronted with disorder and anarchy. Real liberty for all could not exist under the operation of a principle which recognizes the right of each individual person to use his own, whether in respect of his person or his property, regardless of the injury that may be done to others.[60]

Despite the similarities just articulated between sterilization and vaccination, it may be objected that smallpox is a disease that spreads but that child maltreatment is not a disease that spreads. This objection betrays a bias against the power of psychological harm and is revealing in other ways. First, child maltreatment is often physical. It is directly physical in cases of abuse, and it often has residual physical effects in cases of neglect. Second, it can be deadly; thousands of children die from maltreatment each year. Third, sometimes maltreatment is the result of a disease, sometimes physical, sometimes psychological, and sometimes both. Fourth, child maltreatment does spread, and it does so in a largely cyclical fashion. Fifth, unlike smallpox, child maltreatment often causes permanent psychological harm, an increased chance of

not becoming an ISJ, and an increased likelihood to destroy the most important informal social bonds, including trust, in society. Sixth, the exercise of
the police power seems justified in both cases when considering *Jacobson v.
Com. of Massachusetts*, "Upon the principle of self-defense, of paramount necessity, a community has the right to promote itself against an epidemic of
disease which threatens the safety of its members."[61] Though not perfect, a
strong analogy between smallpox and child maltreatment exists.

It may be objected that sterilization was later ruled unconstitutional in
Skinner v. Oklahoma (1944). Though true, sterilization was ruled unconstitutional on equal protection grounds because the law in question laid "an unequal hand on those who have committed intrinsically the same quality of offense"[62] (the person in question was convicted for a third time of a felony
involving moral turpitude but other equally serious crimes did not have the
punishment of sterilization). Therefore, contrary to later treatment of the
case,[63] *Skinner* did not overturn *Buck v. Bell* nor did it rule sterilization unconstitutional outside this particular equal protection case. Likewise, it may
be objected that sterilization is cruel and unusual punishment. However, sterilization is not being used as a punishment, certainly not punishment for a
crime. This is important because it is traditionally held that the Eighth
Amendment, which disallows cruel and unusual punishment, only applies to
those convicted of a crime. Furthermore, many psychologically healthy people voluntarily undergo sterilization, so the practice is not obviously cruel or
unusual. If forced sterilization is deemed cruel and unusual punishment, then
it seems that mandatory vaccinations are also cruel and unusual punishment.

In *Cook v. Oregon* (1972), it was argued, "The state's concern for the welfare of its citizenry extends to future generations and when there is overwhelming evidence, as there is, here, that a potential parent will be unable to
provide a proper environment for a child because of his own mental illness or
mental retardation, the state has sufficient interest to order sterilization."[64] It
may be argued that such a statement is irrelevant to licensing parents because
the subject is one who is mentally ill or mentally retarded. This neglects the
fact that many of those who will be denied licenses in my system will be mentally ill or mentally retarded. Yet for some reason coercively sterilizing the
mentally retarded, at least the severely mentally retarded, is not as controversial as coercively sterilizing those who are not mentally retarded. In fact, most
of those sterilized coercively today are mentally retarded. This is revealing.
The major justification for sterilizing some of those who are mentally retarded is that there is overwhelming evidence that they will be unable to provide an environment for children to be properly nurtured. Note that this justification is identical to that previously articulated in child dependency cases.
Again, the focus is the potential environment of the child. If we are able to

predict with 90 percent accuracy that a person will maltreat his children, this seems like overwhelming evidence that he will be unable to provide a proper environment for his children to be nurtured. If we strictly examine the welfare of children, then there should be no difference between the case of the severely mentally retarded person and the non-retarded person who is predicted to have a 90 percent chance of providing the same unacceptable environment for his children. The only major difference between the two is that the non-retarded individual presumably has a wider set of liberty interests. As such, it is sometimes argued, he should not be sterilized. This demonstrates the common intuition that, ultimately, the liberty interests of adults should trump the well-being interests of children. However, I hope to have shown that such a trend is dangerous and unjust.

CONCLUSION

It is unclear what the Founding Fathers would have thought about licensing parents and the role of state intervention in the family. However, because vast government intervention in the family took place around them, seemingly without much alarm on their part, I think it is unfair to assume that they would have categorically opposed it. If they had, it is possible that they would have been wrong to oppose it. There is no convincing case that licensing parents would necessarily be deemed a constitutional measure if it were to appear before the Supreme Court. In fact, I suspect that if it were put forth before the Supreme Court today it would be ruled unconstitutional. This would likely be true in a Court that is narrowly conservative, which should be surprising considering the conservative majority in cases like *Lehr v. Robertson* and *Lassiter v. Department of Social Services*, the conservative dissent in a case like *Santosky v. Kramer*, and Justice Rehnquist's conservative dissent in *Zablocki v. Redhail*.[65]

My goal was not to demonstrate that licensing parents follows necessarily from the Constitution. Rather, it was to show that precedent and justification exist to make it plausible as a constitutionally acceptable practice. Considering what I have identified as pervasive ageism in America, finding any precedent might be surprising to some. I have merely tried to demonstrate that licensing parents is compatible with the American system. Though seemingly innocuous, this is important. I suspect that much resistance to licensing parents manifests from a reluctance to give up some of our adult liberty. This is not unprecedented, as it took considerable time for blacks and women to gain the rights that they deserved. These changes required important losses of liberty to those already with such rights, and I suspect that this is partly why these things took a long time to achieve. Yet there is no fundamental difference between white adults, black adults, male adults, and female adults, at least differences that merit significantly different rules to apply to them. However, children *are* fundamentally different from all adults. Merely according children the same legal protection of adults is to treat them as adults, and to do this is to treat them unjustly and make them vulnerable to great harm. It took a long time for people to recognize that blacks and women deserve equal rights *and* be willing to lose some of their own liberty to secure the rights of these groups. Consequently, I suspect that a paradigm shift is necessary for us to understand that to grant children equal rights is sometimes unjust and that we should forgo some of our liberties for their benefit and for the benefit of society. With this in mind, it is imperative to recall that the preamble to the Constitution does not merely seek to "secure the Blessings of Liberty to ourselves;" it seeks to "secure the Blessings of Liberty to ourselves and our Posterity." The law sometimes treats children differently than adults, but in the most important case, parenting, a *laissez-faire* approach is taken and prior restraint is often deemed inappropriate because it is paternalistic. It is paternalistic, but it is not paternalistic in a bad way, especially once we consider that we accept prior restraint in many other cases and that it is not as radical as we commonly think.

The rights of adults always trump the rights, interests, and well-being of children insofar as *all* people are permitted to parent. I do not seek the converse, where the rights, interests, and well-being of children always trump the rights of adults. Rather, I merely seek a middle ground where we seriously consider adults and children. When we know that a prospective parent will maltreat his children, permitting him to parent does not seem to be granting the children of such a parent much value. Children do not consent to being born, do not consent to their parents, and are unable to defend themselves, and the harm that they will experience will often be deep and irreparable. Furthermore, if not protected from such abuses, these children will often not mature properly and may pose serious threats to themselves and to society.

One can object to the use of prior restraint, but if we are consistent with our other licensing practices this objection does not carry much weight. It can be objected that the potential for virtue is decreased in licensing parents, but this needs to be balanced by considerations about the actualization of vice. It can be objected that the government should not interfere with pre-political institutions, especially the very intimate association of the family. Yet we accept many restrictions on marriage, often presumably for the sake of children. It may be objected that some adults may be *potentially* harmed by being prevented from parenting even though they would not have maltreated their children, but this must be balanced by the fact that many children are *actually* harmed right now. Likewise, it is important to compare the relative harms of not being able to parent (while able to do everything else freely, including having sex and getting married), to the harm suffered by children from maltreatment. When these factors are considered, the claim that licensing parents is only justified when near-certainty is attained concerning which potential parents will maltreat their children should seem less forceful. It should seem less forceful because, in recognizing that we need to balance the rights, interests, and well-being of children, we are dealing with two parties, children and adults.

NOTES

1. I am aware that lawyers *argue* and judges write *opinions*. However, I am not merely interested in decision outcomes or opinions; I am interested in the reasoning and arguments of judges. Therefore, I will refer to the reasoning provided by judges as arguments. I am also aware that it is not always fair or helpful to label judges as conservative or liberal. However, there seems to be a clear difference between what is decided by liberal and conservative judges in family law cases. I note this only to help guide the reader; I do not believe that contemporary conservative or liberal Supreme Court justices would permit licensing parents, but I believe that conservative judges on the Supreme Court would be committed to doing so based on precedent.

2. I have yet to articulate how licensing parents would be implemented. I assume that it would be implemented by the states, not the federal government. I also assume that most states would implement the policy to avoid interstate enforcement problems. By "the state," I am referring to states, not the federal government. I examine Supreme Court cases to show that precedent exists to allow states the power to adopt the policy of licensing parents.

3. I cite this while recognizing, per *Jacobson v. Com. of Massachusetts* 197 U.S. 11 (1905), that the preamble to the Constitution is not a source of power for the federal government.

4. 262 U.S. 390.
5. 316 U.S. 535.
6. 345 U.S. 528.
7. 321 U.S. 158.
8. 455 U.S. 745. See also *Quilloin v. Walcott* 434 U.S. 246 (1978), *Smith v. Organization of Foster Families* 431 U.S. 816 (1977), *Moore v. East Cleveland* 431 U.S. 494 (1977), *Cleveland Board of Education v. Lafleur* 414 U.S. 632 (1974), *Pierce v. Society of Sisters* 268 U.S. 510 (1925), and *Meyer v. Nebraska*.
9. 410 U.S. 113. See also *Griswold v. Connecticut* 381 U.S. 479 (1965) and *Eisenstadt v. Baird* 405 U.S. 438 (1972).
10. 405 U.S. 438.

11. 497 U.S. 217.

12. 442 U.S. 584.

13. The Tenth Amendment states, "The powers not delegated to the United States by the Constitution, nor prohibited by it to the States, are reserved to the States respectively, or to the people." State authority over domestic matters has largely been a matter of tradition, but it has also sometimes been articulated as such explicitly, "there is no federal law of domestic relations, which is primarily a matter of state concern," *De Sylva v. Ballentine* 351 U.S. 570 (1956).

14. *Chapsky v. Wood* 26 Kan. 650 (1881).

15. *Chapsky v. Wood.*

16. *Whalen v. Olmstead* 61 Conn. 263; 23 A 964 (1889).

17. Raymond O'Brien, "An Analysis of Realistic Due Process Rights of Children Versus Parents," *Connecticut Law Review*, 26 (1993–1994), 1217 n. 35.

18. "Developments in the Law: The Constitution and the Family," *Harvard Law Review*, 93 (1979–1980), 1223.

19. Douglas Rendieman, "Parens Patriae: From Chancery to the Juvenile Court," *South Carolina Law Review*, 23 (1971), 211. See also Stefan A. Risenfield's "The Formative Era of American Public Assistance Law," *California Law Review,* 43 (1955).

20. 497 U.S. 417, my emphasis.

21. 463 U.S. 248.

22. *Lochner v. New York* 198 U.S. 45 (1905).

23. 410 U.S. 113.

24. 410 U.S. 113.

25. I am aware that the issue is not simply one whereby contemporary liberal justices embrace substantial due process and contemporary conservative justices reject substantial due process. Justices Thomas and Scalia are known for rejecting the doctrine of substantive due process, except when they do not. Consequently, the issue seems to be about the proper scope and applicability of substantive due process.

26. 455 U.S. 745. The Due Process Clause reads, "nor shall any State deprive any person of life, liberty, or property, without due process of law."

27. 455 U.S. 745. See also *New York Trust Co. v. Eisner* 256 U.S. 345 (1921).

28. 98 U.S. 145.

29. 125 U.S. 190. Also, "Other contracts may be modified, restricted, or enlarged, or entirely released upon by the consent of the parties. Not so with marriage. The relation, once formed, law steps in and holds parties to various obligations and liabilities. It is an institution, in the maintenance of which in its purity the public is deeply interested, for it is the foundation of the family and society," *Maynard v. Hill.*

30. 434 U.S. 374.

31. 434 U.S. 374.

32. 321 U.S. 158.

33. *Lehr v. Robertson* 463 U.S. 246.

34. 455 U.S. 745.

35. 441 U.S. 418.

36. 441 U.S. 418.

37. 455 U.S. 745.

38. See *Matthews v. Eldridge*, 424 U.S. 319 (1976).

39. 1211.

40. *Santosky v. Kramer* 455 U.S. 745.

41. 441 U.S. 418.

42. 455 U.S. 475, my emphasis.

43. 452 U.S. 18, my emphasis.

44. 316 U.S. 535.

45. This point is important to counter the objection that the law sufficiently protects children because courts today use a "best interests of the child" test to determine child custody cases that include parental termination proceedings that are a result of child maltreatment. This objection overlooks the fact that if the "best interests of the child" standard has to be applied, then the child's best interests obviously have not been sought or secured because the child has *already* often suffered irreparable harm.

46. 452 U.S. 18.

47. 32 Ohio Misc. 65, 288 N.E. 2d 343, 61 O.O. 2d 38, 61 O.O. 2d 108.

48. It seems that even libertarians can accept this. Nozick writes, "*If* some injuries are not compensable, they would not fall under a policy of being allowed so long as compensation is paid," 65–66. See also Nozick's fascinating, yet extremely complicated, discussion of preventive restraint in *Anarchy, State and Utopia* (New York: Basic Books, 1974), 142–46. And what follows, I think, is a libertarian defense of prior restraint by Mill.

49. Mill, 175.

50. Mill, 175.

51. Mill, 166.

52. In this case, I follow *Prince v. Com. of Massachusetts*, "Parents may be free to become martyrs themselves. But it does not follow that they are free, in identical circumstances, to make martyrs of their children before they have reached the age of full and legal discretion when they can make that choice for themselves," 321 U.S. 158.

53. For more on preemption in this sense, see Alan M. Dershowitz's *Preemption: A Knife that Cuts Both Ways* (New York: Norton, 2006). He says, "although preventive confinement has always been and will always be practiced, no systematic and widely accepted jurisprudence of preventive intervention has ever been developed," 56.

54. Cesare Bonesana, Marquis of Beccaria, *An Essay on Crimes and Punishments* (Philadelphia: Nicklin, 1819), 148. William Blackstone and Oliver Wendell Holmes, Jr., also seem to follow Beccaria and the tradition of preventive justice. Blackstone writes, "preventive justice is upon every principle, of reason, of humanity and of sound policy, preferable in all respects to punishing justice," and he notes, "if we consider all human punishments in a large and extended view, we shall find them all rather calculated to prevent future crimes, than to expiate the past," *Commentaries on the Laws of England* (Oxford: Clarendon Press, 1769), vol. 4, 248 and 249. Holmes writes that prevention is the "chief and only universal purpose of punishment," *The Common Law* (Boston: Little, Brown, 1881), 43.

55. Immanuel Kant, *Metaphysical Elements of Justice* (Indianapolis, IN: Hackett, 1999), 138.

56. Dershowitz, 32.

57. 274 U.S. 200.

58. 274 U.S. 200.

59. 197 U.S. 11.

60. 197 U.S. 11.

61. 197 U.S. 11.

62. 316 U.S. 535.

63. See John Lawrence Hill, "What Does it Mean to Be a 'Parent'? The Claims of Biology as the Basis for Parental Rights," *New York University Law Review*, 66 (1991), "While the case [*Skinner v. Oklahoma*] was decided on equal protection grounds, it since has been incorporated unofficially into substantive due process analysis as part of the privacy right elaborated later in *Griswold v. Connecticut* and its progeny," 366.

64. 9 Ore. App. 224; 495 P. 2d 768.

65. Consistency seems to dictate that conservative Justices would be bound to permit licensing parents, but it could be argued that *DeShaney v. Winnebago* 489 U.S. 189 (1989) would enable them to strike down parental licensing because it was argued in that case that the Due Process Clause protects against state action only. However, licensing parents is built upon more than an argument of due process.

8

Unintended Consequences, Trust, Stability, Evil, and Utopia

A large part of this book concerns how society might attain more trust and stability. However, it may be objected that my proposed solution in the last half of the book would result in less trust and stability. In this chapter, I examine this and other potential unintended effects that might question the prudence of licensing parents. I then review Tocqueville and Sumner's warnings about the danger of state intervention and their theories that policies enacted with the intent to reduce vice or increase equality often promote vice, inequality, and tyranny. These considerations lead to an analysis of whether licensing parents is futile or dangerous because it seemingly seeks to do the impossible: eliminate all evil, pain, and suffering. Some object that licensing parents is a utopian or dystopian scheme; however, this caricature is unfair. I conclude by surveying influential utopian works. By demonstrating how the family is treated in utopian works, I will show that licensing parents is not utopian, even though it seems to share much in common with utopian proposals.

1. PROTECTING OURSELVES INTO OBLIVION[1]

Earlier I claimed that an increase in trust would help enable our mostly well-ordered society to approach a completely well-ordered society. Likewise, concerning the current status of trust, Laurence Thomas laments,

> For all practical purposes, a young person today is raised not to trust any adult stranger and to view with suspicion any display of social warmth, even if that social warmth comes from someone who occupies a role that might not naturally

occasion concern. Elementary school teachers may not hug a child; and college professors trip all over themselves to make sure that their conversations with a student are not behind closed doors.[2]

The "better safe than sorry" policy to protect children from adults harming them has had the unintended consequence of trust and social warmth being decreased. The observation that we can protect children too much leads Thomas to claim, "If fewer children are harmed by horrendous adult behavior, that is obviously a good thing. But if the way in which we protect children squeezes social warmth out of society, then that, alas, is bad," and "The well-being of society requires both that the innocent be protected and that good will, respect, and trust be nourished."[3] The overarching question of this chapter stems from these claims: can licensing parents successfully protect children while nourishing goodwill, respect, trust, and stability?

Thomas nicely articulates the tension between protecting children and maintaining social warmth, but he does not provide a solution to the problem. Trusting *all* people with the responsibility of rearing children is imprudent and immoral. This is true if we hold the following: "trust involves the expectation that the one trusted has both good will and competence."[4] I take this to describe *healthy trust* if the expectation in question is reasonably justified. We do not believe that we should trust all people to parent, and this is evident in our practice of licensing adoptive parents. Likewise, we do not believe that we should trust just anyone to care for our children because we are careful about who babysits our own children. In both cases, competence matters even if the other shows goodwill. Generally speaking, if we do not know the intentions, character, or competence of a person, then granting that person trust is imprudent. It is sometimes reasonable to grant trust in situations where the stakes are small. This may enable one to assess the character and competence of the other after a few trials, thereby enabling trust with things of higher value to be justified later. Trusting another in a matter of high stakes may be only imprudent, not immoral, if the only harm posed by the trust is to oneself. However, granting trust when trust is unjustified and may negatively affect others seriously, as is the case of allowing another responsibility to care for a child, is imprudent *and* immoral. If the state is to trust citizens to parent, it should apply some kind of healthy trust standard. Just as verifying goodwill and competence are necessary conditions that should be met before responsible parents allow others to care for their children, the state should first inquire into the goodwill and competency of potential parents. Licensing parents does this, and trust is given to those who meet the minimal standards.

The healthy trust system fits nicely as a mean between two extremes. One extreme is a categorical lack of trust. This would mean a world that always assumes an absence of goodwill and where chances for goodwill and trust disappear accordingly. At the state level, this would entail the state disallowing *all* people to raise children or for the state to raise children (or for the state to monitor parents constantly). At the family level, this would entail *never* allowing another person to care for one's child and *never* letting one's child out of sight until the child is eighteen years old. Neither of these extremes promotes safety for children in a manner that maintains goodwill, respect, and trust. The other extreme is yielding trust promiscuously. At the family level, this perspective would entail that the family exercises no discretion when determining who may care for children, foregoing any oversight of a child's activities, and having no oversight over the child's associations. Neither of these extremes promotes safety for children while maintaining goodwill, respect, and trust.

Trust can be healthy or unhealthy. In most cases, either not trusting at all or trusting without knowledge of the others' goodwill or competence is unhealthy. The first experiences that children have are with their parents. Those children raised properly will naturally trust their parents in a healthy manner. This is largely why child maltreatment by parents is so developmentally devastating; it vitiates the very foundation of healthy trust. Children are then taught to trust other people close to them, such as extended family and friends of the family. This then extends to teachers, doctors, policemen, etc. The extension of trust is not arbitrary and given to others simply because of their role as an extended family member or teacher. Trust is extended for good reason. Parents know members of their family well, and they know that they will likely demonstrate goodwill and competence. For those family members without goodwill or competence, decent parents are careful to disallow their children to be with them or they oversee their children when with untrustworthy family members. It is usually justifiable for parents to teach their children to trust members of their extended family and family friends. Parents can also foster within their children a sense of healthy trust of acquaintances and strangers. For example, parents can assist children to develop a gradual sense of trust in teachers or the police by helping them to discern the proper amount of trust and when it may or may not be warranted, as well as the importance of not trusting promiscuously. Children need to trust, but not to the extent that they take candy from strangers or get into a car with strangers. If we taught children to trust this way, trust would be violated often and an ethos of distrust would quickly emerge. If the gradual process of trust is successfully completed, then the adults who emerge from it are likely to have a good foundation to trust others in society in a healthy sense. Healthy trust does not mean blindly putting faith in others at all times regardless of what is at stake; it means extending oneself in way that demonstrates goodwill and competence with the expectation that others will reciprocate. This is usually done gradually, and healthy trust is earned. This process parallels Rawls's developmental moral psychology as articulated in chapters 1 and 2 of this book, and it shows why the family is the foundation of individual and societal trust.

It may still be objected that licensing parents would cause instability because the state would diminish a sense of respect and trust in its citizens. If we question a person before letting him do something or demand that he demonstrate some kind of competence, then we are often said to disrespect or distrust him. These are not clear cases of distrust or disrespect. One clear case of distrust or disrespect would be to preclude someone from ever having an opportunity to demonstrate goodwill or competence. This would be unjustified distrust or disrespect. Justified disrespect would be preventing an individual who has had an opportunity to demonstrate goodwill or competence but has proven to be incapable or to lack goodwill from doing something. It is the second way in which we trust people to drive or practice medicine only after demonstrating competence. Licensing procedures are imperfect, and some who drive cars or practice medicine may prove to be incompetent. Yet by meeting some condition they demonstrate that others are justified in trusting them, as opposed to a system in which any person could practice medicine or drive without providing some kind of reason why we should trust him. This standard exists even with jobs that do not require licensing, as some kind of demonstration of knowledge, skills, or apprenticeship is required before a person is permitted to practice his job or practice his job independently. We do not distrust people in a categorical sense before being able to prove themselves. Rather, because healthy trust is contingent upon reasonable belief in goodwill and competence in others, we accept such tests to prevent chaos and prevent harm.[5]

Perhaps the objection is something more like this: not *assuming* that people will parent decently and forcing them to demonstrate that they will parent decently is to distrust or disrespect them, and this will cause social instability and a lack of social warmth. First, as evident in the previous paragraph, we usually accept asking people to demonstrate their goodwill and competence before granting them trust. In fact, not requiring this often demonstrates a lack of *healthy* trust. Second, licensing parents seeks only to preclude permanently the worst potential parents, those who will almost certainly abuse or neglect their children. Roughly 97 percent of eligible potential parents will be able to parent if they seek to parent. It is not as if the state would mostly prohibit the chance to parent. In almost all cases, it will provide affirmation to those who will parent. Third, proof of the state's trust will be manifested clearly because those who are permitted to parent will not have the state watching over them. The state leaves the responsibility of parenting to parents. Fourth, in leaving competent parents alone to parent, the state demonstrates a *healthy* trust in its citizens. It gives great liberty to those who are unlikely to harm other citizens while restricting the liberty of those who have demonstrated that they pose great harm to other citizens, an often deep and irreparable harm to the most vulnerable class of its citizens. Fifth, the instances of child abuse and neglect will decrease because only those judged minimally competent will be able to parent. Consequently, the state will have to intervene less frequently in families and demonstrate a lack of trust by removing children from families. Sixth, the state's test is not overly demanding. It does not require extreme pain, money, extensive training, etc. It asks only for what is, in proportion to the responsibility involved in parenting, a minimal gesture that serves as a means of being justified to trust that person. Seventh, having the ability to prevent maltreatment but not then also preventing it could cause distrust. For example, what are we to say to a girl who discovers, after being raped by her father throughout her childhood, that such abuse was preventable? It was preventable because the state had the means to know, with high probability, that her father was likely to abuse her and could have prevented her maltreatment but it did not do so. She might not fault the state for her maltreatment, and in even rarer cases she might not wish that the state licensed parents because she believes that the effects of licensing would be more harmful than what she experienced. Nonetheless, the maltreatment that she suffered will likely entail that she will never be able to trust in a fully healthy sense. She may be overly careful not to trust people so that she does not get hurt again. She may lack carefulness and grant trust where she often should not do so in order to attain something that she lacked. However, she is unlikely to trust in a healthy sense, which is compounded by a sense of unfairness if she recognizes that licensing is pervasive in other aspects of society, such as with drivers and doctors.

Perhaps the objection is that licensing parents will inadvertently cause parents to be less responsible for their children. It could be argued that parents will no longer think that it is *their* job to raise their children because the implementation of licensing parents will cause them to think that it is primarily the state's job to care for children. Yet the very thing that is emphasized in licensing parents is that it *is* the duty of parents to take care of their children. Furthermore, after passing the test, the state would not intervene in the family any more than it does now. A related argument has more force: those who have a parental license might believe that their license proves that they are good parents; therefore, parents will use their license as a shield to protect them from criticism about their parenting. This will sometimes happen. However, these parents have already been deemed likely competent parents, and a competent parent is unlikely to act in such a manner. Besides, there are reasons to believe that licensing parents would cause parents to become more responsible. Margaret Battin believes that reversible sterilization would "reverse the default mode, so to speak, in human reproduction, so that having a child would require a *deliberate* choice," and "Our ways of thinking about pregnancy and childbearing would undergo radical change—from something one accepts or rejects when it happens to something one chooses to begin."[6] It can be objected that every time a person has sex that the decision to have sex implicitly entails a duty to care for the child if a pregnancy results. Yet it does not follow that those who have sex will be able to care for a child adequately, regardless of whether the parties involved deliberately sought to create a child. Furthermore, it does not follow that children should have to be the ones who suffer from this. Licensing parents would require procreation to be deliberate. As such, following Peg Tittle, "No longer could parents say they can't be blamed, they didn't know . . . their license proves that they did."[7]

Even if licensing parents would not yield as much trust as I think that it would, there are other things to consider, such as well-being. The well-being of children, and more controversially the well-being of adults, would be improved. It may be objected that to disallow a person to parent is to disrespect that person. However, it is odd to say that people who do not have a right to parent (because unable to fulfill a duty) have been disrespected if they are prevented from parenting. The main objection has been about not trusting or respecting potential parents. Yet trust and respect is also important for children. Knowingly allowing people to harm children deeply is, in an important sense, to disrespect or inadequately value children. Some might still be bothered by the trust and respect objection. Consequently, I will put forth a hypothetical solution that grants adults the respect and trust that they deserve, at least according to the objections considered thus far. The solution is not to sterilize anybody or implement any coercive licensing scheme. The state would merely provide a licensing test to anyone who sought it in case they cared to know if they would likely maltreat their children. This scheme has many problems. It allows for extremely apathetic people, who are not likely to be decent parents, to avoid the system altogether. Those who are likely to be good parents will want to make sure that their children will be treated properly, and they will likely take the test. However, those who are apathetic, too busy, or feel as though taking a test would be demeaning (or reveal their worst fears) could still have children. Also, there is still the problem of unwanted children. As long as the sterilization element is removed, many unwanted children will continue to be born. Some children who were originally unwanted do well because their parents come to want and love them after pregnancy and the recognition that it is the parents' duty to care for the child. However, such transformations do not always happen. The egalitarian concern of this essay is not addressed; the most important inequality in society will not be improved. Finally, there is the problem of allowing a person to maltreat his child when such maltreatment could be prevented.

There are other possible unintended consequences of licensing parents. Perhaps the most important is the slippery slope objection that society would seek to prevent *all* harm. If this were to happen, then it would be harmful enough to outweigh the good produced by licensing parents. Yet if slippery slope objections to theses were always decisive, then very few, if any, theses in public policy or political philosophy could ever be accepted.

It might be objected that promiscuity would increase among those sterilized and that sexually transmitted diseases would be an insufficient disincentive to keep promiscuity from being rampant. I take this objection seriously because a high number of sexual partners is often linked to many other negatives, and detaching love from sex can arguably put a strain on monogamous marriages. However, parents in the world under consideration would be decent parents, and their children would be more likely to respect them. Consequently, if the family and society made it clear that promiscuity is dangerous, then children would be more likely not to be promiscuous. This may seem detached from reality and demonstrate a lack of understanding teenage hormones or the hormones of people in general. However, promiscuity is largely a function of family structure.[8] Even if promiscuity increased, then this vice would largely be the result of choice among sexually mature individuals. This differs fundamentally from the vice of child maltreatment, which is imposed without choice upon children.

There are also black market concerns. A market might develop for babies to be bought, or some doctors may offer black-market de-sterilizations. Assuming that the de-sterilization process was not too medically complicated, these are legitimate concerns. Yet these are secondary concerns. A major reason why I have advocated the state overseeing licensing parents is that government bureaucracy often leads to inefficiencies in time and money.[9] These are generally bad, but with respect to licensing parents they are virtues. They are virtues because the bureaucracy demands that parents deliberately choose to parent, beyond merely choosing to have sex. A waiting period can be an excellent thing, and most states still require a waiting period for marriage licenses. If people are unwilling to endure the bureaucracy involved in being permitted to parent, then that process alone will weed out many bad parents. Likewise, going on the black market to procure a child or to become de-sterilized would demonstrate that such people deeply want to rear children. The mere want or ability to procure children does not entail that one will be a good parent, but it indicates a likelihood of good parenting.

The social stigma of being denied a license is also important. Those without children might be viewed with some suspicion. However, because more people might choose not to rear children because they need not rear children due to having unintended pregnancies, this may be less of a problem. Even if it is a problem, another instance of stigmatization will be decreased. That is, the stigma of child maltreatment. Those who have been maltreated often feel as though, in some sense, they deserved their maltreatment. Also, especially in rape cases, those who have been abused are often ashamed of being maltreated and fear what others in society might think about them if their maltreatment is discovered. Of course, those who failed parental licensing tests would not need to tell others that they failed. It is also unclear that most parents who maltreat their children are important threats to other children.[10] If society were made aware of this, then less suspicion and stigma would be cast on couples without children or people who failed a licensing test.

2. STATE INTERVENTION AND EVIL

In this section, I examine whether licensing parents harms society by focusing on the well-being of children and whether I am confronting a problem that has no solution. The first concern is articulated by Tocqueville at the end of *Democracy in America*.[11] He argues that democracies are prone to tyranny when they seek more stability or equality, particularly when rights are sacrificed in seeking to secure more stability or equality. He writes,

> It is therefore above all in the democratic times we are in that the true friends of freedom and human greatness must constantly remain on their feet and ready to prevent the social power from lightly sacrificing the particular rights of some individuals to the general execution of its designs. In these times there is no citizen so obscure that it is not very dangerous to allow him to be oppressed, nor are there individual rights of so little importance that one can deliver them with impunity to arbitrariness. The reason for this is simple: when one violates the particular right of an individual in a time when the human spirit is pervaded by the importance and sanctity of rights of this kind, one does harm only to whomever one strips of it; but to violate a right like this in our day is to corrupt national mores profoundly and to put society as a whole in peril, because the very idea of these sorts of rights constantly tends to be distorted and lost among us.[12]

A typical reading of this, in the context of licensing parents, is that licensing parents is unjustified because it violates the rights of parents and this will further cause other rights to be ignored for the sake of overall social improvement. This reading demonstrates ageism and a fetish with adult liberty. The typical reading also generally assumes that *all* potential parents have rights to rear children. If this is assumed, it can then be argued that parental rights are being sacrificed for the sake of a better society. However, this does not follow because it was shown earlier that not all potential parents have rights to rear children. It is also not true that denial of a parental license is an act of "arbitrariness." Licensing parents employs a systematic testing procedure that yields highly accurate predictions. Besides, the practice of allowing any person to procreate is far more arbitrary than a licensing procedure. The rights and well-being of children are also ignored on the typical reading. This interpretation ignores the rights and well-being of children. It only values the rights of adults and fails to consider that permitting all individuals to parent arbitrarily ignores the well-being and the rights of children. But suppose, for the sake of argument, that all potential parents have a right to rear children. If true, it would still not justify thinking *only* about the adults being harmed in the example. Children should still be a part of the picture, and their rights and interests should be considered. I understand Tocqueville's concern about the danger of giving the state more power and trying to increase equality and stability. However, as was demonstrated in the first part of this book, society is largely unstable because a set of citizens are not treated as they should be. Also, Tocqueville's general concerns about too much equality being dangerous, outside the scope of the above quotation, would have served to justify opposition to many things that we cherish today as just, such as equal rights for blacks and women. Such advances made society less stable in some senses and caused others to lose liberties, but society became more just. Justice is also something that supports stability, and a stability that exists alongside injustice is not worth much.

William Graham Sumner expresses concerns similar to Tocqueville's, but from a libertarian perspective. He writes,

> The type and formula of most schemes of philanthropy or humanitarianism is this: A and B put their heads together to decide what C shall be made to do for D. The radical vice of all these schemes, from a sociological point of view, is that C is not allowed a voice in the matter, and his position, character, and interests, as well as the ultimate effects on society through C's interests are entirely overlooked. I call C the Forgotten Man.[13]

and

> [T]he characteristic of all social doctors is, that they fix their minds on some man or group of men whose case appeals to the sympathies and the imagination, and they plan remedies addressed to the particular trouble; they do not understand

that all the parts of society hold together, and that forces which are set in action
act and react throughout the whole organism, until an equilibrium is produced
by a re-adjustment of all interests and rights.[14]

In terms of licensing parents, it could be argued that C becomes the set of all
adults, or perhaps those who are prohibited from rearing children. This becomes complicated quickly because it seems that A, B, and C are adults, and
children are D. According to Sumner, C is not allowed a voice in the matter.
Yet all adults have *some* voice in society, and the policy proposed is about
adults and decided by adults. If we restrict the set to those who will be precluded from parenting, then more of a voice is still had. As long as C is considered an adult, C has more of a voice in any policy matter than any child.
No matter how little of a voice the Forgotten *Man* has, it is more than the
voice of Forgotten *Children*. Consequently, it might be more appropriate to
think of children as C (and adults as A, B, and D), especially because allowing just any person to parent often ignores the interests of children. It is fair
to object that I am playing the role of a social doctor and fixing my mind on
a group of people that appeals to one's sympathy and imagination. However,
unlike many proposals that use children merely as a sympathetic prop to sway
emotions in support of a policy, I focus on children because of their vulnerability and because they play a fundamental role in families and in society. I
do not pretend that helping children comes without a cost; I never made this
claim. I accept Sumner's theory about the social equilibrium needing to read-
just interests and rights. Helping children and families by licensing parents
comes at the cost of limiting adult liberty and freedom. For some, this is
a clear demonstration that licensing parents is unjustified; however, I am
unconvinced.

   In addition to arguing that state attempts to help a certain group inevitably
cause harm to other groups, Sumner argues that legislative efforts to prevent
vice actually protect and promote vice: "Almost all legislative effort to prevent vice is really protective of vice, because all such legislation saves the vicious man from the penalty of his vice. Nature's remedies against vice are terrible. She removes the victims without pity. A drunkard in the gutter is just
where he ought to be, according to fitness and tendency of things."[15] I agree
that government efforts to remove vice generally do more harm than good.
Furthermore, just as I saw little reason or justification for the state to restrain
a man from walking across a dangerous bridge in Mill's example (when by
himself), I generally find little reason or justification for the state to try to
help a man out of the gutter. Yet like the case of Mill's bridge, there is more
to consider. Sumner claims that nature removes the victims of vice without
pity, and he has little problem with this because the victims of vice are at

some point responsible for their vice. However, the victims of vice in child maltreatment cases are not responsible for the origin of the vice, their own maltreatment. Furthermore, the vice committed by parents when they mal-treat their children does not directly harm parents. Nature, fitness, and the ten-dency of things do not entail that if we leave the abusive parent alone that his vice will remove him without pity. The abusive parent will survive and per-petuate vice, and his vice will be felt by his children. Government attempts to prevent vice often promote vice, and vice usually takes care of itself if left alone, but it is unclear that this is applicable to the special case of child maltreatment.

Extrapolating from Sumner's last concern, it may be objected I am trying to prevent evil from existing in the world. I am trying to minimize one type of evil, but I am not trying to prevent all evil. Trying to prevent all evil would be futile, and it is unclear that it would be good if evil were eliminated. We sometimes appreciate life most after experiencing bad things because it forces us to appreciate things in a way that we did not previously. Negative things would continue to exist if we licensed parents. People would still lose jobs, relationships would still involve pain, loved ones would still die, people would still be injured, crime would still exist, war would be a possibility, etc. To those who object that there would not be enough negative things left in life, I ask why they need more than this.

I seek to minimize the instances of one particular evil: child maltreat-ment. I choose child maltreatment because humans develop gradually and are vulnerable and malleable in their early years. What humans experience in their early years largely forms who they are and of what they are capa-ble. Love is that which best enables humans to develop properly. Develop-ment rooted in love generally produces decent human beings, and this is good for these human beings and for the society of which they are a part. I do not claim that child maltreatment is the most painful experience that a person can experience, although it probably ranks among the most painful. Rather, among all other things, child maltreatment is the most efficacious in thwarting proper human development. If a person is parented decently and is provided with the love that humans need, then that person will still con-front pain in a world in which parents are licensed. However, he will be equipped to deal with others and pain in a way that is unlikely to be de-structive to himself or others. For those concerned with equality, there does not seem to be anything more important than to ensure that children receive nurturance. The chasm between those who receive proper parental nurtu-rance and love and those who do not is the most important inequality today. This is not to say that a world in which all children received proper nurtu-rance would not yield many inequalities in other aspects of life; inequality will always remain. Yet the most important equality of opportunity will have been secured through licensing parents.

It may be objected that the existence of child maltreatment is a good thing insofar as it is necessary for us to sometimes fully appreciate life. This objection is sometimes made in tandem with the observation that some people who have experienced severe child maltreatment have flourished. Some have flourished despite being maltreated, but that is not the end of the story. First, no matter how much such people flourish in particular aspects of their lives, I remain skeptical that these people are able to trust in a fully healthy way. Second, these cases are exceptions to the rule; that is what makes their stories so remarkable. Likewise, many remarkable stories of flourishing have arisen from the Holocaust, but that is not an argument that the Holocaust was good or necessary. It certainly does not follow that we should allow events like the Holocaust to happen.

Similarly, some who have been maltreated claim that if they could have lived a life without being maltreated as children, all other things being equal, they would choose to live the life that included maltreatment. This also proves little. First, this often betrays a coping mechanism. They *had* to deal with the maltreatment and, in one way or another, physically and/or psychologically had to adjust to survive the maltreatment. One way to do this is to repress the pain or the memory of it, although that is only a short-term solution. Another way is to acknowledge the maltreatment while believing that it was not that harmful. To contextualize this outside of child maltreatment, consider the child of a single parent. Single parents can provide good or bad experiences. Suppose that in this case the former is true. If asked if one would have preferred having two loving parents to one loving parent, it is not unreasonable for a person to claim that he would choose to have only one loving parent, as he did in actuality. This makes sense because the person apparently did well for himself and might even take pride in the fact that he flourished despite sometimes having to struggle where a struggle would not have been necessary if he had a second parent. Yet if he had a second loving parent, and all other things were equal, he would have almost surely had a preferable life. He may not be able to see this or understand this fully because he cannot compare the life that he had with one that he did not have, and he might choose to have only one parent out of a sense of gratefulness to the parent that he did have. However, at least on the model articulated in this book, he should choose to have two loving parents. Some may object that this demonstrates an unjustified two-parent bias, but it is generally the case that we wish children to have two decent parents rather than only one, if possible.[16] Furthermore, many children of decent two-parent families see this, especially those who had two decent parents but then lost one of their parents.

In any case, when we celebrate the exceptions to the rule who flourish despite being maltreated, it is important to remember that many do not flourish. In fact, about a third of those who are maltreated perpetrate abuse to their children. There is a large cost for the existence of the few who flourish despite being maltreated, and that cost is that many others flounder deeply.

3. UTOPIA VS. LICENSING PARENTS

Licensing parents is not a utopian or dystopian program, but it can be easily caricaturized as such. Consequently, it will be helpful to examine some common elements of dystopian works. I will consider four here: Plato's *Republic*, Yevgeny Zamyatin's *We*, Aldous Huxley's *Brave New World*, and Lois Lowry's *The Giver*.[17] Two common features of dystopias have already been discussed in this chapter. The first is that society has ridded itself of *all* things unpleasant. For example, in *Brave New World* the savage (who is from the non-dystopian world) observes,

> You got rid of them [flies and mosquitoes]. Yes, that's just like you. Getting rid of everything unpleasant instead of learning to put up with it. Whether 'tis better in the mind to suffer the slings and arrows of outrageous fortune, or to take arms against a sea of troubles and by opposing end them. . . . But you don't do either. Neither suffer nor oppose. You just abolish the slings and arrows. It's too easy.[18]

I agree; it is too easy. However, as should be clear from the last section, I do not seek to eliminate *all* things unpleasant. The second feature of dystopias that has already been discussed is a desire for complete stability. This is also evident in *Brave New World*,

> "Stability," insisted the Controller, "stability. The primal and the ultimate need. Stability. Hence all this." With a wave of his hand he indicated the gardens, the huge building of the Conditioning Centre, the naked children furtive in the undergrowth or running across the lawns.[19]

I do seek more stability. However, I do not seek a stability that requires the abolishment of all unpleasant things. I only seek stability insofar as it is compatible with justice.

A common feature of dystopias is that the government controls sex. Zamyatin, for example, reflects upon how society *used* to be, "isn't it absurd that a government (it had the nerve to call itself a government) would let sexual life proceed without the slightest control? Who, when, however much you wanted.

. . . Completely unscientific, like animals."[20] The Sexual Bureau calculated a certain number of sex days for each of its citizens and granted them a book of tickets to use when they had sex with others (because each had a right of access to others as a sexual product).[21] Licensing parents does not restrict sex. It controls who will be able to *procreate* insofar as it ensures that those who will likely maltreat their children will not bear children. However, licensing parents does not intervene with who may have sex with whom, it does not assign sex days, and it does not guarantee sexual access to other citizens.

Another feature of dystopias is that the government selects only the *best*, or best combination, of parents to reproduce. Lowry writes, "Even the Matching of Spouses was given such weighty consideration that sometimes an adult who applied to receive a spouse waited months or even *years* before a Match was approved and announced. All of the factors—disposition, energy level, intelligence, and interests—had to correspond and interact perfectly."[22] Similarly, Socrates observed, "there is a need for the best men to have intercourse as often as possible with the best women, and the reverse for the most ordinary women; and the offspring of the former must be reared but not that of the others, if the flock is going to be of the most eminent quality."[23] Licensing parents does not require that potential parents correspond and interact "perfectly." The bar is low, and all who are expected to raise children without maltreating them will be able to parent. Likewise, licensing parents does not seek to produce children of the "most eminent quality." The goal is to provide children with a reasonable opportunity to be decent human beings after having decent parents rear them.

The most important difference between a society that licensed parents and the societies depicted in dystopias is that families in my system are the heart of political society. In dystopias, families are unknown or reduced to a structure that we would not recognize as a family. Concerning Rawls's question of whether the family should be abolished, dystopias favor abolishment. In the *Republic* Socrates says, "the possession of women, marriage, and procreation of children must as far as possible be arranged according to the proverb that friends have all things in common."[24] Consequently, "All these women are to belong to all these men in common, and no woman is to live privately with any man. And the children, in their turn, will be in common, and neither will a parent know his offspring, nor a child his parent."[25] The problem of stability was addressed in the *Republic* by seeking unity via commonality, which would help to ensure a bond among citizens. However, as I noted in chapter 4, Aristotle correctly diagnosed the problem of this. That is, at least in human relationships, a belief of "my own" is important and helps to ensure that we provide the needed care for others. In a communal environment, the "my own" does not exist. It is likely that people will assume that others are fulfilling obligations. This cannot happen with childrearing because children need a consistent and stable care-taker, ideally one who cares for them narrowly and in an exclusive sense. In particular, children need parental love; it is insufficient that their basic needs are provided by other caretakers. A result of Plato's communal childrearing is that parental love is lost. Parental love is lost because the family is lost.

In *Brave New World*, the very concept of the family had been forgotten by most people. The D.H.C. asked a group of children if they knew what a parent was:

> There was an uneasy silence. Several of the boys blushed. They had not yet learned to draw the significant but often very fine distinction between smut and pure science. One, at last, had the courage to raise a hand.
> "Human beings used to be . . ." he hesitated; the blood rushed to his cheeks. "Well they used to be viviparous."
> "Quite right." The director nodded approvingly.
> "And when the babies were decanted. . . . "
> "'Born,'" came the correction.
> "Well, then they were the parents—I mean, not the babies, of course; the other ones." The poor boy was overwhelmed with confusion.
> "In brief," the Director summed up, "the parents were the father and mother." The smut that was really science fell with a crash into the boys' eye-avoiding silence. "Mother," he repeated loudly rubbing in the science; and, leaning back in his chair. "These," he said gravely, "are unpleasant facts; I know it. But then most historical facts *are* unpleasant."[26]

Huxley also shows how the ancient concept of a "family" is explained to a group of children:

> Mothers and fathers, brothers and sisters. But there were also husbands, wives, lovers. There were also monogamy and romance.
> "Though you probably don't know what those are," said Mustapha Mond.
> They shook their heads.
> Family, monogamy, romance. Everywhere exclusiveness, a narrow channeling of impulse and energy.[27]

Huxley's *Brave New World* actualized Plato's goal of unity. In doing so, he eliminated the family. In eliminating the family, he eliminated the possibility for the most intimate relationships. The exclusiveness and narrow channeling of impulse and energy, which is perhaps best exemplified as parental love, was precluded because privacy was eliminated. Privacy was eliminated to support the unity thesis, which supposedly entails stability. Stability is had, but its cost is removing love from society, thereby rendering society empty. This is relevant to when Socrates said that privacy destroys the city when "they don't utter such phrases as 'my own' and 'not my own' at the same time in the city, and similarly with respect to 'somebody else's'?"[28] Licensing parents precludes some privacy, but it does not preclude the type of privacy that would cause a sense of "my own" to be lost. Rather, it would help foster a more robust and healthier sense of "my own" if tied to a sense of duty, a change that would benefit children, parents, and society. The only privacy lost in licensing parents is in the process of sterilization and in the process of taking a licensing test. No other infringements upon privacy are made once potential parents are permitted to parent. This allows families the privacy that they need to establish and nurture intimate relationships with their children, relationships where exclusiveness is manifested from parental love. It would be less likely that the privacy of families would serve as a prison for children who are maltreated by their parents. Citizens could trust their fellow citizens' parenting skills because parents will have already demonstrated competence.

It was noted before that love was lost in Huxley and Plato. This is also true in Zamyatin, who wrote, "once Hunger had been vanquished. . . . One State mounted an attack on that other ruler of the world, Love. Finally, this element was also conquered."[29] Even in a society where the family still existed, though nominally, love is noticeably absent. The main character in *The Giver*, a boy named Jonas (who had been "chosen" to have the history of man passed down to him, unlike all other members in society) was introduced to the concept of love, and he was briefly able to feel it though the Giver (the sensation was transferred to him). After experiencing this, he hesitatingly asks his parents, "Do you love me?"[30] The response is revealing,

There was an awkward silence for a moment. Then Father gave a little chuckle. "*Jonas*. You, of all people. Precision of language, *please!*"

"What do you mean?" Jonas asked. Amusement was not at all what he had anticipated.

"Your father means that you used a very generalized word, so meaningless that it's become almost obsolete," his mother explained carefully.

Jonas stared at them. Meaningless? He had never before felt anything as meaningful as the memory.

"And of course our community can't function smoothly if people don't use precise language. You could ask, "Do you enjoy me?" The answer is 'Yes,'" his mother said.

"Or," his father suggested, "Do you take pride in my accomplishments?' And the answer is wholeheartedly 'Yes.'"

"Do you understand why it's inappropriate to use a word like 'love'?" Mother asked.

Jonas nodded. "Yes, thank you, I do," he responded slowly.

It was his first lie to his parents.[31]

Lowry beautifully captures the importance of parental love. Jonas's world has complete stability. Yet upon being able to experience what people once experienced, the thing he desired most was parental love. Some things should not be sacrificed while seeking trust and stability by means of trying to minimize child maltreatment. The foremost of these is parental love and the structure that provides it at its best, the family. Society will never be able to ensure *optimally* loving families for *all* children, and attempts to do so are likely to lead to the repugnant dystopias described above. However, I put forth a weaker question: if we can significantly reduce the incidence of child maltreatment by ensuring that children have *minimally decent* parents, should we do it? This is posed after giving great weight to this kind of observation by Socrates: "Don't you know that the beginning is the most important part of every single work and that this is especially so with anything young and tender? For at that stage it's most plastic, and each thing assimilates itself to the model whose stamp anyone wishes to give it."[32] If Socrates and most who have followed him about the fragility of children are correct, then how children are reared in political society is not trivial. If children are not reared well, and if child maltreatment is a paradigm case of bad parenting, then we can expect that those who have been maltreated, as well as their society, will suffer serious harm. Preventing child maltreatment does have a price, but it is unclear that we cannot afford it.

CONCLUSION

In the *Republic*, Socrates seeks to construct a city that meets *all* the demands of justice. However, he ultimately observes,

> [Unless] the philosophers rule as kings or those now called kings and chiefs genuinely and adequately philosophize, and political power and philosophy coincide in the same place, while the many natures now making their way to either apart from the other are by necessity excluded, there is no rest from ills for the cities, my dear Glaucon, nor I think for human kind, nor will the regime we have now described in speech ever come forth from nature, insofar as possible, and see the light of the sun.[33]

Injustice will always exist because regimes can only be improved, not perfected. I have not offered a utopia. I have not sought to meet *all* the demands of justice. I have not tried to eliminate all evil, pain, and suffering. I have not ignored the unintended consequences of licensing parents. I have not disregarded the rights and interests of adults. And I have not overlooked the fact that state solutions to remove vice or promote equality are often dangerous and counterproductive. I have retained the most important institution in society—the family. Furthermore, I have articulated what family structure is required if we seek to become more just and improve society. The family secures the remarkable power of parental love. A certain private space is needed for the intimate nature of parental love and the family to work at its best. Licensing parents respects this space. When this space is respected and children have decent parents, then children have the foundation to flourish, to become ISJs, and to develop a healthy sense of trust. These are secured while nourishing goodwill, respect, trust, and stability. The importance of parental duties to children must be recognized if we seek to create a better society or a society that provides genuine equality of opportunity. The clearest violation of parental duty is child maltreatment, and child maltreatment is that which is most efficacious in hindering healthy child development. Decent families and decent parents are necessary for children and society. If we are willing to secure these things, it will require us to sacrifice some adult liberty. However, in sacrificing some of this liberty, we might gain so much more in well-being, opportunity, stability, trust, and justice.

NOTES

1. I borrow this title from a posting by Laurence Thomas at www.moralhealth.com on August 5, 2005. Its original title was "Protecting Ourselves into Oblivion: Avoiding Pain and Trust is a Lose-Lose Situation," at www.moralhealth.com/blog/_archives/2005/8/5/1110624.html (6 Apr. 2008).

2. Thomas, "Protecting Ourselves."

3. Thomas, "Protecting Ourselves."

4. Amy Mullin, "Trust, Social Norms, and Motherhood," *Journal of Social Philosophy*, 36 (Fall 2005), 317. Mullin is paraphrasing Annette Baier's account in "Trust and Antitrust," *Ethics*, 96 (1986), 259.

5. It may be objected that parenting is not a "job"; therefore, the above analogies are unfair. Yet being a driver is not a job, and it fits the analogy. The objection that parenting is not a "job" is a red herring. What clearly ties the licensing of drivers, doctors, and parents together is that all entail considerable responsibility because competence is needed to perform each of them. If the responsibility to act is given to someone who is incompetent in the task in question, then serious harm can result to himself or others. This concept is also applicable in non-licensing schemes, such as security checkpoints, where threat levels are assessed before trust is granted.

6. "Sex and Consequences: World Population Growth vs. Reproductive Rights," *Philosophic Exchange*, 27 (1997), 17 and 30, my emphasis.

7. "Introduction," in Peg Tittle, ed. *Should Parents Be Licensed? Debating the Issues*, (Amherst, NY: Prometheus, 2004), 16.

8. For example, see R. L. Collins, M. N. Elliott, S. H. Berry, D. E. Kanouse, D. Kunkel, and S. B. Hunter, "Watching Sex on Television Predicts Adolescent Initiation of Sexual Behavior," *Pediatrics*, 114 (2004); C. Cubbin, J. Santelli, C. D. Brindis, and P. Braveman, "Neighborhood Context and Sexual Behaviors Among Adolescents: Findings from the National Longitudinal Study of Adolescent Health," *Perspectives on Sexual and Reproductive Health*, 37 (2005); C. E. Kaestle and C. T. Helpern, "Sexual Activity Among Adolescents in Romantic Relationships with Friends, Acquaintances, or Strangers," *Archives of Pediatric and Adolescent Medicine*, 159 (2005).

9. It may be objected that corruption is another feature of government bureaucracy. I already addressed this earlier in the book. Besides, the corruption objection is not clearly decisive because significant corruption also exists in the current system whereby just anyone can parent. If corruption did not exist, there would be no problem of child maltreatment in the first place.

10. This anticipates a related objection that people who abuse their own children will abuse children no matter what; therefore, if they cannot have children of their own, then they will actively seek out children of other people to abuse. This seems unlikely. First, almost all child maltreatment happens within the family. Second, most child abuse is not premeditated and does not result from a desire to maltreat children. Third, child maltreatment is strongly correlated with stress. If a person does not have the additional stress of raising a child, then it seems reasonable to assume that the likelihood of maltreating goes down accordingly. Fourth, not having children will enable those who are forbidden from parenting to take better care of their own lives.

11. See especially, Vol. 2, Part 4, chapters 2–8. At the other extreme, Socrates notes that democracies are prone to tyranny when too much liberty is sought, "Too much freedom seems to change into nothing but too much slavery, both for private men and city . . . tyranny is probably established out of no other regime than democracy—the greatest and most savage slavery out of the extreme of freedom," Plato, *The Republic*, Book VIII, 564a2–7. Rousseau has similar worries.

12. Tocqueville, 670.

13. *What Social Classes Owe to Each Other* (New York: Harper and Brothers Publishers, 1911), 123.

14. *What Social Classes Owe*, 123–24.

15. *What Social Classes Owe*, 131.

16. Likewise, we generally believe that it is better to be able to see or hear than to not be able to see or hear. Yet there is a movement in the deaf community that rejects the use of cochlear implants (and I suspect that a similar movement will eventually take place in the blind community). This is understandable, although according to the above argument it proves little.

17. I consider all of these to be dystopias, not utopias. The *Republic* is more complicated because Socrates puts his model forth as an ideal while recognizing that it will never be attainable.

18. Huxley, *Brave New World* (New York: Perennial Classics, 1998), 238.

19. Huxley, 43.

20. Yevgeny Zamyatin, *We*, trans. Clarence Brown (New York, Penguin, 1993), 14.

21. Zamyatin, 10 and 22. The latter feature was to eliminate envy.

22. Lowry, *The Giver* (New York: Laurel Leaf, 1993), 48.

23. V, 459d6–e1. Also, "they will take the offspring of the good and bring them into the pen to certain nurses who live apart in a certain section of the city. And those of the worse, and any of the others born deformed, they will hide away in an unspeakable and unseen place, as is seemly," V, 460c1–5.

24. IV, 423e6–424a1.

25. V, 457c11–d3.

26. Huxley, 23–24.

27. Huxley, 40.

28. *The Republic*, V, 462c3–8.

29. Zamyatin, 22.

30. Lowry, 127.

31. Lowry, 127.

32. II, 377a11–b3.

33. V, 473c10–e2.

Epilogue

I decided to write a book on licensing parents after reading Hugh LaFollette's "Licensing Parents" and finding his conclusion that we should license parents repugnant to my moral sensibilities. I originally sought to articulate precisely where and why he was wrong. This became increasingly difficult after extensive research and contemplation revealed that LaFollette was more right than wrong and that my initial objections were founded mostly on unjustifiable dogmatic assumptions. My project then shifted to providing a comprehensive justification of licensing parents. I believe that this attempt is useful because putting forth the strongest possible arguments for all positions to assess their merits in an intellectually honest manner is integral to philosophy. I am willing to concede that licensing parents may not be the best solution to the problems discussed in this book, and I am not wedded to the idea that we should license parents. Yet I hope to have shown how licensing parents might be permissible. I genuinely hope that a less invasive but equally effective solution is possible, and I would favor such an alternative were it proposed. Unfortunately, effective alternatives do not seem prevalent, especially if we recognize the severe and irreparable harm often posed by child maltreatment. If one is unconvinced by my solution, I shift the burden of proof and ask why licensing parents is unjustified and what solution would be less invasive but equally effective as a solution to the problems posed in this book.

Even if one were to disagree with my solution but be unable to provide an alternative, I hope I have raised awareness regarding the danger that child maltreatment poses—both for children and for the stability of society. With the latter, it may be helpful to realize why I raised the subject of child maltreatment. My other concerns were to increase an equality of opportunity and create more political stability by moving from a mostly well-ordered society towards a completely well-ordered society. Assuming that a formally well-ordered society exists insofar as rights are mostly secured properly, I asked how to improve the informal well-ordering of society by inquiring how to improve the character of citizens. Before discussing this further, I recognize that some may object to my conclusion because they are satisfied with the *status quo*. They may concede that we live in an imperfect society, but that some attempts to make the world better yield greater harm than that which they seek to overcome. Such harm is possible, but this book asks what should be done *if* we sought to improve society. The objection that the *status quo* is all that we can hope for may be true, but it is a position that itself requires justification because of the amount of harm to children that exists today. Furthermore, that objection is not a direct objection to this book.

In focusing on the informal well-ordering of society, I took the problem of psychological stability seriously. Furthermore, I inquired how to increase societal trust and cooperation. The solution is to ensure that there are more decent and fewer indecent people in society. This requires citizens who are not easily prone to Rawlsian envy and who have a sufficiently robust self-respect to preclude them from harming others. Some people harm from a conscious and free choice, but others harm because, in an important sense, they are unable to choose the morally appropriate action. Consequently, I have argued that it is important to foster ISJs who desire to act according to the dictates of justice and who possess the self-respect to make this desire efficacious. The problem is then how to allow humans to develop into ISJs, and the solution is to provide children with parental love. Parental love is a tremendous force, and its role needs to be better appreciated in political philosophy. If parental love is not a necessary condition for healthy psychological and moral development, then it is the closest thing to a necessary condition that exists. Yet parental love is an insufficient condition for healthy child development. Parents must also be competent. It is of the utmost importance that political philosophy takes families, as well as how parents love and treat their children, seriously. Public affirmation of rights and liberties is important, but the private affirmation of love is more important—especially once the public affirmation of rights and liberties is secured. Likewise, equal rights and liberties provide an excellent space for those with self-respect to flourish. Yet equal rights and liberties will not help those without self-respect. A free society requires that citizens have good character, fellow feeling, and trust. These things are influenced greatly in childhood.

The key to producing ISJs is to nurture children properly, and the surest way to create non-ISJs is to maltreat children. This does not mean that children who are maltreated will necessarily become non-ISJs, but families have the most important influence over how humans develop—for better or worse.

Conservatives are often focused on securing the traditional nuclear family to such an extent that they overlook the fact that family structure is irrelevant for the well-being children if the parents are incapable of decent parenting. Liberals tend to be more tolerant of all family structures, and they tend to leave adults free to do as they choose so long as their liberty is consistent with a similar liberty for (adult) others. Yet not all family structures are acceptable for decent childrearing. This tolerance for all family structures is also in tension with a liberal desire to remove inequalities in life that are not a result of irresponsibility. I advocated the neo-nuclear family because it provides the kind of love, stability, privacy, and intimacy that is needed to develop the self-identity requisite to become an ISJ. Rather than abolish the family for the sake of equality, I argued that we should seek to promote the family in a healthy form. If we are to ensure some kind of share at the beginning of life that is capable of providing a significant foundation that lasts throughout one's life regardless of one's later luck in life, ensuring a good family is even more important than providing financial and educational assistance. Living in poverty with good parents is unlikely to yield significant harm, but maltreated children are likely to be harmed regardless of their economic status. Securing excellent parents for all children is impossible. I advocated a more realizable goal: providing children with minimally decent parents. What is minimally decent may seem controversial, but I located something that all people find indecent—child maltreatment. Child maltreatment is also important because it is the most efficacious means of thwarting healthy human development. The most important equalisandum is minimally decent parents for children, hence my advocating family egalitarianism. Licensing parents is a mechanism to implement family egalitarianism.

The necessary conditions for justifiable implementation of the system of licensing parents have been met. First, I demonstrated that the problem of child maltreatment is sufficiently destructive to be a compelling interest of the state. Second, I ensured that the kind of intimacy and privacy that are important within the family remain untouched; it also remains the duty of families, not the state, to rear children. Third, I put forth the plausibility of a test that can predict which potential parents will likely maltreat their children with reasonable precision. Fourth, I articulated a means to implement the policy effectively. Fifth, I demonstrated that prospective parents do not necessarily have an indefeasible right to parent. Sixth, I showed that no other less invasive solutions seem to yield the similar desired effects of licensing parents. Furthermore, precedent for licensing parents exists in our adoption practices, as well as our practice of licensing things that require a certain competence so as not to impose a serious danger to oneself or others. These speak to a further concern about prior restraint.

Licensing parents can successfully protect children while nourishing goodwill, respect, trust, and stability. Similarly, licensing parents can help promote healthy trust while better balancing the rights and duties between adults and children, as well as balancing equality and liberty. A major concern throughout this book was to expose the danger of thinking about the parent-child relationship only in terms of rights. When duties and obligations are taken seriously, the ethical and political status of the family changes considerably. This is particularly true when the asymmetrical relationship between adults and children is understood and the vulnerability of children is exposed. Decent childrearing is important for children to develop properly, but the opportunity to rear children is also central to the lives of most adults. Childrearing plays a major role in the lives and life plans of children and adults. We should give those who seek to rear children the opportunity to parent if they demonstrate that they are competent to parent. If a person deeply seeks to rear children but fails a licensing test, then we should give him opportunities to retake the test because people can change. However, if a person cannot or will not ever take and pass a licensing test, then the risk of permitting such a person to parent is too high to children and society. The negative aspect of this book, precluding a few people from parenting, should not overshadow the positive: parental love is one of the most powerful gifts that can be given, and when this gift is given by a competent parent then his child has a secure foundation to be a decent human being and citizen. Licensing parents does not eliminate the family, the love, or the intimacy and privacy needed for humans to flourish; it helps secure the possibility of their fruition.

Bibliography

Aaronfreed, Justin. "Moral Development from the Standpoint of a General Psychological Theory." in Bill Puka, ed. *Moral Development: Defining Perspectives in Moral Development*, Vol. 1. New York: Garland Publishing, 1994.

Addington v. Texas, 441 U.S. 418 (1979).

Aiken, William, and Hugh LaFollette, eds. *Whose Child? Children's Rights, Parental Authority, and State Power*. Totowa, NJ: Rowman and Littlefield, 1980.

Ainsworth, Mary D. Salter, Mary C. Blehar, Everett Waters, and Sally Wall. *Patterns of Attachment: A Psychological Study of the Strange Situation*. Hillsdale, NJ: Erlbaum, 1978.

Alston, Philip, Stephen Parker, and John Seymour, eds. *Children and the Law*. Oxford: Oxford University Press, 1992.

Altemeir, William A., Susan O'Connor, Peter Vietze, Howard Sandler, and Kathryn Sherrod. "Prediction of Child Abuse: A Prospective Study of Feasibility." *Child Abuse and Neglect* 8 (1984).

Anderson, Elizabeth. "Is Women's Labor a Commodity?" *Philosophy and Public Affairs* 19 (1990).

———. "What Is the Point of Equality?" *Ethics* 109 (1999).

Anderson, Stephen C., and Michael L. Lauderdale. "Characteristics of Abusive Parents: A Look at Self-Esteem." *Child Abuse and Neglect* 6 (1982).

Anthony, E. James, and Bertram J. Cohler. *The Invulnerable Child*. New York: The Guilford Press, 1987.

Archard, David. *Children: Rights and Childhood*. London: Routledge, 2004.

Aries, Phillippe. *Centuries of Childhood: A Social History of Family Life*. New York: Vintage, 1962.

Aristophanes. *Lysistrata*. Ed. Jeffrey Henderson. Oxford: Oxford University Press, 1990.

Aristotle. *Nicomachean Ethics*. Trans. Martin Ostwald. Englewood Cliffs, NJ: Prentice Hall, 1962.

——. *Politics.* Trans. T. A. Sinclair. London: Penguin Books, 1992.

Arneson, Richard. "Equality and Equality of Opportunity of Welfare." In Louis Pojman and Robert Westmoreland, eds. *Equality: Selected Readings.* New York: Oxford University Press, 1997.

——. "Equality and Equal Opportunity for Welfare." *Philosophical Studies,* 56 (1989).

Axinn, W. G., and A. Thornton. "The Relationship Between Cohabitation and Divorce: Selectivity or Causal Influence?" *Demography* 29 (1992).

Ayoub, Catherine, Marion M. Jacewitz, Ruth G. Gold, and Joel S. Milner. "Assessment of a Program's Effectiveness in Selecting Individuals 'At Risk' for Problems in Parenting." *Journal of Clinical Psychology* 39 (1983).

Baier, Annette. "Trust and Antitrust." *Ethics* 96 (1986).

Battin, Margaret P. "Sex and Consequences: World Population Growth vs. Reproductive Rights." *Philosophic Exchange* 27 (1997).

Bonesana, Cesare, Marquis of Beccaria. *An Essay on Crimes and Punishments.* Philadelphia: Nicklin, 1819.

Becker, Gary. *A Treatise on the Family.* Cambridge, MA: Harvard University Press, 1981.

Becker, Gary S., and Nigel Tomes. "Human Capital and the Rise and the Fall of Families." *Journal of Labor Economics* 4 (1986), S1.

Belsky, J. "Child Maltreatment: An Ecological Integration." *American Psychologist* 35 (1980).

Belsky, Jay, Sara R. Jaffee, Judith Sligo, Lianne Woodward, and Phil A. Silva. "Intergenerational Transmission of Warm-Sensitive Parenting: A Prospective Study of Mothers and Fathers of 3-Year Olds." *Child Development* 7 (2005).

Benatar, David. "Why It Is Better Never to Come Into Existence." *American Philosophical Quarterly* 34 (1997).

Benedict, Mary I., Roger B. White, Donald A. Cornley. "Maternal Perinatal Risk Factors and Child Abuse." *Child Abuse and Neglect* 9 (1985).

Benson, Peter L., Anu R. Sharma, and Eugene L. Roehlkepartain. *Growing Up Adopted: A Portrait of Adolescents and Their Families.* Minneapolis, MN: Search Institute, 1994.

Ben-Ze'ev, Aaron. "Envy and Inequality." *The Journal of Philosophy* 89 (1992).

Berger, Lawrence M. "Income, Family Characteristics, and Physical Violence Toward Children." *Child Abuse and Neglect* 29 (2005).

Bergner, Raymond A., Leslie K. Delgado, and Daniel Graybill. "Finkelhor's Risk Factor Checklist: A Cross-Validation Study." *Child Abuse and Neglect* 18 (1994).

Bernick, Michael. "A Note on Promoting Self-Esteem." *Political Theory* 6 (1978).

Bettelheim, Bruno. *The Informed Heart: Autonomy in a Mass Age.* Glencoe, IL: Free Press, 1961.

Blackstone, William. *Commentaries on the Laws of England.* Oxford: Clarendon Press, 1769.

Blustein, Jeffrey. "Childrearing and Family Interests." In Onora O'Neill and William Ruddick, eds. *Having Children: Philosophical and Legal Reflections on Parenthood.* New York: Oxford University Press, 1979.

———. *Parents and Children: The Ethics of the Family*. Oxford: Oxford University Press, 1982.

Bobo, L., and R. A. Smith. "Antipoverty Policy, Affirmative Action, and Racial Attitudes." In Sheldon H. Danziger, Gary Sandefur, and Daniel Weinberg, eds. *Confronting Poverty: Prescriptions for Change*. Cambridge: Cambridge University Press, 1994.

Bolger, Kerry E., and Charlotte J. Patterson. "Developmental Pathways from Child Maltreatment to Peer Rejection." *Child Development* 72 (2001).

Bolger, Kerry E., Charlotte Patterson, and Janis B. Kupersmidt. "Peer Relationships and Self-Esteem among Children Who Have Been Maltreated." *Child Development* 69 (1998).

Booth, A., and D. R. Johnson. "Premarital Cohabitation and Marital Success." *Journal of Family Issues* 9 (1988).

Borders, L. DiAnne, Lynda K. Black, and B. Kay Pasley. "Are Adopted Children and Their Parents at Greater Risk for Negative Outcomes?" *Family Relations* 47 (1998).

Bowlby, John. *Child Care and the Growth of Love*. Baltimore: Penguin Books, 1957.

Bremer, J. D., P. Randall, T. M. Scott, S. Capelli, R. Delaney, G. McCarthy, and D. S. Charney. "Deficits in Short-Term Memory in Adult Survivors of Childhood Abuse." *Psychiatry Research* 59 (1995).

Bremer, J. D., P. Randall, E. Vermetten, L. Staib, R. A. Bronen, C. Mazure, S. Capelli, G. McCarthy, R. B. Innis, and D. S. Charney. "Magnetic Resonance Imaging-Based Measurement of Hippocampal Volume in Posttraumatic Stress Disorder Related to Childhood Physical and Sexual Abuse: A Preliminary Report." *Biological Psychiatry* 41 (1999).

Brennan, Samantha, and Robert Noggle. "The Moral Status of Children: Children's Rights, Parents' Rights, and Family Justice." *Social Theory and Practice* 23 (1997).

Brofenbrenner, U. "Toward an Experimental Ecology of Human Development." *American Psychologist* 32 (1977).

Brown, Jocelyn, Patricia Cohen, Jeffrey G. Johnson, and Suzanne Salzinger. "A Longitudinal Analysis of Risk Factors for Child Maltreatment: Findings of a 17-Year Prospective Study of Officially Recorded and Self-Reported Child Abuse and Neglect." *Child Abuse and Neglect* 22 (1998).

Brown, Susan L. "Family Structure and Child Well-Being: The Significance of Parental Contribution." *Journal of Marriage and the Family* 66 (2004).

Brown, Susan L., and Alan Booth. "Cohabiting Versus Marriage: A Comparison of Relationship Quality." *Journal of Marriage and the Family* 58 (1996).

Brownridge, D. A., and S. S. Halli. "'Living in Sin' and Sinful Living: Toward Filling a Gap in the Explanation of Violence Against Women." *Aggressive and Violent Behavior* 5 (2000).

Brunner, J., and A. Gaston, eds. *Human Growth and Development*. Oxford: Clarendon Press, 1978.

Buck v. Bell, 274 U.S. 200 (1927).

Butler, Samuel. *Fifteen Sermons*. Charlottesville, VA: Lincoln-Rembrandt Publishing, 1993.

Caban v. Mohammed, 441 U.S. 380 (1979).

Campbell, Bernard, ed. *Sexual Selection and the Descent of Man 1871–1971.* Chicago: Aldine Publishing Company, 1972.

Cambell, Tom D. "The Rights of the Minor: as Person, as Child, as Juvenile, as Future Adult." In Philip Alston, Stephen Parker, and John Seymour, eds. *Children and the Law.* Oxford: Oxford University Press, 1992.

Caplan, Gerald. *Principles of Preventative Psychiatry.* New York: Basic Books, 1964.

Chaffin, Mark, and Linda Anne Valle. "Dynamic Prediction Characteristics of the Child Abuse Potential Inventory." *Child Abuse and Neglect* 27 (2003).

Chapsky v. Wood, 26 Kan. 650 (1881).

Chasteen, Edgar R. *The Case for Compulsory Birth Control.* Englewood Cliffs, NJ: Prentice-Hall, 1972.

Chen, Zeng-Yin, and Howard B. Kaplan. "Intergenerational Transmission of Constructive Parenting." *Journal of Marriage and Family* 63 (2001).

Child Maltreatment: U.S. Department of Health and Human Resources, Administration on Children, Youth, and Families. Washington, DC: U.S. Government Printing Office, 2006.

Cicchetti, Dante, and Vicki Carlson, eds. *Child Maltreatment: Theory and Research on the Causes and Consequences of Child Abuse and Neglect.* Cambridge: Cambridge University Press, 1989.

Clayton, Matthew, and Andrew Williams, eds. *The Idea of Equality.* New York: St. Martin's Press, 2000.

Cleveland Board of Education v. Lafleur, 414 U.S. 632 (1974).

Cleveland, Michael J., Frederick X. Gibbons, Meg Gerrard, Elizabeth A. Pomery, Gene H. Brody. "The Impact of Parenting on Risk Cognitions and Risk Behavior: A Study of Mediation and Moderation in a Panel of African American Adolescents." *Child Development* 76 (2005).

Cohen, G. A. "On the Currency of Egalitarian Justice." *Ethics* 109 (1989).

Cohen, Joshua, Martha Nussbaum, and Matthew Howard, eds. *Is Multiculturalism Bad for Women?* Princeton, NJ: Princeton University Press, 1999.

Coie, John, Robert Terry, Kari Lenox, John Lochman, and Clarine Hyman. "Childhood Rejection and Aggression as Predictors of Stable Patterns of Adolescent Disorder." *Development and Psychopathology* 7 (1995).

Coleman, Rebecca A., and Cathy Spatz Widom. "Childhood Abuse and Neglect and Adult Intimate Relationships: A Prospective Study." *Child Abuse and Neglect* 28 (2004).

Collins, R. L., M. N. Elliott, S. H. Berry, D. E. Kanouse, D. Kunkel, and S. B. Hunter. "Watching Sex on Television Predicts Adolescent Initiation of Sexual Behavior." *Pediatrics* 114 (2004).

Conger, K. J., M. A. Rutter, and R. D. Conger. "The Role of Economic Pressure in the Lives of Parents and Their Adolescents: The Family Stress Model." In Lisa J. Crockett and Rainer K. Silbereisen, eds. *Negotiating Adolescence in Times of Social Change.* New York: Cambridge University Press, 2000.

Conger, R. D., K. J. Conger, G. H. Elder, F. O. Lorenz, R. L. Simons, and L. B. Whitbeck. "A Family Process Model of Economic Hardship and Adjustment of Early Adolescent Boys." *Child Development* 63 (1992).

Conger, R. D., G. R. Patterson, and X. Ge. "It Takes Two to Replicate: A Mediational Model for the Impact of Parents' Stress on Adolescent Adjustment." *Child Development* 66 (1995).

Cook v. Oregon, 9 Ore. App. 224; 495 P. 2d 768 (1972).

Cowen, E. L., P. A. Wyman, W. C. Work, J. Y. Kim, D. B. Fagen, and K. B. Magnus. "Follow-Up Study of Young Stress-Affected and Stress-Resilient Urban Children." *Development and Psychopathology* 9 (1997).

Crockett, Lisa J., and Rainer K. Silbereisen, eds. *Negotiating Adolescence in Times of Social Change*. Cambridge: Cambridge University Press, 2000.

Cubbin, C., J. Santelli, C. D. Brindis, and P. Braveman. "Neighborhood Context and Sexual Behaviors Among Adolescents: Findings from the National Longitudinal Study of Adolescent Health." *Perspectives on Sexual and Reproductive Health* 37 (2005).

Daly, Martin, and Margo Wilson. "Discriminative Parental Solicitude: A Biological Perspective." *Journal of Marriage and the Family* 42 (May 1980).

Daniel, Jessica H., Eli H. Newberger, Robert B. Reed, and Milton Kotelchuck. "Child Abuse Screening: Implications of the Limited Predictive Power of Abuse Discriminants from a Controlled Family Study of Pediatric Social Illness." *Child Abuse and Neglect* 2 (1978).

Danziger, Sheldon H., Gary Sandefur, and Daniel Weinberg, eds. *Confronting Poverty: Prescriptions for Change*. Cambridge: Cambridge University Press, 1994.

Darwall, Stephen L. "Two Kinds of Self-Respect." *Ethics* 88 (1977).

De Bellis, Michael D. "Developmental Traumatology: The Psychobiological Development of Maltreated Children and Its Implications for Research." *Development and Psychopathology* 13 (2001).

De Bellis, M. D., A. S. Baum, B. Birmaher, M. S. Keshavan, C. H. Eccard, A. M. Boring, F. J. Jenkins, and N. D. Ryan. "Developmental Traumatology Part I: Biological Stress Systems." *Biological Psychiatry* 45 (1999).

De Bellis, M. D., and F. W. Putnam. "The Psychobiology of Childhood Maltreatment." *Child and Adolescent Psychiatric Clinics of North America* 3 (1994).

De Bellis, M. D., M. Keshavan, D. B. Clark, B. J. Casey, J. Giedd, A. M. Boring, K. Frustaci, and N. D. Ryan. "A.E. Bennett Research Award. Developmental Traumatology Part II: Brain Development." *Biological Psychiatry* 45 (1999).

Deigh, John. "Shame and Self-Esteem: A Critique." *Ethics* 93 (1983).

DePanfilis, Diance. *Child Neglect: A Guide for Prevention, Assessment, and Intervention*. U.S. Department of Health and Human Services Administration for Children and Families. www.childwelfare.gov/pubs/usermanuals/neglect/neglect.pdf (2006).

Dershowitz, Alan M. *Preemption: A Knife that Cuts Both Ways*. New York: Norton, 2006.

DeShaney v. Winnebago, 489 U.S. 189 (1989).

De Sylva v. Ballentine, 351 U.S. 570 (1956).

"Developments in the Law: The Constitution and the Family." *Harvard Law Review* 93 (1979–1980).

Dillon, Robin S., ed. *Dignity, Character, and Self-Respect*. New York: Routledge, 1995.

Djerassi, Carl. "Birth Control After 1984." *Science* 169 (Sept. 1970).

——. "Prognosis for the Development of New Chemical Birth-Control Agents." *Science* 166 (October 1969).

Disbrow, M. A., H. Doerr, and C. Caulfield. "Measuring the Components of Parents' Potential for Child Abuse and Neglect." *Child Abuse and Neglect* 1 (1977).

Douglass, Frederick. *Narrative of the Life of Frederick Douglass: An American Slave, Written By Himself*. Ed. Benjamin Quarles. Cambridge, MA: Harvard University Press, 1988.

Dugan, Timothy F., and Robert Coles, eds. *The Children of Our Times: Studies in the Development of Resilience*. New York: Brunner/Mazel, 1989.

Duncan, Greg J., and Katherine Magnuson. "Promoting the Healthy Development of Young Children." In Isabell Sawhill, ed. *One Percent for the Kids: New Policies, Brighter Futures for America's Children*. Washington, DC: The Brookings Institution, 2003.

Eisenstadt v. Baird, 405 U.S. 438 (1972).

Ekelaar, John. "The Importance of Thinking that Children Have Rights." In Philip Alston, Stephen Parker, and John Seymour, eds. *Children and the Law*. Oxford: Oxford University Press, 1992.

Ermisch, John F. *An Economic Analysis of the Family*. Princeton, NJ: Princeton University Press, 2003.

Éthier, Louise S., Jean-Pascal Lemelin, and Carl Lacharité. "A Longitudinal Study of the Effects of Chronic Maltreatment on Children's Behavioral and Emotional Problems." *Child Abuse and Neglect* 28 (2004).

Eyal, Nir. "'Perhaps the Most Important Primary Good': Self-Respect and Rawls's Principles of Justice." *Politics, Philosophy & Economics* 4 (2005).

Fagan, Patrick F. "The Child Abuse Crisis: The Disintegration of Marriage, Family, and the American Family." Backgrounder, No. 1115. Washington, DC: Heritage Foundation, June 3, 1997.

Fagan, Patrick F., Kirk A. Johnson, and Jonathan Butcher, "The Map of the Family," The Heritage Foundation. www.heritage.org/Research/Family/upload/76145_1.pdf

Farson, Richard. *Birthrights*. New York: Macmillan, 1974.

Faudin, Jr., James M., Norman Polansky, Allie C. Kirkpatrick, and Paula Shilton. "Family Functioning in Neglectful Families." *Child Abuse and Neglect* 20 (1996).

Feinburg, Joel. "The Child's Rights to an Open Future." In William Aiken and Hugh LaFollette, eds. *Whose Child? Children's Rights, Parental Authority, and State Power*. Totowa, NJ: Rowman and Littlefield, 1980.

Festinger, Leon. "A Theory of Social Comparison Processes." *Human Relations* 7 (1954).

Finkelhor, David, and Angela Browne, "Assessing the Long-Term Impact of Child Sexual Abuse: A Review and Conceptualization." In Gerald Hotaling, David

Finkelhor, John T. Kirkpatrick, and Murray A. Straus, eds. *Family Abuse and Its Consequences: New Directions in Research*, London: Sage Publications, 1988.

Forste, R., and K. Tanfer. "Sexual Exclusivity among Dating, Cohabiting, and Married Women." *Journal of Marriage and the Family* 58 (1996).

Fox, Claire L., and Michael J. Boulton. "Friendship as a Moderator of the Relationship Between Social Skills Problems and Peer Victimization." *Aggressive Behavior* 32 (2006).

Freeman, Michael D. A. "Taking Rights More Seriously." In Philip Alston, Stephen Parker, and John Seymour, eds. *Children and the Law*. Oxford: Oxford University Press, 1992.

Freidrich, William N., and Jerry Boriskin. "The Role of the Child in Abuse: A Review of the Literature." *American Journal of Orthopsychiatry* 46 (1976).

Freud, Anna, Joseph Goldstein, and Albert Solnit. *Before the Best Interests of the Child*. New York: The Free Press, 1979.

Galambos, Nancy L., Erin T. Barker, and David M. Almeida. "Parents *Do* Matter: Trajectories of Change in Externalizing and Internalizing Problems in Early Adolescence." *Child Development* 74 (2003).

Galston, William. "Two Concepts of Liberalism." *Ethics* 105 (1995).

Gauthier, David. "Political Contractarianism." *The Journal of Political Philosophy* 5 (1997).

Gelles, Richard J. "Child Abuse as Psychopathology: A Sociological Critique and Reformulation." *American Journal of Orthopsychiatry* 43 (1973).

George, C., and M. Main. "Social Interactions of Young Abused Children: Approach, Avoidance, and Aggression." *Child Development* 50 (1979).

George, R. M., and B. G. Lee. "Poverty, Early Child Bearing, and Child Maltreatment: A Nominal Analysis." *Children and Youth Services Review* 21 (1999).

Gerhardt, Sue. *Why Love Matters: How Affection Shapes a Baby's Brain*. New York: Brunner-Routledge, 2004.

Gerstein, Robert. "Intimacy and Privacy." *Ethics* 89 (1978).

Giovannoni, Jeanne M., and Rosina M. Becerra. *Defining Child Abuse*. New York: The Free Press, 1979.

Goldman, Jill, and Marsha K. Salus. *A Coordinated Response to Child Abuse and Neglect: The Foundation for Practice*. U.S. Department of Health and Human Services Administration of Children and Families. See www.childwelfare.gov/pubs/ usermanuals/foundation /foundation.pdf (2003).

Gordon, Michael, and Susan Creighton. "Natal and Non-natal Fathers as Sexual Abusers in the United Kingdom: A Comparative Analysis." *Journal of Marriage and the Family* 50 (1998).

Griswold v. Connecticut, 381 U.S. 479 (1965).

Hagan, Kristine Amlund, Barbara J. Meyers, and Virginia H. Mackintosh. "Hope, Social Support, and Behavioral Problems in At-Risk Children." *American Journal of Orthopsychiatry* 75 (2005).

Hamilton, Alexander, James Madison, and John Jay. *The Federalist*. Ed. Jacob E. Cooke. Hanover, NH: Wesleyan University Press, 1961.

Harlow, H. F., R. O. Dodsworth, and M. K. Harlow. "Total Social Isolation in Monkeys." *Proceedings of the National Academy of Sciences* 54 (1965).

Haskett, Mary E. and Janet A. Kistner. "Social Interactions and Peer Perceptions of Young Physically Abused Children." *Child Development* 62 (1991).

Haskett, Mary E., Susan Smith Scott, and Kellie D. Fann. "Child Abuse Potential Inventory and Parenting Behavior: Relationships with High-Risk Correlates." *Child Abuse and Neglect* 19 (1995).

Hedman, Carl. "Three Approaches to the Problem of Child Abuse and Neglect." *Journal of Social Philosophy* 31 (2000).

Helferin, Ray. "Review of the Concepts and a Sampling of the Research Relating to Screening for the Potential to Abuse and/or Neglect One's Child." Presented at a workshop sponsored by the National Committee for the Prevention of Child Abuse, 3–6 December 1978.

Higgins, Daryl J. "The Importance of Degree Versus Type of Maltreatment: A Cluster Analysis of Child Abuse Types." *The Journal of Psychology* 138 (2004).

Higgins, Daryl J., and Marita P. McCabe. "Multiple Forms of Child Abuse and Neglect: Adult Retrospective Reports." *Aggression and Violent Behavior* 6 (2001).

Hildyard, Kathryn L., and David A. Wolfe. "Child Neglect: Developmental Issues and Outcomes." *Child Abuse and Neglect* 26 (2002).

Hill, Lawrence. "What Does it Mean to Be a 'Parent'? The Claims of Biology as the Basis for Parental Rights." *New York Law Review* 66 (1991).

Hill, Thomas. "Servility and Self-Respect." *Monist* 57 (1973).

Hodgson v. Minnesota, 497 U.S. 217 (1990)

Hoffman-Plotkin, Debbie, and Craig T. Twentyman. "A Multimodal Assessment of Behavioral and Cognitive Deficits in Abused and Neglected Preschoolers." *Child Development* 55 (1984).

Holmes, Jr., Oliver Wendell. *The Common Law*. Boston: Little, Brown, 1881.

Holt, John. *Escape From Childhood: The Needs and Rights of Children*. New York: Ballantine Books, 1974.

Horowitz, R., ed. *Review of Child Development Research*. Vol. 4. Chicago: University of Chicago Press, 1975.

Hotaling, Gerald, David Finkelhor, John T. Kirkpatrick, and Murray A. Straus, eds. *Family Abuse and Its Consequences: New Directions in Research*. London: Sage Publications, 1988.

Howe, Tasha R., and Ross D. Parke. "Friendship Quality and Sociometric Status: Between Group Differences and Links to Loneliness in Severely Abused and Nonabused Children." *Child Abuse and Neglect* 25 (2001).

Howes, Carollee. "Abused and Neglected Children with Their Peers." In Hotaling, Gerald, David Finkelhor, John T. Kirkpatrick, and Murray A. Straus, eds. *Family Abuse and Its Consequences: New Directions in Research*. London: Sage Publications, 1988.

Hudson, Stephen. "The Nature of Respect." *Social Theory and Practice* 6 (1980).

Huesman, L. Rowell, Leonard D. Eron, Monroe M. Lefkowitz, and Leopold O. Walder. "Stability of Aggression Over Time and Generations." *Developmental Psychology* 20 (1984).

Hume, David. *A Treatise on Human Nature*. 2nd Edition. Ed. P. H. Nidditch and index by L. A. Selby-Bigge. Oxford: Oxford University Press, 1978.

Huston, Aletha C., ed. *Children in Poverty: Child Development and Public Policy*. New York: Cambridge University Press, 1991.

Huxley, Aldous. *Brave New World*. New York: Perennial Classics, 1998.

In re East, 32 Ohio Misc. 65, 288 N.E. 2d 343, 61 O.O. 2d 38, 61 O.O. 2d 108 (1972).

Irvine, William B. *Doing Right By Children: Reflections on the Nature of Childhood and the Obligations of Parenthood*. St. Paul, MN: Paragon House, 2001.

——. *The Politics of Parenting*. St. Paul, MN: Paragon House, 2003.

Ito, Yukata, Carol A. Glod, and Erika Ackerman. "Preliminary Evidence for Aberrant Cortical Development in Abused Children: A Qualitative EEG Study." *The Journal of Neuropsychiatry and Clinical Neurosciences* 10 (1998)

Ito, Yukata, Martin H. Teicher, Carol A. Glod, David Harper, Eleanor Magnus, and Harris A. Gelbard. "Increased Prevalence of Electrophysiological Abnormalities in Children with Psychological, Physical, and Sexual Abuse." *Journal of Neuropsychiatry and Clinical Neurosciences* 5 (1993).

Jackson, Nicky Ali. "Observational Experiences of Interpersonal Conflict and Teenage Victimization: A Comparative Study Among Spouses and Cohabitors." *Journal of Family Violence* 11 (1996).

Jacobson v. Com. of Massachusetts 197 U.S. 11 (1905).

James, William. *Principles of Psychology*. Vol. 1. New York: Dover, 1950.

Jones, David P. H. "The Untreatable Family." *Child Abuse and Neglect* 11 (1987).

Kaestle, C. E., and C. T. Helpern. "Sexual Activity Among Adolescents in Romantic Relationships with Friends, Acquaintances, or Strangers." *Archives of Pediatric and Adolescent Medicine* 159 (2005).

Kane, Andrea, and Isabell Sawhill. "Preventing Early Childbearing." In Isabell Sawhill, ed. *One Percent for the Kids: New Policies, Brighter Futures for America's Children*. Washington, DC: The Brookings Institution, 2003.

Kant, Immanuel. *Metaphysical Elements of Justice*. Indianapolis, IN: Hackett, 1999.

Kaplan, Sandra J., David Pelcovitz, and Victor Labruna. "Child and Adolescent Abuse and Neglect Research: A Review of the Past 10 Years. Part I: Physical and Emotional Abuse and Neglect." *Journal of the American Academy of Child and Adolescent Psychiatry* 38 (1999).

Katz, L. F., and J. F. Gottman. "Patterns of Marital Conflict Predict Children's Internalizing and Externalizing Behaviors." *Developmental Psychology* 29 (1993).

Katz, Sanford N. *When Parents Fail: The Law's Response to Family Breakdown*. Boston: Beacon Press, 1971.

Kaufman, Joan, and Edward Zigler. "Do Abused Children Become Abusive Parents?" *American Journal of Orthopsychiatry* 57 (1987).

——. "The Intergenerational Transmission of Child Abuse." In Dante Cicchetti and Vicki Carlson, eds. *Child Maltreatment: Theory and Research on the Causes and Consequences of Child Abuse and Neglect*. Cambridge: Cambridge University Press, 1989.

Kavka, Gregory. *Hobbesian Moral and Political Theory*. Princeton, NJ: Princeton University Press, 1986.

Kent, James. *Commentaries on American Law*. New York: O. Halstead, 1832.
Kent, M., and J. Rolf., eds. *Primary Prevention of Psychopathology: Social Competence in Children*. Hanover, NH: University Press of New England, 1979.
Kilpatrick, Kym L. "The Parental Empathy Measure: A New Approach to Assessing Child Maltreatment Risk." *American Journal of Orthopsychiatry* 75 (2005).
Kinard, E. M. "Emotional Development in Physically Abused Children." *American Journal of Orthopsychiatry* 50 (1980).
Knutson, John F., David S. DeGarmo, and John B. Reid. "Social Disadvantage and Neglectful Parenting as Precursors to the Development of Antisocial and Aggressive Child Behavior: Testing a Theoretical Model." *Aggressive Behavior* 30 (2004).
Koenig, Amy L., Dante Cicchetti, and Fred A. Rogash. "Moral Development: The Association Between Maltreatment and Young Children's Prosocial Behaviors and Moral Transgressions." *Social Development* 13 (2004).
Kotelchuck, Milton. "Child Abuse and Neglect: Prediction and Misclassification." In Raymond H. Starr, Jr., ed. *Child Abuse Prediction: Policy Implications*. Cambridge, MA: Ballinger Publishing, 1982.
Kukathas, Chandran. "Are There Any Cultural Rights?" *Political Theory* 20 (1992).
Kymlicka, Will. *Liberalism, Community, and Culture*. Oxford: Clarendon, 1989.
LaFollette, Hugh. "Licensing Parents." *Philosophy and Public Affairs* 9 (1980).
Lassiter v. Department of Social Services, 452 U.S. 18 (1981).
Lehr v. Robertson, 463 U.S. 248 (1983).
Liao, S. Matthew. "The Idea of a Duty to Love." *Journal of Value Inquiry* 40 (2006).
———. "The Right of Children to Be Loved." *The Journal of Political Philosophy* 14 (2006).
Lochner v. New York, 198 U.S. 45 (1905).
Locke, John. *Some Thoughts Concerning Education and Of the Conduct of the Understanding*. Ed. Ruth W. Grant and Nathan Tarcov. Indianapolis, IN: Hacking Publishing Company, 1996.
———. *Two Treatises of Government*. Cambridge: Cambridge University Press, 1996.
Long, Janis V. F., and George E. Vaillant. "Escape From the Underclass." In Timothy F. Dugan and Robert Coles, eds. *The Children of Our Times: Studies in the Development of Resilience*. New York: Brunner/Mazel, 1989.
Lowry, Lois. *The Giver*. New York: Laurel Leaf, 1993.
Luthar, S. "The Culture of Affluence: Psychological Costs of Material Wealth." *Child Development* 74 (2003).
Luthar, S. S., and B. E. Becker. "Privileged but Pressured: A Study of Affluent Youth." *Child Development* 73 (2002).
Luthar, S. S., and K. D'Avanzo. "Contextual Factors in Substance Abuse: A Study of Suburban and Inner-City Adolescents." *Development and Psychopathology* 11 (1999).
Luthar, S. S., and Shawn J. Latendresse. "Comparable 'Risks' at the Socioeconomic Status Extremes: Preadolescents' Perception of Parenting." *Development and Psychopathology* 17 (2005).
Magdol, Lynn, Terrie E. Moffitt, Avshalon Caspi, and Phil A. Silva. "Hitting Without a License: Testing Explanations for Differences in Partner Abuse Between Young Adult Daters and Cohabiters." *Journal of Marriage and the Family* 60 (1998).

Manning, Wendy D., Pamela J. Smock, and Debarum Majumdar. "The Relative Stability of Cohabiting and Marital Unions for Children." *Population Research and Policy Review* 23 (2004).

Manser, Marilyn, and Murray Brown. "Marriage and Household Decision-Making: A Bargaining Analysis." *International Economic Review* 21 (1980).

Margolin, Leslie. "Child Abuse by Mothers' Boyfriends: Why the Overrepresentation?" *Child Abuse and Neglect* 16 (1992).

Massey, Stephen J. "Is Self-Respect a Moral or Psychological Concept?" *Ethics* 93 (1983).

Matthews v. Eldridge, 424 U.S. 319 (1976).

May v. Anderson, 345 U.S. 528 (1953).

Maynard v. Hill, 125 U.S. 190 (1888).

McClennen, Edward F. "Justice and the Problem of Stability." *Philosophy and Public Affairs* 18 (1989).

McCord, Joan. "A Forty Year Perspective on Child Abuse and Neglect." *Child Abuse and Neglect* 7 (1983).

McIntire, Roger W. "Parenthood Training or Mandatory Birth Control: Take Your Choice." *Psychology Today* 34 (Oct. 1973).

McKinnon, Catriona. "Basic Income, Self-Respect and Reciprocity." *Journal of Applied Philosophy* 20 (2003).

McLoyd, V. C., T. E. Jayaratne, R. Ceballo, and J. Borquez. "Unemployment and Work Interruptions among African-American Single Mothers: Effects on Parenting and Adolescent Socioemotional Functioning." *Child Development* 65 (1994).

McLoyd, V. C., and L. Wilson. "The Strain of Living Poor: Parenting, Social Support, and Child Mental Health." In Aletha C. Huston, ed. *Children in Poverty: Child Development and Public Policy*. Cambridge: Cambridge University Press, 1991.

McNary, Scot, and Maureen M. Black. "Use of the Child Abuse Potential Inventory as a Measure of Treatment Outcome." *Child Abuse and Neglect* 27 (2003).

Meyer v. Nebraska, 262 U.S. 390 (1923).

Mill, John Stuart. *On Liberty*. London: Penguin Books, 1985.

Milner, Joel S. "Development of a Lie Scale for the Child Abuse Potential Inventory." *Psychological Reports* 50 (1982).

Milner, Joel S., and Catherine Ayoub. "Evaluation of 'At-Risk' Parents Using the Child Abuse Potential Inventory." *Journal of Clinical Psychology* 36 (1980).

Milner, Joel S., Ruth G. Gold, Catherine Ayoub, and Marion M. Jacewitz. "Predictive Validity of the Child Abuse Potential Inventory." *Journal of Consulting and Clinical Psychology* 52 (1984).

Milner, Joel S., and Kevin R. Robertson. "Development of a Random Response Scale for the Child Abuse Potential Inventory." *Journal of Clinical Psychology* 41 (1985).

Milner, Joel S., and Ronald C. Wimberly. "Prediction and Explanation of Child Abuse." *Journal of Clinical Psychology* 35 (1980).

Moller Okin, Susan. *Justice, Gender, and the Family*. New York: Basic Books, 1989.

Montague, Philip. "The Myth of Parental Rights." *Social Theory and Practice* 26 (2000).

Moody-Adams, Michele M. "Race, Class, and the Social Construction of Self-Respect." In Robin S. Dillon, ed. *Dignity, Character, and Self-Respect*. New York: Routledge, 1995.

Moore v. East Cleveland, 431 U.S. 494 (1977).

Moriarty, Jeffrey. "Rawls, Self-Respect, and the Living Wage." *Unpublished draft*.

Mulgan, Tim. "Debate: Reproducing the Contractarian Debate." *The Journal of Political Philosophy* 10 (2002).

Mullin, Amy. "Trust, Social Norms, and Motherhood." *Journal of Social Philosophy* 36 (Fall 2005).

Murphy, Lois Barclay, and Alice E. Moriarty. *Vulnerability, Coping, and Growth: From Intimacy to Adolescence*. New Haven, CT: Yale University Press, 1976.

Murphy, Solbritt, Bonnie Orkow, and Ray M. Nicola. "Prenatal Prediction of Child Abuse and Neglect: A Prospective Study." *Child Abuse and Neglect* 9 (1985).

Murray, Velma McBridge, Gene H. Brody, Anita Brown, Joseph Wisenbaker, Carolyn E. Cutrona, and Ronald L. Simons. "Linking Employment Status, Maternal Psychological Well-Being, Parenting, and Children's Attributions About Poverty in Families Receiving Government Assistance." *Family Relations* 51 (2002).

National Center on Child Abuse and Neglect. *Third National Study of Child Abuse and Neglect*. Washington, DC: US Department of Health and Human Resources, 1996.

Nelson, Charles A., and Floyd E. Bloom. "Child Development and Neuroscience." *Child Development* 68 (1997).

New York Trust Co. v. Eisner, 256 U.S. 345 (1921).

Nock, Stephen L. "A Comparison of Marriages and Cohabiting Relationships." *Journal of Family Issues* 16 (1995).

Nozick, Robert. *Anarchy, State and Utopia*. New York: Basic Books, 1974.

Nussbaum, Martha. *Women and Human Development: The Capabilities Approach*. Cambridge: Cambridge University Press, 2001.

Oates, R. Kim, and Douglas Forrest. "Self-Esteem and Early Background of Abusive Mothers." *Child Abuse and Neglect* 9 (1985).

Oates, R. Kim, Douglas Forrest, and Anthony Peacock. "Self-Esteem of Abused Children." *Child Abuse and Neglect* 9 (1985).

O'Brien, John D., Daniel J. Pilowsky, and Owen W. Lewis, eds. *Psychotherapists with Children and Adolescents: Adapting the Psychodynamic Process*. Washington, DC: American Psychiatric Association, 1992.

O'Brien, Raymond. "An Analysis of Realistic Due Process Rights of Children Versus Parents." *Connecticut Law Review* 26 (1993–1994).

O'Neill, Onora. "Begetting, Bearing, and Rearing." In Onora O'Neill and William Ruddick, eds. *Having Children: Philosophical and Legal Reflections on Parenthood*. New York: Oxford University Press, 1979.

——. "Children's Rights and Children's Lives." In Philip Alston, Stephen Parker, and John Seymour, eds. *Children and the Law*. Oxford: Oxford University Press, 1992.

O'Neill, Onora, and William Ruddick, eds. *Having Children: Philosophical and Legal Reflections on Parenthood*. New York: Oxford University Press, 1979.

Orkow, Bonnie. "Implementation of a Family Stress Checklist." *Child Abuse and Neglect* 9 (1985).

Otnow Lewis, Dorothy, Catherine Mallouh, and Victoria Webb. "Child Abuse, Delinquency, and Violent Criminality." In Dante Cicchetti and Vicki Carlson, eds. *Child Maltreatment: Theory and Research on the Causes and Consequences of Child Abuse and Neglect.* Cambridge: Cambridge University Press, 1989.

Parham v. J.R., 442 U.S. 584 (1979).

Parker, Jeffrey G., and Steven R. Asher. "Peer Relations and Later Personal Adjustment: Are Low-Accepted Children At Risk?" *Psychological Bulletin* 102 (1987).

Passmore, Nola L., Gerard J. Fogarty, Carolyn J. Bourke, and Sandra F. Baker-Evans. "Parental Bonding and Identity Style as Correlates of Self-Esteem Among Adult Adoptees and Nonadoptees." *Family Relations* 54 (2005).

Pears, Katherine C., and Deborah M. Capaldi. "Intergenerational Transmission of Abuse: A Two-Generational Prospective Study of an At-Risk Sample." *Child Abuse and Neglect* 25 (2001).

Peters, H. Elizabeth, and A. Sinan Ünür. "Economic Perspectives on Altruism and the Family." In Arland Thornton, ed. *The Well-Being of Children and Families: Research and Data Needs.* Ann Arbor: University of Michigan Press, 2004.

Phillips, Derek. *Toward a Just Social Order.* Princeton, NJ: Princeton University Press, 1986.

Pierce v. Society of Sisters, 268 U.S. 510 (1925).

Plato. *The Republic.* Trans. Allan Bloom. New York: Basic Books, 1991.

Pojman, Louis, and Robert Westmoreland, eds. *Equality: Selected Readings.* New York: Oxford University Press, 1997.

Prince v. Com. of Massachusetts, 321 U.S. 158 (1944).

Pruitt, Doyle L., and Marilyn T. Erickson. "The Child Abuse Potential Inventory: A Study of Concurrent Validity." *Journal of Clinical Psychology* 41 (1985).

Puka, Bill, ed. *Moral Development: Defining Perspectives in Moral Development,* Vol. 1. New York: Garland Publishing, 1994.

Purdy, Laura. *In Their Best Interest? The Case Against Equal Rights for Children.* Ithaca, NY: Cornell University Press, 1992.

Quilloin v. Walcott, 434 U.S. 246 (1978).

Quinton, David, and Michael Rutter. *Parenting Breakdown: The Making and Breaking of Intergenerational Links.* Aldershot, UK: Aveburg, 1988.

Raskin White, Helene, and Cathy Spatz Widom. "Intimate Partner Violence Among Abused and Neglected Children in Young Adulthood: The Mediating Effects of Early Aggression, Antisocial Personality, Hostility and Alcohol Problems." *Aggressive Behavior* 29 (2003).

Rawls, John. "The Sense of Justice." *The Philosophical Review* 72 (1963).

——. *A Theory of Justice.* Revised Edition. Cambridge, MA: Harvard University Press, 2000.

Reidy, Thomas J. "The Aggressive Characteristics of Abused and Neglected Children." *Journal of Clinical Psychology* 33 (1977).

Rendleman, Douglas. "Parens Patriae: From Chancery to the Juvenile Court." *South Carolina Law Review* 23 (1971).

Reynolds v. U.S., 98 U.S. 145 (1878).

Risenfield, Stefan A. "The Formative Era of American Public Assistance Law." *California Law Review* 43 (1955).

Roback Morse, Jennifer. *Love and Economics: Why the Laissez-Faire Family Doesn't Work*. Dallas: Spence Publishing Company, 2001.

———. "No Families, No Freedom: Human Flourishing in a Free Society." *Social Philosophy and Policy* 16 (1999).

Robertson, John A. *Children of Choice: Freedom and the New Reproductive Technologies*. Princeton, NJ: Princeton University Press, 1994.

Robitaille, Joanne, Eleanor Jones, Ruth G. Gold, Kevin R. Robertson, and Joel S. Milner. "Child Abuse Potential and Authoritarianism." *Journal of Clinical Psychology* 41 (1985).

Roe v. Wade, 410 U.S. 113 (1973)

Rohner, R., and E. Rohner. "Antecedents and Consequences of Parental Rejection: A Theory of Emotional Abuse." *Child Abuse and Neglect* 4 (1980).

Rousseau, Jean-Jacques. *Emile, or On Education*. Trans. Allan Bloom. New York: Basic Books, 1979.

———. *The Social Contract*. Ed. Maurice Cranston. London: Penguin Books, 1968.

Rutter, Michael. "Early Sources of Security and Competence." In J. Brunner and A. Gaston, eds. *Human Growth and Development*. Oxford: Clarendon Press, 1978.

———. "Intergenerational Continuities and Discontinuities in Serious Parenting Difficulties." In Dante Cicchetti and Vicki Carlson, eds. *Child Maltreatment: Theory and Research on the Causes and Consequences of Child Abuse and Neglect*. Cambridge: Cambridge University Press, 1989.

———. "Protective Factors in Children's Responses to Stress and Disadvantage." In M. Kent and J. Rolf, eds. *Primary Prevention of Psychopathology: Social Competence in Children*. Hanover, NH: University Press of New England, 1979.

———. "Resilience in the Face of Adversity: Protective Factors and Resistance to Psychiatric Disorder." *British Journal of Psychiatry* 147 (1985).

Sachs, David. "How to Distinguish Self-Respect from Self-Esteem." *Philosophy and Public Affairs* 10 (1981).

Sack, William H., Robert Mason, James E. Higgins. "The Single-Parent Family and Abusive Child Punishment." *American Journal of Orthopsychiatry* 55 (1983).

Salmivalli, Christina. "Feeling Good about Oneself, Being Bad to Others? Remarks on Self-Esteem, Hostility, and Aggressive Behavior." *Aggression and Violent Behavior* 6 (2001).

Salzinger, Suzanne, Richard S. Feldman, Muriel Hammer, and Margaret Rosario. "The Effects of Physical Violence on Children's Social Relationships." *Child Development* 64 (1993).

Sameroff, A., and M. Chandler. "Reproductive Risk and the Continuum of Caretaking Causality." In F. Horowitz, ed. *Review of Child Development Research*, Vol. 4. Chicago: University of Chicago Press, 1975.

Sameroff, Arnold J., and Robert N. Emde, eds. *Relationship Disturbances in Early Childhood*. New York: Basic Books, 1989.

Santosky v. Kramer, 455 U.S. 745 (1982).

Saudmire, Michael J., and Michael S. Wald. "Licensing Parents—A Response to Claudia Mangel's Proposal." *Family Law Quarterly* 24 (1990).

Sawhill, Isabell, ed. *One Percent for the Kids: New Policies, Brighter Futures for America's Children*. Washington, DC: The Brookings Institution, 2003.

Scanlon, T. M. "The Diversity of Objections to Equality." In Matthew Clayton and Andrew Williams, eds. *The Idea of Equality*. New York: St. Martin's Press, 2000.

Scheler, Max. *Ressentiment*. Milwaukee, WI: Marquette University Press, 1998.

Schmidtz, David, and Robert E. Goodin. *Social Welfare and Individual Responsibility*. Cambridge: Cambridge University Press, 1998.

Schoeck, Helmut. *Envy: A Theory of Social Behavior*. Indianapolis, IN: Liberty Fund, 1987.

Schoeman, Ferdinand. "Rights of Children, Rights of Parents, and the Moral Basis of the Family." *Ethics* 91 (1980).

Schrag, Francis. "Justice and the Family." *Inquiry* 19 (1976).

Schumacher, Julie A., Amy Slep, and Richard E. Heyman. "Risk Factors for Neglect." *Aggression and Violent Behavior* 6 (2001).

Schwartz, Joshua. "Rights of Inequality: Rawlsian Justice, Equal Opportunity, and the Status of the Family." *Legal Theory* 7 (2001).

Seltzer, Judith A. "Families Forced Outside of Marriage." *Journal of Marriage and the Family* 62 (2000).

Sen, Amartya. *Inequality Reexamined*. Cambridge, MA: Harvard University Press, 2001.

Shafran, R. B. "Children of Affluent Parents." In John D. O'Brien, Daniel J. Pilowsky, and Owen W. Lewis, eds. *Psychotherapists with Children and Adolescents: Adapting the Psychodynamic Process*. Washington, DC: American Psychiatric Association, 1992.

Shields, Ann, and Dante Cicchetti. "Reactive Aggression among Maltreated Children: The Contributions of Attention and Emotion Dysregulation." *Journal of Clinical Child Psychology* 27 (1998).

Shields, Ann M., Dante Cicchetti, and Richard M. Ryan. "The Development of Emotional and Behavioral Self-Regulation and Social Competence Among Maltreated School-Age Children." *Development and Psychopathology* 6 (1994).

Shue, Henry. "Liberty and Self-Respect." *Ethics* 85 (1975).

Skinner v. Oklahoma, 316 U.S. 535 (1942).

Smetana, Judith G., and Mario Kelly. "Social Cognition in Maltreated Children." In Dante Cicchetti and Vicki Carlson, eds. *Child Maltreatment: Theory and Research on the Causes and Consequences of Child Abuse and Neglect*. Cambridge: Cambridge University Press, 1989.

Smith v. Organization of Foster Families, 431 U.S. 816 (1977).

Smith, Adam. *The Theory of Moral Sentiments*. Amherst, NY: Prometheus Books, 2000.

Smith, Dorothy W., and Laurie Nels Sherwen. *Mothers and Their Adopted Children: The Bonding Process*. New York: Tiresias Press, 1983.

Snook, I.A., ed. *Concepts of Indoctrination: Philosophical Essays*. London: Routledge & Kegan Paul, 1972.

Solheim, Barbara P. "The Possibility of a Duty to Love." *Journal of Social Philosophy* 30 (1999).

Spinetta, J., and D. Rigler. "The Child-Abusing Parent: A Psychological Review."
Psychological Bulletin 77 (1972).

Spitz, René. "Hospitalism: An Inquiry Into the Genesis of Psychiatric Conditions in
Early Childhood." *The Psychoanalytic Study of the Child* 1 (1945).

Spitz, R. A., and K. M. Wolf. "Anaclitic Depression: An Inquiry Into the Genesis of
Psychiatric Conditions in Early Childhood." *The Psychoanalytic Study of the Child*
2 (1946).

Sroufe, Alan. "Relationships, Self, and Individual Adaptation," In Arnold J. Sameroff
and Robert N. Emde, eds. *Relationship Disturbances in Early Childhood*. New
York: Basic Books, 1989.

Stanley v. Illinois, 405 U.S. 645 (1972).

Starr, Jr., Raymond H. "A Research-Based Approach to the Prediction of Child
Abuse." In Raymond H. Starr, Jr., ed. *Child Abuse Prediction: Policy Implications*.
Cambridge, MA: Ballinger Publishing, 1982.

—— ed., *Child Abuse Prediction: Policy Implications*. Cambridge, MA: Ballinger
Publishing, 1982.

Stowman, Stephanie A., and Brad Donohue. "Assessing Child Neglect: A Review of
Standardized Procedures." *Aggression and Violent Behavior* 10 (2005).

Straus, Murray A. "The Marriage License as Hitting License: A Comparison of Assaults in Dating, Cohabiting and Married Couples." *Journal of Family Violence* 4
(1989).

——. "Stress and Physical Child Abuse." *Child Abuse and Neglect* 55 (1983).

Straus, Murray A., and Glenda Kaufman Kantor. "Definition and Measurement of Neglectful Behavior: Some Principles and Guidelines." *Child Abuse and Neglect* 29
(2005).

Sumner, William Graham. *What Social Classes Owe to Each Other*. New York:
Harper and Brothers Publishers, 1911.

Survey of Consumer Finance, 2001.

Thomas, Laurence. *The Family and the Political Self*. Cambridge: Cambridge University Press, 2006.

——. "Gratitude and Social Equality." *The Hedgehog Review* 3 (Spring 2001).

——. *Living Morally: A Psychology of Moral Character*. Philadelphia: Temple University Press, 1989.

——. "Morality and Human Diversity: A Review of Owen Flanagan's *Varieties of
Moral Personality*." *Ethics* 103 (1992).

——. "Morality and a Meaningful Life." *Philosophical Papers* 34 (2005).

——. "Morality and Our Self-Concept." *Journal of Value Inquiry* 12 (1978).

——."Protecting Ourselves into Oblivion: Avoiding Pain and Trust is a Lose-Lose
Situation," www.moralhealth.com/blog/_archives/2005/8/5/1110624.html

——. "Rawlsian Self-Respect and the Black Consciousness Movement." *The Philosophical Forum* 9 (1978–1979).

——, "Self-Respect: Theory and Practice" In Robin S. Dillon, ed. *Dignity, Character, and Self-Respect*. New York: Routledge, 1995

Thornton, Arland, ed. *The Well-Being of Children and Families: Research and Data Needs*. Ann Arbor: University of Michigan Press, 2004.

Tittle, Peg. "Introduction" In Peg Tittle, ed. *Should Parents Be Licensed? Debating the Issues*. Amherst, NY: Prometheus Books, 2004.

Tocqueville, Alexis de. *Democracy in America*. Ed. and trans. Harvey C. Mansfield and Delba Winthrop. Chicago: University of Chicago Press, 2002.

Trivers, Robert L. "Parental Investment and Sexual Selection." In Bernard Campbell, ed. *Sexual Selection and the Descent of Man 1871–1971*. Chicago: Aldine Publishing Company, 1972.

Tsujimoto, Richard N., and Dale E. Berger. "Predicting Child Abuse: Value of Utility Maximizing Cutting Scores." *Child Abuse and Neglect* 12 (1988).

United States Census: Adopted Children and Stepchildren—Census 2000 Special Report. U.S. Department of Commerce, 2004.

van Doornick, W. J., P. Dawson, P. M. Butterfield, and H. I. Alexander. "Parent-Infant Support Through Lay Health Visitors." Final Report Submitted to the Bureau of Community Health Service, National Institute of Health, Department of Health, Education, and Welfare, 1980.

Van Parijs, Philippe. "Why Surfers Should Be Fed: The Liberal Case for an Unconditional Basic Income." *Philosophy and Public Affairs* 20 (1991).

Velleman, J. David. "Family History." *Philosophical Papers* 34 (2005).

Vopat, Mark. "Contractarianism and Children." *Public Affairs Quarterly* 17 (2003).

Wald, Michael S. "State Intervention on Behalf of Endangered Children—A Proposed Legal Response." *Child Abuse and Neglect* 6 (1982).

Werner, E. E. "High Risk Children in Young Adulthood: A Longitudinal Study from Birth to 32 Years." *American Journal of Orthopsychiatry* 59 (1989).

Werner, Emmy E., and Ruth S. Smith. *Vulnerable But Invincible: A Longitudinal Study of Resilient Children and Youth*. New York: Adams, Barrister, Cox, 1998.

Westman, Jack C. *Licensing Parents: Can We Prevent Child Abuse and Neglect?* New York: Insight Books, 1994.

Whalen v. Olmstead, 61 Conn. 263; 23 A 964 (1889).

Whelan, Robert. *Broken Homes and Battered Children: A Study of the Relationship between Child Abuse and Family Type*. London: Family Education Trust, 1993.

Williams, Gertrude J. "Management and Treatment of Parental Abuse and Neglect of Children: An Overview." In Gertrude J. Williams and John Money, eds. *Traumatic Abuse and Neglect of Children at Home*. Baltimore, MD: The Johns Hopkins University Press, 1982.

Williams, Gertrude J. "Toward the Eradication of Child Abuse and Neglect in the Home" In Gertrude J. Williams and John Money, eds. *Traumatic Abuse and Neglect of Children at Home*. Baltimore, MD: The Johns Hopkins University Press, 1982.

Williams, Gertrude J. and John Money, eds. *Traumatic Abuse and Neglect of Children at Home*. Baltimore, MD: The Johns Hopkins University Press, 1982.

Wu, Samuel S., Chang-Xing Ma, Randy L. Carter, Mario Ariet, Edward A. Feaver, Michael B. Resnick, and Jeffrey Roth. "Risk Factors for Infant Maltreatment: A Population-Based Study." *Child Abuse and Neglect* 28 (2004).

Wyman, P. A., E. L. Cowen, W. C. Work, L. Hoyt-Meyers, K. B. Magnus, and D. B. Fagan. "Caregiving and Developmental Factors Differentiating Young At-Risk Urban Children Showing Resilient Versus Stress-Affected Outcomes: A Replication and Extension." *Child Development* 70 (1999).

Yanal, Robert J. "Self-Esteem." *Noûs* 21 (1987).

Yllo, Kersti, and Murray A. Straus. "Interpersonal Violence Among Married and Cohabiting Couples." *Family Relations* 30 (1981).

Young, W. Jean, Miriam R. Linver, and Jeanne Brooks-Dunn. "How Money Matters for Young Children's Development: Parental Investment and Family Processes." *Child Development* 73 (2002).

Zablocki v. Redhail, 434 U.S. 374 (1978).

Zamyatin, Yevgeny. *We*. Trans. Clarence Brown. New York, Penguin, 1993.

Zigler, Edward, and Nancy W. Hall. "Physical Abuse in America: Past, Present, and Future." In Dante Cicchetti and Vicki Carlson, eds. *Child Maltreatment: Theory and Research on the Causes and Consequences of Child Abuse and Neglect*. Cambridge: Cambridge University Press, 1989.

Zhou, Qing, Nancy Eisenberg, Sandra H. Losoya, Richard A. Fabes, Mark Reiser, Ivanna K. Guthrie, Bridget C. Murphy, Amanda J. Cumberland, and Stephanie A. Shepard. "The Relations of Parental Warmth and Positive Expressiveness to Children's Empathy-Related Responding and Social Functioning: A Longitudinal Study." *Child Development* 73 (2002).

Zimmerman, M. A., D. A. Salem, and K. I. Maton. "Family Structure and Psychosocial Correlates Among Urban African-American Adolescent Males." *Child Development* 66 (1995).

Index

Trivers, Robert, 66–69
trust: healthy versus unhealthy, 55,
188–92, 210; ISJs and, 3, 8, 14, 29,
63, 70, 81, 92, 98, 179–80;
maltreatment and, 41, 48, 55,
179–80, 198; psychology and, 8,
13–14, 32, 36n2, 93, 97–99, 204;
society and, 3–4, 29, 34, 92, 107,
110, 128, 187–88, 203, 208, 210;
steward or, 140, 145, 162–63

Velleman, David, 150
Vopat, Mark, 143

Wald, Michael, 109
well-ordered society, 1–14, 17–18, 28,
34–36, 41–47, 54, 65–70, 81–82,
90–92, 107, 110, 118,   127, 159,
187, 207–8
Werner, Emmy, 57
Westman, Jack, 123–25

Yanal, Robert, 35

Zablocki v. Redhail, 166–67, 181
Zamyatin, Yevgeny, 199–200, 202
Zigler, Edward, 52

About the Author

Michael T. McFall received his Ph.D. in philosophy from Syracuse University. He is currently an IHUM Postdoctoral Fellow and Stanford University.

Breinigsville, PA USA
30 June 2010
240907BV00002B/2/P